THE HOLY FOREST

The publisher gratefully acknowledges the generous contribution to this book provided by the Humanities Endowment Fund of the University of California Press Foundation.

THE HOLY FOREST

Collected Poems of Robin Blaser

Revised and Expanded Edition

Edited by Miriam Nichols

Foreword by Robert Creeley

With a new afterword
by Charles Bernstein

University of California Press

Berkeley Los Angeles London

University of California Press, one of the most distinguished
university presses in the United States, enriches lives around
the world by advancing scholarship in the humanities, social
sciences, and natural sciences. Its activities are supported by
the UC Press Foundation and by philanthropic contributions
from individuals and institutions. For more information,
visit www.ucpress.edu.

University of California Press
Berkeley and Los Angeles, California

University of California Press, Ltd.
London, England

The first edition of *The Holy Forest* (Coach House Press),
© Robin Blaser, 1993. *Wanders* (Nomados Press) © Robin
Blaser, 2003.

Library of Congress Cataloging-in-Publication Data

Blaser, Robin.
    The holy forest: collected poems of Robin Blaser / Robin
Blaser ; edited by Miriam Nichols ; foreword by Robert
Creeley ; with a new afterword by Charles Bernstein. —
Rev. and expanded ed.
        p. cm.
    Includes index.
    ISBN-13 978-0-520-24593-8 (alk. paper)
    ISBN-10 0-520-24593-8 (alk. paper)
    I. Nichols, Miriam. II. Title.
    PS3552.L37H65   2006
    811'.54—dc22   2006040497

Manufactured in the United States of America

15   14   13   12   11   10   09   08   07   06
10   9   8   7   6   5   4   3   2   1

This book is printed on New Leaf EcoBook 50, a 100%
recycled fiber of which 50% is de-inked post-consumer
waste, processed chlorine-free. EcoBook 50 is acid-free and
meets the minimum requirements of ANSI/ASTM D5634-01
(*Permanence of Paper*).

CONTENTS

FOREWORD

For a reader to begin here may well prove displacing if one expects to find either a simple explanation or some securing directions. I have read Robin Blaser's consummate poetry for years, but I cannot predicate its authority on any sense that it has answered the questions which compelled it or come to the conclusion of what it thought to say. What has to be recognized is that these poems are not a defining "progress," or a skilfully accomplished enclosure. Above all else I must emphasize a sense often echoed here, that the "unfolded fold" to be found in his work—the turn, the bend in the road, the "twist" of Charles Olson's preoccupation—is the nexus of its life and the life it has made so movingly eloquent. No one is going anywhere—as if to get "there" were the sole possibility.

Reading these poems, one finds a life that is inexorably human, the adamant given of our common fact. Yet Descartes's curiously meagre proposition, "I think, therefore I am," can nonetheless empower the imagination, and "Only the imagination is real," as William Carlos Williams insisted to anyone who would listen. All else lives by the fate of its active being, its seemingly unreflective fact. But our human life yields a double, its acts and the thinking coincident. Who knows which more proves our determining world?

I first knew Robin Blaser as one of an almost mythic band, a triad composed of himself and his fellow poets Robert Duncan and Jack Spicer. In his valuable essay "The Practice of Outside," which serves as his defining proposition for the value of Jack Spicer's own poetry, he speaks with great clarity and power of that poēsis he shared with Spicer, recognizing how malevolent the stable "discourse" had become:

> Where the poēsis reopens the real and follows its contents, the presuming discourse imposes form and closes it, leaving us at the mercy of our own limit. . . . It may be argued that the push of contemporary poetics towards locus, ground, and particularity is a remaking of where we are. . . . From Pound's hierophanies and Williams's ground to Olson's cosmology and Spicer's narrative of the unknown, a remaking of the real is at stake. One needs only to notice how much of it is a common experience and also something regained, rather than an invention.
>
> —from *The Collected Books of Jack Spicer*, ed. Robin Blaser (1975)

Blaser's company was not just persons of the "San Francisco school" but survivors from a legendary Berkeley, where learning for oneself and discovering the appropriate teacher (Ernst Kantorovich is such an instance) had still a singular value. Robin was the quiet one, as my mother might say, certainly the modest one, and it was he, one guessed, who kept the bridge between Duncan and Spicer secure, though it was always precarious. I think of those brothers in the old stories, of the magic that protected them, of the complex trials they had to undergo, especially the youngest, least recognized, most at risk—who again I proposed to myself as Robin.

> I am taking the occasion of Jack's book to speak of the battle for the real of poetry in which all contemporary poetry in America is engaged. It began with Pound and continues. For me, it moves West and becomes a fateful meeting of three men—Jack Spicer, Robert Duncan and myself in 1946.
>
> —from *The Collected Books of Jack Spicer*

No doubt I compound it all with my own story, but a poem of his from *The New American Poetry* (1960), our first meeting place, made actual where we were and had to be:

Herons

I saw cold thunder in the grass,
the wet black trees of my humanity, my skin.

How much love lost hanging there
out of honesty.
              I catch at those men who chose
to hang in the wind
                  out of honesty.
It is the body lies with its skin—

Robed in my words I say the snake
changes its skin out of honesty.

And they
          hanged there with some symmetry
died young
              like herons proud in their landscape.
Now it is age crept in, nobody younger knows
the quick-darting breath is
  our portion of honesty.

A wryly attractive biographical note in the same collection contin-
ues aptly: "Born in 1925. Tied to universities from 1943–1959:
Northwestern, College of Idaho, Berkeley, California as a student;
Harvard as a librarian from 1955–1959. Now free and hoping to
remain that way. But it's doubtful. Money!"

There were to be subsequent employments of similar nature,
but with his moving from San Francisco to Vancouver in the mid-
sixties and his transforming presence at Simon Fraser University
(1966–1986), Robin Blaser became a source for poetry's author-
ity beyond any simplifying place or time. It is not at all that his
work is transcendent or beyond the obvious limits of common
life. Quite the contrary. In this still shifting edge of that West
which is his first place of origin, he enters upon his own power
without distraction or compromise, and comes to the substantiat-
ing community of his own need and recognition. In this respect
only Robert Duncan finds a place of similar order, while their
peers, such as Spicer and Olson, too often are battered by increas-
ing isolation and overt rejection. So the last words said by Jack
Spicer to his old friend echo with poignant emphasis: "*My vocabu-
lary did this to me. Your love will let you go on.*" These words have no sim-
ple reason, such as Blaser's initial Catholicism or Spicer's
determined Calvinism, to explain them. What is realized is what
has always been, that our words are literally our world, that their
permission, what they lead us to, is all we have.

Jack Spicer's own genius was his clear sight, a sometimes ruthlessly grounded specificity. It was he, for example, who recognized that Blaser would follow his emotions with a shifting rhythm, led by feeling to pattern. Together they proposed a "serial poetry" far more the fact of what might *now* happen rather than any presumed method for gaining generalized continuity, however defined. Therefore one can come to this actuating place of Blaser's powers without need for static containment or to think to summarize its information finally. The point seems clear enough in the titles of several of the books, for example: *Image-Nation* (in its continuing parts), *Streams*, *Syntax*, *Pell Mell*. What he has written about his poetics proves a basic advice:

> It seems to me that the whole marvellous thing of open form is a traditional and an American problem. . . . The whole thing came in a geography where the traditional forms would no longer hold our purposes. I was very moved when, some years ago, I was reading a scholarly book by Jo Miles in which she is making an argument for the sublime poem . . . and she begins to talk about the narrative of the spirit. I think the key word here is narrative—the story of persons, events, activities, images, which tell the tale of the spirit.
>
> I'm interested in a particular kind of narrative—what Jack Spicer and I agreed to call in our own work the serial poem—this is a narrative which refuses to adopt an imposed story line, and completes itself only in the sequence of poems, if, in fact, a reader insists upon a definition of completion which is separate from the activity of the poems themselves. The poems tend to act as a sequence of energies which run out when so much of a tale is told. I like to describe this in Ovidian terms, as a *carmen perpetuum*, a continuous song in which the fragmented subject matter is only apparently disconnected. Ovid's words are:
>
>> to tell of bodies
>> transformed
>> into new shapes
>> you gods, whose power
>> worked all transformations,
>> help the poet's breathing,
>> lead my continuous song
>> from the beginning   to the present world
>>
>> —from *The Fire* (1967)

Put it that one is to *be* somewhere in this transforming, accumulating poetry—not simply *be* led to a conclusion, but *be* taken by just such a magical *carmen perpetuum* to all the *image-nations* of this remarkable, revivifying world. How lovely that neither concept nor any other obligating pattern can enclose us, if we can "come into the world," as Charles Olson put it, recognizing that "we do what we know before we know what we do." The authority in any act is rooted here.

What comes then to be in the complexly layered "song" of these poems is an increasingly familiar presence, a person quite literal to any life. There is no fact of a didactic history, however much a particularizing story has been told and told again. Time folds and unfolds ("dépli") continuously all that is said, and the person each one presumes to know has momently to be recognized anew:

in the tree tops,

> the child, the child of the big shot, invalid's child, labourer's
> child, child of the fool, child of railroads, child of trees,
> child that is deiformed, child of fireworks, child of colour-
> lessness, child of damask, Mage's child, the child born with
> twenty-two folds at least   his or her concern is only to
> unfold herself or himself, curious   one or the other's life
> is, then, complete   under that form he or she dies there's
> no fold left for one or the other to undo

in the land of magic

—from *Exody* (1990–1993)

Bringing this extensive and multifaceted "song" now together, remembering all that these poems constitute as a presence, makes in turn a vivid and enduring evidence of the human in the fact of that, *itself*. Much as a tree might grow in beloved intention, or anything of fragile possibility find continuing if unexpected time, so this poet's life is manifest as a complex of perceptions, of reflections, ironies, humor, things learned, things forgotten, person become substance of its own potential. Robin Blaser makes clear the heroes of his determining order, found particularly in the sections *Great Companions* but everywhere echoing in quotation and allusion whether Robert Graves or Pindar, or Robert Duncan, or the measuring instance of Robin Blaser's concept of justice, Hannah Arendt. Or his belief in a hierarchic premise for human order such as Hermann Broch's *The Death of Virgil*. These are all *lintels*, as Blaser says, those supporting beams over any door's opening that so make possible the door. We enter by their provision into *The Holy Forest* (for us / for our rest) itself.

One soon realized that Robin Blaser was an immensely literate poet but never confiningly bookish or contesting in what he knew. One saw him shifting in circumstance, from the harshly exposed yet determined poet of "Herons" to the confidence and openhanded recognitions and accommodation of a much later work such as the wondrous "Image-Nation 24 ('Oh, pshaw,.'" Or yet these amazing lines:

> *How can a body be made from the word?*—language, a shivaree
> of transparence—jigsaw—glass immensity
> > —from "Image-Nation 25 (Exody,"

Reading them, a younger poet wrote as a tag now left in this copy of Robin's manuscript: *wow, does this make me want to be poured through Blaser's work, like clear water through a glass pitcher. . . .* As through a glass darkly—or brightly, as the case may be. Robin Blaser has become a touchstone for all his company, a bond in mind and heart. What does one ever want a poetry to be other than the sounding that reaches through all the fact of our variousness, brings to a common apprehension and presence whatever we have known, feel, or have felt? It is such a simple yet subtle art, this saying things in time. So there is time, it is time, to read.

Robert Creeley
Waldoboro, Maine
August 11, 1993

A NOTE ON THE TEXT

This revised edition of Robin Blaser's *The Holy Forest* is based on the
1993 collection of the same title, edited by Stan Persky and
Michael Ondaatje and published by Coach House Press. New to
this edition are some poems that were hiding in back drawers in
1993: these have been interpellated into the text in chronological
order and marked by an asterisk in the table of contents. Most of
the new additions, however, consist of poems written between
1994 and 2004. The serial books *Notes, Wanders, So,* and *Oh!* appear
here as part of *The Holy Forest* for the first time. (*Wanders* was re-
leased as a chapbook by Nomados Press in 2003.) The order of
the whole, like that of the first edition of the *Forest*, is as nearly
chronological as possible. In exception, I have placed the long
poem "Great Companion: Dante Alighiere" (1997) after *Notes*
(1994–2000) to signal a distinction between the serial run of the
former and the latter as a singular work.

On typographical conventions, I have retained original spell-
ings, which shift from American to Canadian, and Blaser's prefer-
ence for single quotation marks. Over the years, some poems have
been dated and others not. Where Blaser has dated the poems, I
have preserved the dates in the manner recorded—most often by
year, but sometimes more specifically by day and month as well.
In front and back materials, I have followed U.S. conventions of
spelling and punctuation.

Many thanks to University of California Press editor Rachel
Berchten for shepherding the manuscript through the production
process, to Ellen F. Smith for her careful copyediting, and to Peter
Quartermain for his work in preparing the manuscript of the new

additions. A special thanks as well goes to Charles Bernstein and Peter Gizzi for reading the manuscript in its early stages and to Robert Creeley and Charles Bernstein for contributing to this collection. Creeley's Foreword is reprinted here from the first edition of *The Holy Forest*; Bernstein's Afterword was written for the occasion of this new release. Peter Gizzi's editorial advice for this volume and for its companion, *The Fire: Collected Essays of Robin Blaser*, has been crucial.

Miriam Nichols

AUTHOR'S NOTE

These poems follow a principle of *randonée*—the random and the given of the hunt, the game, the tour. Poems called *Image-Nations* come and go throughout, as I come upon them. *Great Companions* of the art of poetry, a series which here consists of Pindar, Robert Duncan, and Dante Alighiere, will continue as I go on rereading the others and fold them in. And what of the "mere pals," my friend Peter Quartermain asked, pinching the pretension? They are here from the start, folded in and innermost. They are—men and women—there by friendship and their own attentions, aspects of the 'you' who appears in the poems.

Some of these poems appeared in *Measure, Locus Solus, Paris Review, Open Space, The Nation, Pacific Nation, Caterpillar, Line, Capilano Review, O-blēk,* and *West Coast Line*. Some have appeared as chapbooks or books, published by Open Space, Four Seasons, Ferry Press, Cobblestone, Talonbooks, Fissure, Coach House Press, and Nomados. I am grateful for their attention.

I want to thank my editors of the first edition of this collection (Coach House, 1993), Michael Ondaatje and Stan Persky, for the initial gathering and editing of *The Holy Forest*, and Miriam Nichols for her work on this revised version. David Farwell has helped in every way—more than I can say.

The whole thing: just trying to be at home. That's the plot.

Robin Blaser
Vancouver

THE HOLY FOREST

The Boston Poems

1956–1959

for Cleo Adams

Two Astronomers with Notebooks

Character I.   'Mirage
                  O everywhere.
                              The air
          very steady,'
                      said the astronomer.
              Notebook 1:   fd. 1 meteor.
              Notebook 2:   No meteors. The horizon had
                            a sharp edge to it.
              Notebook 3:   No meteors, but there are
                            apparitions unrecorded because
                            visible only in an uncivilized
                            country.
              Notebook 4:   They being invisible, added a
                            lens.
              Notebook 5:   The stars are where they always
                            are.
              Notebook 6:   They streamed crosswise, specific
                            as when a man dies.
              Notebook 7:   Advised to keep to the subject —
                            scholars are encouraged to study
                            the history of meteors
              Notebook 8:   No celestial event.
              Notebook 9:   Japan, A.D. 1037, 9th month, 16th
                            day: *masses were said in 8 provinces*
                            owing to the meteors.
                            the emperor was present at one
                            of them.
          Notebook 10:   fd. 1 meteor

Character II.   Notebook 1:
                              Watched all night
          the glow of morning
                              in my sleep —
          the sun pretend to seek
                              the leaf.

Heard the words twist
                    until
they were tall
            as
                dignity

Notebook 2:
            I began by insisting (in my
sleep, mind you), 'Gimme one a them stars
and I'll put your eyes out with it.' —
Woke up long before daylight.

Notebook 3:
            Watched all night
a telescope
                trained on the image
as when
            a bird stirs in the eaves
The sound becomes
                    full-bodied.

Notebook 4:
            Intolerable
the mind's likeness
                to the sky
as when
        certain particulars
catch the eye:
                a meteor
and its form
                as someone said
like a sword
                shorn of the man
who
    manipulates it.

War for Those Who Are Not Soldiers

How curious to create their blood,
record heroics in historical dimension
and still want to touch the wound's blood.

The soldier marches, his heart furious,
moves singular when his eyes blink.
These are not false heroes.   How curious:

We have made them tall like trees,
green things to bend to the water's edge.
On their green hearts we often seize.

To want war that these, our figurines,
may take on wings and soar—
we do not remember they are not what they seem.
How curious to want war.

2

An Answer

It isn't our smallness that counts so much as our
size when like tall trees we bend to an idea.

My mind mismatched the questions, like that hallu-
cinated wife who created on herself the wound her
husband bore.   'A bayonet in the belly,' she said,
'scored him.'   She remembered that splendid thing,
the body, the flesh all over.   A red rose on his
belly.

Ah, it is a cold wind to bend to, insisting that a
man fight for his colours in spite of brighter ideas
that shine above the battle—Aphrodite about to
make me Diomede.

But then it takes a knife to open the pomegranate,
the jewelled centre, the ruby-glow of paradise and
promised change.

Changes, if you see them, qualify.   Insist upon the
idea. Grab Proteus and he becomes a snake, an eel,
a bear, a crow.   Touch him, he insists upon changes—
and only a herdsman of seacows.

We ask splendour.   We insist on opposition to clear
the air.   We might cut across the face the president
or prince who makes these battles.   Lop an ear for
retribution.

Sweet princes, remember us for this dissatisfaction.
We told your fortunes in a soldier's entrails
when his gut spilled them.   May your faces change
like the flesh he wore.

It is the wind freezing the rain and the rice pools.
It is the hills burned barren.   It is the dead weather-
ing.

And splendour?   It is as if, in the political action,
in the decision given us, we wore a lion's claw.

And when I pay death's duty
a few men will come to mind
and 1 or 2 objects shine like buttons.

 And when I pay death's duty
my dry mouth will swallow up
                    INDIGNITY
and old hands crack its wedding cup.

And when I pay death's duty, the big question
is what will it feel like with eyes wide open.
It won't be complete darkness because there
isn't any. One thing will stop and that's this
overweening pride in the peacock flesh. That's
a negative definition. More to the point is that
the skin wrinkles and the muscles weaken. And
what I think is that there's a sparrow in an old
man's heart and it flies up—

                                        Thus
in the wrinkling flesh the discovery of disgust.

What is the word for completion.   A steel girder?
A building going up?

And when I pay death's duty
the love I never conquered
when young will end as such.

A 4 Part Geometry Lesson

1   I teach how we cheat the young:
that is,

        to know how tall a tree is
        I must fall from the top;
that is,

        to have caught all this talk
        of eternity, I must stop;
that is,

        desire burns.

2   Now let me give you experience.
Listen carefully to lies.   They
have charm.

        I'm young
you say

        and those words
make me pay

        $10.

            Two words more
and I'll pay 20.

        (If I were 20
I'd say forget decrepitude,
it's more than a mile away.)

3   I would speak for all my skin
that part which is serpentine:
that is,

      now

        you

      sleep

        as
    though

youth

were

   a

    point

    whose

    definition   i

        s

     that

    at

   least

  '2

exist

  and

   2 suffice to de termine

             a

            line

            of

            de

4 That's it. All those dead children.
What calm eyes. A machine gun
tore them out of the ġrass.   velop
        Our eyes
like leaves on aspens twist
       in the wind,   ment'
desire continu
    ING.

     for Sylvia Townsend Warner

Poem

O dark heaven . This chaos
to my ears.

          Men and women cry out.

O chimney-sweep whom Blake
saw conquered.
I have done nothing to ring out.

No sleep.

         Unwritten poems
in humdrum wonder at such pain

is here in Boston streets. Winter
blossoms. Soot specks the snow.
The salted ice is black with shapes
reaching out.

         Lost Nijinski
followed for a guide unhurried drops of blood
in his hallucinated snow.

Recognized, the poor
who wear such multicolor—
all stolen goods,
attachments of the flesh, as leaves—
walk crisply in my frozen arms.

         1957

Herons

I saw cold thunder in the grass,
the wet black trees of my humanity, my skin.

How much love lost hanging there
out of honesty.
                      I catch at those men who chose
to hang in the wind
                    out of honesty.
It is the body lies with its skin—

Robed in my words I say the snake
changes its skin out of honesty.

And they
          hanged there with some symmetry
died young
          like herons proud in their landscape.
Now it is age crept in, nobody younger knows
the quick-darting breath is
our portion of honesty.

For years I've heard
others speak like birds.
                        The words
clicking.
        One day I spoke
articulate
        the words tic-ed
in my throat.
                It was
as if love woke
                after anger.
The words
        sure—
                Listen.
(CHURRR)
        Love wakes
at the breakfast table.
                    (CHURRR)
Not that
        the language itself has wings.
(CHURRR) Not that
                    (CHURRR)
unfortunate skill.
                Listen.
The words
        sure as a scream.

Poem by the Charles River

It is their way to find the surface
when they die.
                        Fish feed on fish
and drop those beautiful bones
                                        to swim.
I see them stretch the water to their need
as I domesticate the separate air to be my
breath.
            These fish die easily.

I find my surface in the way they feed.
Their gathering hunger is a flash like death.
No agony
            as if
                        my mind had eaten death.

Letters to Freud

((*When I*—
                        yes, sleep, Mr Freud.
                                        A crushed dog on West 9th.
Sounds like a man.
                                        Yes
Mr Freud, if—
                        Mr Freud, if—
Oh, damned words. Yes, Mr Freud,
                                        damned descriptive.
My dear Mr Freud, *when I lie in the sun, a bird passes*
over and the wings grow on me.   Yes,
                                Mr Freud
this is
                my image.   I chose—yes, Mr Freud
the wings.   Yes.
                Men.
                Yes . . .

                Mr Freud, *the face of love* . . . Yes,
Mr Freud,
                can be a monument.   Damned words.
Mr Freud—descriptive.
                                Yes, Mr Freud,
there is, Yes, Mr Freud, *a dead dog.*   Yes
on my yes street.   Yes,
                        (spit.)
                                Yes,
                                I killed,
Yes,
        Mr Freud, I chose
                a monument.
                                Well
the dog died when I strangled him.   Yes,
                                Mr Freud—

my dear Mr Freud,
                    I killed.
                                        Well,

Mr Freud,
            he was suffering.))
My dear Mr Freud,
                    I hear perfectly men who suffer for
words.   *Begin a poem.*
                        Death.
                                    Begin a poem.
                                                Death,
you are an image complete as my face.
                                    Continue.
Death, you forbid a better image.
                                    Begin over.
Too much pride in an easy harvest.
My dear Mr Freud,
                    it is consistently a small
victory.
Dear Mr Death,
            I am proud to death.
((Dear Mr Freud,
                    I know a postman.   This message.
Like water, the sound,
                        Mr Freud.   The moon there
is love, is absolute like a planet.   My dear Mr
Freud,
        I mean the flesh,
                        the golden earth.   Yes,
like wheat.   I mean, yes
                        what I have touched.))
My dear Mr Freud,
                    the sound of the earth.   Yes.
Begin a poem.   Light
                    has the sound of a swallow.

My dear Mr Freud,

          Begin over.

                    Words

of the poem.   Man

            in the mind.

                        The moon there

is—

((My dear Mr. Freud,

                A dog is.

                    On West 9th.

I strangled.   *Begin*

            a poem.

                Death.   Yes,

Mr Freud,

          I chose   YES   stopping the sound.

My dear Mr. Freud,

            I'll begin over.))

My dear Mr Freud,

            simply no longer.   *Yes.*   *Light*

yes is after all yes like yes

            an image in flight.

P.S.   yes.

                        9/30/56

The Hunger of Sound

I

I asked a man to consider poetry.
I said
Begin then with this image:
A child's head bends in the light,
slips like a star across a man's mentality.
He and his guardian cat reach for a word.

Among stars, a man becomes a giant.
Take this image:
                    the masked face of a child,
insatiable of light.
                    A word found,
a child's voice—
                    this hunger of gulls
that fish from the broken edge of ice.

The child says, 'Draw me,'
and my hand trembles like a tree
first planted in chaos.
Hear the words sound a child's joy.
    What is uprooted.
Hear the wind howl at a world of exact proportions.
    A shape that was like him.
Hear the sound inhabit the mind,
bells in an orchard.
The words knock against chaos.

How measured a time that childhood,
joy and terror counted like marbles.
Beyond endurance, 10 fingers.
How measured the growth of the limbs upward.
Each word counted. The returning birds
or the new leaves counted.
    On 10 fingers

the flowering peach of the orchard,
each blossom counted and named.
    A child's voice
with the hunger of pigeons,
                        '10,000'

2

A lesson in speech, perhaps.
                        The grasp
d stone.
            A tink in the silence.
We heard it.
            Part of a man
worn away in his clarity.
                        This poem
skin-tight for his black body
                        (white
in the daylight).
            A night sound.
He is not against
                even the chaos.
Bird
        turned up
        shouted out
                wakes him.
                        He
tastes the joy of a flexed tongue.
                        Left
to his own devices,
                speech is given
to the fish of the water
                (in silence, speech)
to the snake by the highway
                (sound in the dry earth).
Decisions, part his

as we teach him
        the household,
           object,
the taste of milk,
     and the returning
breast
   the mind seeks.
As if
The Man unsaid what he should say,
uncertain, kept it simple, direct
and downright, licking stones
to improve their colour.   Not the first time
; as if
The Wife damned his words
out of which came a new sound,
damned the long glass mirror
he could lie upon.

      What to teach
even a boy about
    household objects.
          Red lacquer
flowers—a Persian symmetry—
       on a brass spout.
Or a candy dish,
    gold, with a hanging bird,
green and blue lacquer.
       Both in this house.
They bought him a toy sax
    for a household object.
A lesson in speech,
   perhaps.   A darting tongue
of courage.
   Read Dante without words.
(By Doré.)
   I try now to remember

what I thought of hell.

                          A small head
bent over the big pages.

                        And now
borrowed the terrible trees

                  and
the whole image of Dante.

                        His assertion:
that he did not invent Beatrice.

                     He invented
nothing.

               Bent to return the torn leaves
and cracked bark

             to their wounds.

                     What to teach
                     of bright
bowls, of books, of fire,

               the magic salamander,
that a child may have there sounds stuck
in his growing throat.

                          That
from among the Germans, we chose a whore
to fill her womb with bullets

                          That
we tossed coins.

             (glint in the air)
before we split a man's belly.

                          That
we had courage to stand in sub-zero air
and piss on the machine gun to unfreeze
it   'Tomorrow,'
the child says,

            'take me to the sea.'
A boatman calls,

            'A good catch.
A day's work

and well done.'
Sound
      lapping at edges.
            A hand
on the quick-silver.
          A man
returns each day with his labour.
               What to teach
of the process
         of the unsounded chaos
or the thief of speech.
         From the mouth
a stone has dropped.
         We begin a monument.
Unsaid and uncertain.
         It is time
to begin the alphabet.
         The lesson:
             (if
the mouth blossom)
        words so accurate
of agony
      of chaos
        of joy
          we need not
fear the cat
      will suck the child's breath.
Words
    like our daily bread.
         Words
so sure
      that if stolen
         they will call back:
as if   (the word yelled, caught in the car window)
'A Bread-Bandit,' a first lover,
the wind beginning in the East,

the snake of the morning,
a quick uncurling light
on the body, and this man,
a monument to deeds of men,
hanged bloody now,
hanged here between mornings,
among these deeds
stiff-legged like a heron,
stole bread.

Listen.

3

I asked a man to consider poetry.
He said, 'There is no joy in it.'
I was unsure in these sounds
and unable to knock against chaos.
Across clear sound the boatman sings
like a star in our firmament.
He bends to an outward journey.

I said: there is joy in this image:
10,000 blossoms to one tree in the orchard
counted and named.   The measure of childhood
was how many trees stood shining and white,
stood bare to the rain, naked and wet.
And joy in the small face reflecting
the white surface of the trees.

It was joy to tear at the earth like a scorpion.
The insect blood turned man or child god.
The small face shown   a jewel
or a leaf turning windward.   This child's head
twists.   A broken branch
on the dark wet grass.

I said:

      My emblem became a tree.   Stood
tall and could both bend and straighten.   Rode
on the hills of New Hampshire   a great hunter.
Ice-caught gestures of the trees
turn inward.

This is a gesture. The words stopped
there—part of the forest.
'I, poet,' the man said, and the child
measured his fortune.
                    I said:
It was the damp earth.   Rot
killing the young pines.   Rot
feeding the star flowers.   White cover
of my childhood, like gathering stars.
White rot in the wood.

The words killed there in the blossoming mouth
are uncounted. The light of the body bends over us,
out of the bestial torment,   Dante's head.
The word becomes a star
or the image of a star
or star-fire in our limbs.

A child's head twists in the night
like snakes.
                 'Goodnight.
Your saxophone is by your bed.
Think of starlings and their sharp quick sounds.
            Goodnight.'

for Lars Balas

Quitting a Job

I

Nothing to it. I counted my money. There wasn't much.

I took a cup of wild courage out of the Charles River.
Yellow iris perched like canaries on the shore.

Climb out of the rocks, I said. With thirty-three years,
you have a few left. Whatever the fortune-teller in Chicago
said, you won't die strangled.

The tea leaves sparkle.

O, I expect the joy to last all summer. I'll hang on to it
with a gull's beak.

The hot Boston summer. The sweating thighs. The slow, building
irritation with the wilted people. Streets. Subways. Window-
ledges.

Dusty sparrows dart among the red-legged pigeons, winning bread.

Last week I quit my job. It is a geographical necessity, I said,
to find an image for this century. Crowded. Speechless. I need
time.

Whatever it is. Here, where it isn't, the blue-winged flies are
almost beautiful.

I think of Lawrence's angry poems.

What have they done to you, men of the masses,
creeping back and forth to work!

Ah, the people, the people!
surely they are flesh of my flesh!

2

The dancer completes a turn. Stands waiting to resume.
Rhythmic. Sexual. Begins again on Cambridge Street.

The arms lift away from the body, for balance.
The hands close, breathless, touching the air
as a cat paws at unimagined beasts.

Look at it!
The joy will outlast summer.
I quit my job.
I abolished money.

The moon shines through the straggly body of a
tree of heaven. (They grow out of gutters, drainpipes
among the falling bricks, between vacant
houses.)

The stars are like leaves this summer.
I've tasted their sweat.

I think of Tu Fu's rabbit pounding bitter herbs.
The seeding grass. And yes, this blue (O, inward)
mountain.

1959

Cups 1–12

1959–1960

I

Inside I brought
willows, the tips
bursting,
               blue
iris (I forget
the legend of long life
they represent)
and the branch of pepper tree
whose pink seeds
lack the passion of most fruit.

On my hands a perfume of pepper.

Outside the rain walks.

There were two.
Their posture
taken out of the wall-
paper (a ghost story)
Jack talked.   His
determined privacy against
my public face.   The poem
by dictation.   A
disturbance in the cone
of weather.
                    Neither of these
is not making.   The comic
is a matter of style
as yellow hands mark the worker.

The clown of dignity sits in a tree.
The clown of games hangs there too.
Which is which or where they go—
the point is to make others see
that two men in a tree is clearly
the same thing as poetry.

2

The window washer
returns,
stepping out of his shame.
He was not rich.

There, in the dark window
the African bus-driver
unfolds the black petals
of that season.

Across town.   Out.
Sacramento
into the bargain.   The surface
is only manhood.
If he does not masturbate,
the promise is a second chance.

There were two.   They both fell down
into the clover where love abounds.
One imagined an African king.
The other, divers treasures
without being rich.
The poem they gathered
was made of four leaves.
1 for the lip of Amor's crown.
1 for the tree they ran around.
1 for the bed where they lay down.
1 for the comical physical union
their arms like briars
wrapped around.

3

Unnamed objects.   The fear
dispersed like the sound
of angry peacocks.

The white ones.   So still
in the aviary.

We opened the rock.   This
time I saw the god
offer with out-stretched hand
the heart to be devoured.   The
lake flowed into my hands.
Dante would say the lake
of the heart.

Two men sit in a tree
and wink and spit.
Now this is the tree
where Amor sits.
He gave them each
a trinket of flesh.
The rules, he sighed,
are in the wrinkled grass
when the wind goes by
seeking itself or jealousy.

One imagined two small windows
cut in his skin.   His breasts
look out upon the tree.
The other thought the shape
of his tongue was poetry.

The word, he said,
drawn like an arrow,
so fits
into the body of the bird it hits.

4

The shadow of the fish lies
among the rocks.   The
shadow of the sagebrush
turns the hill blue.   The
shadow of the mountain
includes all strangers.

 (The strangulations will appear
in the brush fire.)

The coyotes, burned out of their lairs,
follow the railroad.   Shapes
of poems
                fly out of the dark.

The tree spoke: Love is not love.
Imagine your first stupor.   The
effort to untie the strings
of the loins. The lips endure
the semen of strangers.
                                It is spring
when the shadow of willows is gone.

5

The intensities
of these branches
of willow
open.

What is it
broke the skin?

How lovely
that jewel
of under the skin.

Neither dark nor light
is my true love.

The blood whose beauty crosses
the hand like money
will fight for that true love.

6

Two milk goats tied
to the wheels of the chuckwagon
(here, so far from water
tank trucks bring it in).

He joked that the sheepherder
must use goats for a lover.

I have lain back
and imagine my father.

The hands dip out of the water
the shell or sperm dropped
there in passing.

Two men sit in a tree.
How ugly they are
in the bright eye
of this pageantry.
In service to love
is dignity, one cried,
1, 2, 3, the other replied,
you're out
when the dew falls from imagination's dark.

Amor turned geometer,
briefly, of course,
and cut their bodies into triangular parts.
When reassembled
they hung in that tree,
their genitals placed
where their heads should be.

7

Today, we lost both horses
though they were hobbled.

Two milk goats
tied to the wheels of the chuckwagon
where we came riding a water truck.

 (I have lain back and imagine my father.
He joked that the sheepherder must choose
one goat with a finer pelt than the rest
for a lover.)

This year the herds move
far out into the sagebrush
toward the foothills.
Suddenly, the aspens,
like herds themselves,
fill the gullies.   This
is the darker blue
you see from the highway.

The dew fell from imagination's dark
on to our hands where it stuck like bark.
The wheels of your heart, Amor cried,
roll around the edge of the fire.
You might imagine, in service to love,
your hands dip out of the water
the shell or sperm, dropped there in passing
by some *ashen likeness*.
                    And higher
he seemed than this dark tree
and brighter burned his pageantry.

8

There is no salutation.   The
harvesters with gunny sacks
bend picking up jade stones.

(Sure that Amor would appear
in sleep.   Director.   Guide.)

Secret borrowings fit into their hands.

Cold on the tongue.
White flecks on the water.

These jade pebbles are true green
when wet.

On the seventh night, the branches parted.
                        The other replied,
How photographic.   Amor doesn't appear
on demand.   He's more like a snake skin.
If he fits, he lets you in
or sheds your body against the rocks.

                        I slept in a fort.
My bed pushed up against the log
enclosure.   At 3:00 his ankles pressed
against each side of my head.
When I woke crying for help
he rose near the kitchen door
dressed as a hunter.

                        The other replied,
Amor born like a cup trembles
at the lip.   Superstitions fit
into your hands.

Thou has returned to thy house.

                  The other replied,
Torn loose from the eaves,
the blood trembles at the lips.

Nine fetters on thy feet
Nine crossings of the street

Nine suppers where they meet
Nine words of loss repeat
this and that

Nine hunters cross the field
Nine lovers yield
their right of way

Two came fighting out of the dark.

9

The sour smell of laundry day.
The steamed-up windows,
initialed and etched.

Saving electricity, only the kitchen
at the back lights up,
a shaft across the congoleum
where the Persian pattern
departs from real leaves.

Briefly, the car lights
follow the water drops.
The desert returns
through the shiny glass.

So he stretched for the pear tree
branch.   It was the flower
before the fruit.

Upon that tree there was a ring.
HI   HO   HUM
The ring surrounded the darkest part.
HA   HA   HA
The ring imagined a marriage bout.
FIRE   FIRE   FIRE

Out on the pond, the striders
wander.
                And yonder the sour
bush.

10

High on stilts, the black water tank
leaks.   A pond rises by the railbed.

The tracks sing, they say,
meaning the beat and whirr
the steel carries.

Willows, starwort,
water striders appear in the desert.

The telegrapher's key between thumb
and fingers.   The message
held up to the speeding train
on a willow hoop.

Amor entered disguised as grass.   You both
hoped your seed would fall among the roots
of this tree and there grow up a second tree
and guardian.

WHAT IS THAT WRINKLES UNDER THE ROOT?

SKIN, SEMEN, AN ARM AND A FOOT.

11

The wheat goes unharvested.
The spears broken.

Uncle Mitch wrote westerns.
His sentences broken.   He
liked to whistle between fragments.

There was a large bell which
rang out—the stockade
protected—until what history
calls the Mountain Meadow
Massacre—Black Hawk
died in our house, stabbed
in his savage belly—
Aunt Celestia sat down
with the Indians—the
feast at our table—
the rain—the salt—
falling against the horses—
it was too dark—they
ride out hunting—the bell
rang—
the stockade grew in our hearts—
supperless—we hid
in the brush—the colour
of raspberries—the fire
consumed—

The rider who leads us out ♩♩♩
stops midway ♩♩♩ the flank
of his horse caught fire ♩♩♩♩
discovered their nests ♩♩♩ bunched
and tangled the rattlesnakes ♩♫♩
curled at the edge ♩♩♩
you ride for the dark ♩♪♩♩♩

Where Amor sits, the body renews itself,
twists ♩♩♩ ♩♩♩ ♩♩♩ ♩♩

inhabits the rights of poetry.

1 2

The turbulence.   Replies.
The dark picked up,
deposited.
              A sediment
like what one knows
is there under the starwort.

Plus cuts on the hands
from gardening and such
other grasping
                        as fits
this season.

You take the far side
of the street from the bus-stop
Geary and Presidio
following the car lights,
shop-windows, street-lamps.

So that.   A path emerges
without the necessary guide.

          The breath stutters
in limbs where Amor swings.

The realism he's after cheats and sings.
He drops the steel scales of his body down
where one eye out, the lover turns
round and round.

The Muse requires a politics
where the tongue meets
in the thick of it
the sour sweat.
The milk of her breasts

divides again and again
among the thyrsus bearers
and then among those who wear the hue
of her nipples.   The initiates are few
but they stamp on the ground
where her skin has fallen.

What falls from the tree
renews itself in the guise
of poetry.
                    The guide
rides out of the dark
with a body shaped
from the sluffing bark.

The Park

1960

The Park

Cleo on the Section Gang
75 miles of railroad   Checking
the ties   Repairing the washouts

More than one animal

Duplications tick in the leaves
like insects
sucking the bitter green

The male womb
which links our bodies
in brutal imagination

Cleo swears
                the god-damned rabbits
mate with the sagebrush

Nearly no sound at all

•

The whir of traffic identifies a city
It is night out

The rain starts   A musical
plucking at the windows

I have allowed the stream
of traffic to end here
(Lost River) at my table
where lost,
            I was hunted

Evidence   Footsteps
on the muddy bank
at the edge

Event   The river
flowed into a cave,
disappeared, except for a field
of water-filled pits
where he walked, testing
the grass before each step

A salutation
Obedient to the garden
Out of the spines of that black
flowering tree,
the night noises

•

The soft step is
only the possibility
of entrance
at the door

I am framed
as in a box at the play
Around   Around   Around
To look out   Lookout
Abstractions
(beyond my capacity
to write)
          stop striking
The clock
          Around

So much for what it is
in the heart
steps back

•

He follows   The bird endures
what the bird sings

Between two gates,
The garden   That turn
to the left where the pale

yellow wisteria is falling,
surprisingly

Though it is not the body
attaches there in its quick
movements a what-next
the deed pities my hand
Follow!   And you did
take the next turn,
                              surprising
the water that fell from your fists,
dropped to your thighs,
and were only tokens of a loud knocking

•

Around us, the city imagines
the tourists   The guide books
are full of facts
                              The fountains
play on Monday and Wednesday

A light of desire among
the monuments,

                    wet to the skin

•

She went down cellar to get
the ham (larder, she called
it) but stopped on the last
step and held up her right arm
so the bull snake could come
down off the rafter to greet us
(she said)   She liked to describe
the pull of its body on her skin
Its nature (she said) was to pull
tightly in friendship

•

She beat on the floor with her stick
until I came   She said 'Sing'   Which
I did   She commented that my voice
was thin, but I had enough silliness to
amount to (hesitation) a poet   Old
lady whose false breasts were made of
cambric stuffed with cotton and hung
around her neck on a ribbon, kept a
goldfish bowl full of life-savers to
sweeten the sour breath she was aware of

•

She bent over the drinking fountain
one hand poised to turn the
cock
　　　　and there she remained
(caught up)
until we noticed and called an
ambulance

•

Sights float on the ponds

•

True and false, two sparrows,
chittering,
　　　　fall down the side of the building,
stems of ivy breaking their descent,
locked beaks,
　　　　　then fly up
in the nick of time

•

The idiot gathered her aprons
from the clothes line　　The
wind shaking the sumac,
planted for an 18th birthday,
breaks the red plumes

Crack   (The burned
letters of the alphabet)
We wake hurt,
the sight of ourselves too much
the pattern

Wake up!   The birds dive at the trees,
true enemies of their shapes

Awake   Sophia Nichols says

we are using all this electricity which
escapes upward, gathering to destroy
the world

Telephone   'Many happy returns'   (true
turns of the light, she meant)

•

(Tincans smashed around the heels of our shoes
High heels

(Bill took out the atlas and began to divide
   the world between us   General William Halley
   England, the Americas, Russia   he used his
   own name, so I kept mine, but added Duc of
   Orleans because I held France, China and Africa

(We gave the imaginary kingdoms to the late
   comers   Mu, Atlantis, the Arctics

(Then I held power in a vacant lot where I
   built a tunnel dedicated to their sex play

(Then I built a tunnel in a vacant lot dedicated to history

(where their sex play held power

•

The oath between us
for 1 hour
        to see
nothing that did not appear
in the water

The male womb here caught up
in the beloved sight,
passes quickly over the surface,
darkens among the water plants,
the goldfish more golden
                but 'you'
will form in
          the bell
          We timed
this oath

•

From a high shelf
above the books of pedigree
the clock chimes

Someone called out
against this photographic proof
of ancestors

A flight of sparrows
suddenly drops into a nearby tree
disappearing, though its shape
darkens

a sudden or violent display (of joy,
        delight, etc.

Jessie Whitehead told me they sometimes choose a tree
and kill it, they so mire the branches

The Faerie Queene

1961

An Appearance

Okay   A nightingale
does sing
        outside this window

A mirror of leaves and noise

          This monument
has torn to pieces our guide book
of facts
        This startles

A nightingale,
        the bird so ancient
he (anybody)
        falls back
on his dusty shoes, pointing

The event darkens   So like
our trembling,
        we caught at it
breaking the skin

Metamorphoses

I burn 'your' magnificence in the streets
It is paper

The gods written on paper flare up
suddenly
        in a turn taken up the alley

I turn away from the stars,
roll over,
          it is that falls out of my eye
a pearl of great price
             no tear
The same with the flakes of mica,
                desiring
the tree stands before me of what name

So

.

You speak against the mundane
which is for instance
the sidewalk

and, I suspect, the gods
severed and loose
like architectural adornments

The word means
                worldly
but requiring the mundus

Gloria Swanson used one image to reappear
in the imagination
                the claw,
and Garbo chose white to show that death
works at the convenience of the lady of the
camellias, thus saving Robert Taylor for
later movies—in white flannels, the college
hero out on the town
                I suppose you think the
plots were about Norma Desmond and Mme. Gauthier

You missed the structure they personified

where Dionysus lay sleeping against
the corner stone

the wall broke into pieces of glass

Again and again

I saw myself about to wake him

From a Fortune-Cooky

He is practicing a speech before the glass

There is a slight wind
bitter on the tongue
An image trembles
or floats as in water
The dismemberment happens
like rain against the sidewalk

What rules
is a twist of light

In the arms of these railroads,
no music
               discovers us

The Sphinx

A honk and broken sounds

Rain spills lights
against the window
They have a brief life
of their own

faced into

A rayed machine is before me
devouring my labour   This much,
a dream wherein I read the next morning
that many carry the wands

I am to ask a question
where no question exists

Who stops among the leaves
of this tree I'm married to
in Roman fashion?
                    I piss
into the roots of my love
where words break true

For Gustave Moreau

The streets are my body
or rather the wish
of the skin to put on
the grass in a gold rain

not vice-versa,
the lips twisting to allow
the tongue to play in
the broken mirror on the floor
Catches an arm
a distance
         the light
at the ceiling
           This kills
the lift begged
of a magical hand

I have walked a long way
traced in these pieces
an arm
a crotch   The queen
of faerie guarded
by blue-winged griffins

Untouched by

The Moth Poem

1962–1964

for H.D.

A Literalist

the root and mirror
of a plant
           its shape
and power familiar
iris

the light is disturbed by
the boxwood leaves
shining
            rosemary
green, unblossoming
(the earth is too damp)

the eye catches
almost a tune

the moth in the piano
wherein
           unhammered
the air rings with

an earlier un
ease of the senses
disturbed (by Mrs. Arpan,
wife of a sailor

The Literalist

the wind does not move on
to another place

bends into,
as in a mirror,
                    the
breaking

the moth in the piano
will play on
frightened wings brush
the wired interior
of that machine

I said, 'master'

Between

the morning face of
turns you who
turn

          a complete
interior furniture
flecked with
the children
of the moth
          how
loud you are
against glass

the strings of / play on

this
    that
        now scattered

The Borrower

the one loved is
holding a moth
thin, metallic dark
model with a triangular
crest

what's out and secret
spills
the wind dries
moves on

           the interior
of his body
              red water
with white threads
                 the bone
a ghost of his thigh
                pale
blue gut holding the shit

highway

Awake

in the dark morning you are circled
by loss of sleep you lean forward
from the balcony to see the moth
dying in the window swept by
still wings

loose pieces of air fall
cold and catch your eyelids

the words don't fit you

your back is a mirror your
hand a bowl holding the musical
moth

Supper Guest

leaning over the white
linen which casts

a pale light
over his face,

we are not deprived
the white bowl

must shine
behind our words,

leave us
in a fire of clouds

the tin flowers
the castles

which drift out
of our mouths

whitely
in the cold air,

fantômes
de sentiments

magic juices
on the eyelids,

so it is
what is met

a white moth carries its moth-body
trying the way into corners

The Medium

it is essentially reluctance the language
a darkness, a friendship, tying to the real
but it is unreal

the clarity desired, a wish for true sight,
all tangling

'you' tried me, the everyday which
caught me, turning the house

in the wind, a lovecraft the political
was not my business I could not look

without seeing the decay, the shit poured
on most things, by indifference, the personal

power which is simply that,   demanding a friend
take dullness out of the world (he doesn't know
his lousy emptiness)   I slept
in a fire   on my book bag, one dried wing

of a white moth   the story is of a man
who lost his way in the holy wood

because the way had never been taken without
at least two friends, one on each side,

and I believe my dream said one of the others
always led   now left to acknowledge,

he can't breathe, the darkness bled
the white wing,   one   of the body

of the moth that moved him, of the other
wing,   the language is bereft

O-friend

it was time you came
this night   you were NO

man attached to his opposite,
seen through a gate   or handed

his hat   you were as held
in a vase   orange calendula

and hot pink geraniums in blue
glass   that tropism

made you laugh   and the room,
is it possible you do not exist

separate from that glow
when I turned the flashlight

on the door?   who is there
who came dragging his

bag of tears? and remained
invisible   the whine is

not in me is not part
of the moth who escapes

the cold in my electric
blanket   I suppose

I heard the dark and
with the craft wrought

against memory, it should
have been of no consequence

but the bones breathe,   that
frame of what is contained,

opposites   the Sorrows sit
nearby surely,   cracking

their paws   once,   the I
came on the Lady Bugs' home

at the foot of a redwood
they swarmed in heaps

their shells and loosened wings
flew in the wind of my steps

and once, Proteus, the goldfish,
jumped out of his bowl,   left

the colour of dried orange peel
and so it is a turn of the wheel

you left   a kind of music,
la-de-da   and stink

in the air   held close
with the invisible rose,

O-imaginarie-in-knowledge

Invisible Pencil,

one does not willingly take the honey
sweet plant,   the words are lost, the
holy language simultaneous with this speech

and flatteries, this participation in mirrors,
turns from the streets of some minds
one follows another man who kissed his shadow

now a moth flies overhead to the floorlamp,
stops my reading the *Death of Virgil*,
form fixed and mute,   one element

participates in his travels
more than another,   watery source
as if the hometown river flowed

into the room and out of the heart

Atlantis

draws back from the shine on the water,
the crumbling pieces flow unattached

the cement patches, the fit of the dark
streets around the towers   the wet

touches   spring a trap in personal
history,   interior, riotous   smokers

of poetry bathe among the ruins,
slip off the rocks,   green and

waking with weeds of the sea
the technical movement is made

by the water harp   in *moth-time*
the waves lift the bunched-up

newspaper, full of foam,   then
looking up, I see it run back, *defecate*

to a pure transparency,   the castles,
the lighted cliffs

Atlantis

the light of it, as he felt himself perish,
the *riotous moth,*   back and forth

there is a spilled glass of water, an ocean
spreading on the table

under the shine on the water, the pieces
flow, unattached   it will be that

horseplay the mouth takes for milk,   the
fit of the rivers around the books,

ashtrays, yellow apple and pomegranate
here   the web falls, sticky,   holding

the forehead   the apparent violence
bathed in,   a key to this privacy

he leaned over his poem   a piece
of blood fell out of his head   dazzling

clock sounds, the riotous moth, happiness
and this habit of light   *the sad soul*

wanders about a spirit like an image
this image enters the ghost
                              ly sent iment

My Dear—

        we end with you
circling your garden, allowing
the officials to lead you in,
trivial and cheap at Gump's,
the worthless mention of Snellgrove,
Pomeroy, Hack divided, phony last
suppers, démodé drips on the California
landscape, fake spooks in the upper
right hand corner of the orange machine,
brief agony for the dining room wall
at a price,   you, coming to
ignore this language

which is coloured, takes in slime, is
some centre where one is helpless
even to oneself,   flowers of the mouth,
it is smoke, alive only in the
car lights,   is stationary,

considered as paint full of secrets   flows,
still on the wall like a moth   until
it is pushed, then separating

with an outward stammer, officially
immortal,   to feed itself,   the final
thing
        somebody else's idea

Paradise Quotations

the stairs did not creak, but the snow did
I fixed the telescope and looking through I saw
a stag
         on the way back I saw the traces
of blood, but no longer believed in their
existence

first in translucent lymph with cobweb-threads
the Brain's fine floating tissue swells, and spreads

the marble hand probably from its contact
with the uncharmed harp, had strength to
relax its hold and yield the harp to me

nerve after nerve the glistening spine descends
the red Heart dances, the Aorta bends

the white rose of Eddy-foam, where the stream
ran into a scooped or scalloped hollow of the
Rock in its channel   this Shape, an exact
white rose, was for ever overpowered by the
Stream rushing down in upon it, and still
obstinate in resurrection it spread up into
the Scallop, by fits and starts, blossoming
in a moment into a full Flower

through each new gland the purple current glides,
new Veins meandering drink the refluent tides

for here would be the moonbeams on the ice,
glittering through a warrior's breastplate
   whenever a breeze went by, it swept the old
men's heads, the women's beauty, and all the
unreal throng, into one indistinguishable
cloud   ever-anxious crowd

edge over edge expands the hardening scale,
and sheathes his slimy skin in silver mail

it   it   it   it

a white shadow there on the glass,
the white T-shirt   turns that

are no longer an end
less meaning   leans forward to the

shaping, to find it, a flutter of the
darkness, but it ducks back

from the open slit of the window,
a cinnamon moth enters
and amorous, the lamp takes
it   came from the back

garden planted with pale flowers
that might show in the dark it
mocked, tripped, then toted its
image, having no past, unprepared

the *moth-kiss* has two languages,
the one everyday, dusty, habitual,
and part delight, the other
an *unexpended myth* washes against

the glass, to be abstract, untied
by the friendship,   the moment caught

Salut

you, priest, must know why you strike

tearing, teasing in that silly personality
if you fell, it is the rain falling down
the hanging pot of ivy, each leaf a-light
the grass of my eyes holding to a point,
the dew,   the spring

the piano, it was a gift, a promise of a debt
of music it was a moth under the strings,
frantic to escape, played
    wings eyed like an owl came to the lamp

the cold has come, the moths have gone,
white, grey, cinnamon and one rested
in the sun, wine purple wings, yellow
edged, tacked with the wind's changes,
careened, then, taking flight, hid
in the fig tree

the circles the moon, the stars, the
planets and below, under the earth, the sun
between the earth and the moon, a tone
beyond that, the lyre

asleep, the four oval paintings, stories alive,
the artist of the moth, his foot upon the lion's
paw of the table there is no storm in the
glass, only the white edge of a sleeve, the
form, nothing beyond that I   I

further asleep, there are petunias, white, red,
rose and night, zinnias, red, violet, orange, roses,
silver and yellow, nasturtiums, yellow, pansies, blue,
hollyhocks, pastel and waxy, violets, lilacs, sumac,
castor-bean flowers, flags, purple, white, brown

what is the day, what is the charm, she, her
madness, yours, musical poplars, the mind
nearly destroyed by the presences, the fine
points which have no beginning

restless jewels she is from the light on the rails,
a-light running miles to a point she is
in the house, an old railroad coach placed
on foundations by the railbed among golden-rod
and hop vines she stands in the middle
of the room with arms outstretched, to protect
the bat, which caught, brown and velvet, she
puts to her breast against the yellow apron

this flower which is no flower this new
land the day filled with invisible princes,
Dr. Dolittle, the moon, the flow of rain
lighting the ivy there is no meaning here,
there is all meaning here Fran and Stan
laughing, the blue glass is $9.00, the Houssin
lsadora Duncan, looking more like Rodin's Balzac
is $350 there is nothing here but an intense,
interior monologue with moments of colour, forms
flowing toward beloved plants the cost has
been high   when all the world is loved by the
daimon of mediocrity,   you, unpriestly, among
hierarchs on fire   burned mouth

must know why you strike

C

D

$\flat$E

G

A

$\flat$B

B

D

The Translator: A Tale

first, the pool of water just waking my arms hold
it the circle of the cold morning air

last night's coffee spoon sticks to the drainboard
under it the clear print of a brown moth, made of sugar,
cream, coffee with chicory, and a Mexican spoon of blue
and white enamel

The ashtray is full and should be emptied before working
that translation, *Attis ran to the wooded pastures*
of the weavers of gold, the shadowy place, where as if a
bee stung his brain, he took a flint knife and let the
weight of his cock and balls drop from him, so

when she felt her limbs lose their manhood, still with
fresh blood spotting the ground, she grabbed the drum
with snowy hands, beating the polished hide with soft
fingers, she rose to sing to her companions

the mound of cigarette butts moves, the ashes shift,
fall back on themselves like sand, startle out of
the ashes, awakened by my burning cigarette, a brown
moth noses its way, takes flight

Image-Nations 1–4

1962–1964

Image-Nation I (the fold

the participation is broken
fished from a sky of fire
the fiery lake pouring itself
to reach here

that matter of language caught
in the fact   so that we
meet in paradise   in such
times, the I consumes itself

white trees, rings around them,
wander and roll, the fog breaks,
the sky, blue in the window

sits up there, out of reach
hand full of *beautifuls-uglies,*
justs-unjusts,   halves-doubles,
pull the strings,   I saw the cat

the births begin on the bed,
shaped as it is
by a god,   four kittens
when they are there
she comes to his feet

picked up and held, she
fills his hand with blood
the red pool flows over
his silver ring,   drips
to the floor

the language sticks to
his honey-breath   she is
the path of a tale, a door
to the perishing moonshine,
holes of intelligence
supposed to be in the heart

Image-Nation 2 (roaming

we are journeying in company with the messenger

      but there, it was
there   'you' saw
the head of a horse burn,
its red eye flame   'you' stepped
to the fireplace where the meta-
morphosed log lay without a body
and put 'your' hand over the seeing

turned by that privacy
from such public perils as words
are, we travel in company with the messenger

the name of the bird who fell
from the hands of O-moon
is Naught   if following
angels, shaped tears, nourished by
Sodom apples, we draw darkness,
a kind of mud   (in the moonlight
white blossoms hastening to fall
are cut free)

then we, the apparatus, burned by a night
light, are travelling in company with the messenger

Image-Nation 3 (substance

what if the body goes   the sense
of the word which draws amor
in a body his arrows leafless, shining
steel his meaning in that meeting of
hands, tastes, bitter
filling fountain if that language goes
whose power drank from the body, gave
the body, gave amor a skin,

an act, the worshipped height higher
than what is left
another amor inescapable pouring, holding
that shape here together   all ways,

born through all the elements, the night
singing sparrows are arrows   I define
the dark correct   allowing that I to appear
naked, an unyielding form of I   acting apart,
but it is Naught   the other is that   unlearned,
this fear and charm of words   O shepherd, his way apart,
flower and youth   with an arrow offshot

Image-Nation 4 (old gold

a visit to the Longs
who run the pump house, stoke
its fires, spread the ashes

over a field to burn out
this is a surface of the moon
black and crusted   we ran

out on it, calling
'you're it,' jumped   rang with
laughter, the crust broke, his

bare feet slipped into the burning
coals beneath, what's-his-name,
the mystery that in winter the

snow did not remain in this
place, a black garden, the
surface of the moon, now explained

(Ella Cinders) it is a crust
of cinders over the red coals, a
banked fire over which no Snow

caught her hair   if you walk
unwary, your feet slip into the
fire   of strawberries

Cleo, nearby, picks up agates and
moonstones between railway ties,
works at his wheel to polish and open

well, when the whole place was mud,
a part of it froze in with the
sunset, and these shadows were

only curls in the mud, but
the moonstone   that's a piece
of the cheese fell out of the moonstream

Les Chimères

versions of Gérard de Nerval

1963–1964

for Fran Herndon

The Shadow

I am the Darkness   the Widowed   the Unconsoled,
the Prince of Aquitaine in his broken tower,
my only Star is dead   and my lustrous lute
carries a melancholy black sun

in the night of Death, You who consoled me,
give back the high hill above the Mediterranean,
the flower which pleased my desolated heart so much,
and the arbor where the vine branch unites with the rose

am I Amor or Apollo?
my forehead is still red from the Queen's kiss
I have dreamed in the Grotto where the Siren swims

I have crossed Acheron twice,   a winner,
modulating the sighs of a saint and the cries
of a fairy   turn by turn   on Orpheus' lyre

Myrtho,

I think of the bewitchment
on that hill   without care
shining with a thousand fires,
your forehead overflowing
with eastern lights,
and black grapes
mixed with your golden hair

it is in your wineglass also
that I drank drunkenness,
and in the secret brightening
of your eye when you saw me
worship at the feet of Dionysus,
for Poetry made me a son of Greece

I know why the volcano over there
reopened   only yesterday
you touched it with your quick foot,
and suddenly the sky was clouded
with ashes

since a Norman duke smashed
your gods,
the woody vine with the pale flowers
which do not bear
twines around the green myrtle
with the dark berries
under Virgil's branches of laurel

Horus

the god Kneph's trembling
shook the universe:
then, the mother rose up
on her bed,   Isis,
moved with hatred
toward her savage husband,
and the old fire
burned in her green eyes

she spoke   'Look at him,
this volcanic god and king
of winter is dying,
this old corruption'
she ordered his crooked feet bound
and his crossed-eyes put out
she said   'All the world's cold
passed through his mouth'

she said   'Just now
the eagle flew by   the new
ghost calls me
I put on the robe of Cybele
for him,   the son
loved by Hermes and Osiris'

the goddess fled
in a golden shell
the sea reflected
her image,
the sky shone
under the scarf of Iris

Anteros

you ask why there is rage in my heart
and an untamed head
on a neck that could bend:

because I descend from Antaeus,
I turn the arrows back
against the winning god   yes,

the Requiter breathes on me
he marked my forehead
with his angry lips

I sometimes feel the unquenched
redness of Cain
under Abel's pallor
the paleness is stained

the last defeated by your genius,
God, cried out from the pit
of hell against your power
he is my forebear Belus
or my father Dagon

they dipped me three times
in the waters of Cocytus
    protector
of my plundering mother,
    on my own
I sow again at her feet
the teeth of the old dragon

Delfica

do you understand this old ballad
at the foot of the sycamore,
or under the white laurels,
do you know it, Daphne,
beneath the olive, the myrtle,
or the trembling willows,
this love-song which always
begins again?

do you recognize the Temple
with huge columns,
and the sour lemons
when you bit them,
the cave hiding an unexpected
end, part of the tale of the dragon's
seed?

you shed tears over returning ghosts
we read the sound of an earthquake
for signs

so, the sybil with dark skin
is asleep under the Arch of Constantine
    nothing has troubled the cold gate

Artemis

the Thirteenth returns
still the first
and she is always the only one—
or this is the only moment
but are you queen,
'you', the first and last
are you king
'you', the only or the last lover

love him who loved 'you'
from the cradle to the grave
the only one I loved
loves me dearly still
she is death—or the dead one,
delight torment,
the rose she holds
is the rose-pink hollyhock

Saint of Naples with hands full of fires,
or Rose with a heart of purple,
or Saint Gudula's flower,
did you find your cross in the sky's desert?

I want the white roses to fall
they attack our gods
I want these white phantoms to fall
from their burning sky
    the saint of the abyss is holier in my eyes

Christic among the Olives

god is dead! The sky is empty
weep, children, you no longer have a father
     —Jean-Paul

I

under the holy trees,
the Lord lifted his thin arms
to the sky,   as poets do
after the silence
and the loss of his friends'
belief

he turned toward those
who waited below,   lost
in animal sleep,   dreaming
of themselves as kings,
wisemen, prophets,   but deadened
he began to call,   God
does not exist

they slept

have you heard the news?

I touched my forehead
to the eternal arch
here, sick, broken
and stained for many days
I cheated you in this
abyss, god is missing
from the altar with its victim
God isn't
God is never again

they always slept

2

he began again:
everything is dead
I've wandered over worlds
and lost my flight
in their milky ways
as far as
inventive life bleeds
gold and silver

everywhere the dry ground
bordered by waters
whirlpools stir
the stormy oceans,
a faint breath pushes
the roaming spheres,
but no ghost exists
in this largeness

seeking the eye of God
I saw only a socket,
huge, black and bottomless
where night which inhabits it
sends rays over the world
and always thickens

a strange rainbow
encircles this darkness
door-sill of the old chaos
whose shadow is the emptiness,
a spiral swallowing
the Worlds and the Days

3

you, the fixed End of it,
the mute sentinel,
the cold Necessity,   Chance,
who advances among dead worlds
under everlasting snow,
who chills the whitening universe,
bit by bit,

do you know what you're doing
with your burnt-out suns,
Beginner,
are you sure to transmit
an immortal breath
between one world which dies
and another being born

father, is it you inside me
can you live and conquer death
or have you given up
in a last battle

with that night-time angel
whom the curse struck
        this Myself

the tears and sickness,
    if I die,
everything will die

4

no one heard the grief of the sacrifice,
the sacrificed pour his heart out
to the world vainly
weakening and stooped
he called the only one
awake in Jerusalem

you know the price
they put on me,
sell, and end this bargaining
I have a sickness
here on the world
you have the strength
of a crime, at least,
    in friendship

Judas went away,
brooding and malcontent,
discovered himself poorly paid
for such biting back
when he read his trick
written everywhere on the walls

only Pilate,
who sat watching for Caesar,
turned by chance
and feeling some of it,
ordered his satellites
to find the fool

5

it really was this fool
a madman above us
forgotten Icarus climbing
the sky again
the charioteer destroyed
by lightning
a lovely, murdered Atys
brought back by Cybele

the magician questioned
the entrails of the victim
the earth became drunk
on the precious blood
the unmoved universe
bent on its axes
the gods began to die
for an instant

Caesar called Jupiter Ammon
to answer this new god
forced on the earth—
at least a daimon—
but he invoked
a closed oracle
only one in the world
could open the hiding place
    who gave souls
      to the children of the slime

Golden Poem

everything is alive
   —Pythagoras

free of the dead,
what can be thought
seems to be yours in this world
where it *all coheres*
free to spend some powers,
but the universe is absent
from all your plans

take the ghost stirring
in an animal   each
flower, a piece of light
scattering love's mystery
asleep in metal   alive
the coherence takes power
over you

in the blind wall, you fear
the blindness which sees you
even to matter,   put to
true and false uses,
a word is tied

often, a secret god exists
in the darkness
and like an eye born
with the lids closed,
a real ghost comes to be
under the surface of the stones

Charms

1964–1968

for Stan Persky

Psyche,

the sorrow is sharp
one plays on innocence
the harp silences

'you can pull them up
by their boot-straps'   they
will themselves into your life
the will takes them   a love
at first sight

                        you
have joined the thousand songs
the measure is the step over
the abyss, your love, which would
have eaten them up   they
refused

                about this,
you're cantankerous   the dull
charge of importation   as if
their words hadn't come
from outside   and your

cheapness   elegance of feeling
is a trick
                nothing
can be taken back
                    and
there is nothing on your lips

you live by the round about
between true light and
scattered brightnesses without
knowing the different sounds
of a new house   your false
sleep was to watch over
his shapeless love   in the dark
of his bed you looked for
some cinch, some way to live
entangled and closed in heat
you were even to yourself
an ancient face   preening
before mirrors of comfort
the silent feathers of peacocks,
unangered   among willows
and sharpnesses

in the piecemeal   in the partitions
you could not know his face

Translation

The ash
came from Mt. St. Helens
They all fell
as by the same wind
Rooted in springs
the stone-filled trunks
stretch out

or an oak grows
from the rock bark

I turn   to the fire
on the manzanita branches
where the bees light

buzzing   beside the prehistory

of the ghosts of young
cherry trees,
there is an appearance
on the way back

Winter Words

O fountains, where the throat
is a silent partnership,   part of

the folklore of birds,
the news is

these sorrows
on a dream tree

rigged and actual

(the diaries of friendships
   have almost won a nest for themselves

   the life in art fashions itself,
   returns, gazes upon the traffic

(has the cold caught
   my hand in the game

   torn

an invisible entertainment
somehow
falls upon all things

The Stories

our suppers stunned on the table
hold radios
                hold
flasks of sound,
                      sharp intensities
bottled up for a time

I taste your imagination, authors,
and place it among cotton trees
whose white stuff perches,

cousins of the air

if the manner could be political
the high walls protect against disgust

the lady of blue glass
                      joined by
Pierrot, a griffin,   papers, books,
the chilled correspondence,   and
another woman whose futurist shape
suggests lines of the wind

on my desk

to awaken
the traffic would have to run into the radio

In a Dark

the drive to the spring mountains
rising out of the vineyards, now
yellow with mustard

within a room
the lost quiet of stiff peach trees

the white buildings must be miles back
with invisible windows

where secret birds fall

The Prints

the snail paths glistening underfoot
lead anywhere

                      some other
distance put the story down

of a prince who, tired
of his nobility,
found the cupboards offered
sweet companionship

open and shut

                        'we
take up where left off
all flowers and short steps
among the trees'

the marvellous we had lost
came back   arms,
stone, bristling hair bend
toward the start

Love

the water moved the
false stars

the forest which is
also a wall and a city

is claimed by *specialists*
in *ecstasy,*   short of breath

is obscured by oppositions
of that louder voice

so we move
easily numb to a dark

reading
                a wing
that is alone

                    a black
which traditional sights
like teeth
and old tales   give up   to us

The Private I

the white dog is blind
intent upon its master's
footsteps   walks into
my black dog

the moon is full
the fog is across
her   in motion
a high wind
does not touch our place

the effort has been to make it one
in the teeth of it   the fire that
is bright in one street, a pale striation
in another   gone to be relit

an assurance at the edge of the wood
(the profit)   almost enters
a conjunction of tall glass
buildings and Greek pillared banks

'It's all right, mine's blind' he called   the
white is blind   in public show, the alphabet
washes the sidewalk   the years taught the personal
to stand on a rise of ground within the sign
                out there
water runs in across the fingers

and among silent rings
the wind comes down in a cloth

Song

              in the night
the only brightness
a wisp of smoke
                            a
bird curled out of the leaves
in one shape or another
became the preoccupation
of the string

an accident of distance
where the dark tore
to see

on the way,
                  a horse,
the ground, a gift,
a horse of footsteps

simple

1st Tale: Over

it was not salt   you spoke sweetly
and the child was dumb
(your vocabulary had been praised
beyond your age)
                    that child
patted the dull face of the puddle,
turning back, his head lifted, as

each year a congress of birds collects
to let fall these sounds

the guttural taste upon your tongue
was borrowed and remains
the wings lift,   an advantage

of hallucination,   to set straight
to drop down
                    and remain
inventions

then, taking them up,
to drop shots across curious lands

2nd Tale: Return

the oldest one and his sister and brother were
lost and he thought, telling a story
will keep fear away.   so he began

the right path is further to your left
where the well is.   and he looked
into the water and the water looked
back.   now it is certain that water
is a magical substance.   it will drink
up all things.   and I am told this is
most like love, who stood near the
high way, and because it is one of
the few bare places the world has
ever known, love asked directions,
but the high way ran on.   now it is
certain that the high way is a magical
substance.   it will lead inside the
shape of things.   and I am told this
is most like love, who has an amazing
ability to surprise travellers.   love
asked the first hitch-hiker to spend
the night with him at the side of the
high way, but the hiker went on.   now
it is certain that a hitch-hiker is
a magical substance which moves along.
and I am told this is most like love,
who has an amazing ability to pass on.
love, then, was quite alone the next
morning, and he stood stock-still
trying to understand, because in the
bright sun, the high way appeared to go
straight on without curves, turn-offs
or junctions into a kind of watery
air.   the rule is, walk on the left

side facing traffic if you don't want
to be killed.   this love did
until after a very long time, he
entered the watery air, which I
remember, is when

they were found

: At Last

to be nowhere   as you say

I suppose the trees will lift up
out of nowhere

and that youth in the light-distance
will be seen contrary

against the self-centred equation,
among bunkers at Fort Cronkite,   (your story,
having forgotten youth is that far)

and this one, the mixed mythologies
a dissembler of knowing more

but what is it the repetitious
fascinations of the body make, as
a weaving
                I would tear off
leaving clear, an un
interrupted view of what/where

you keep
company

Aphrodite of the Leaves

                        in
some lie told to draw
you forward

the city is all light the
movement all close
to the skin   you have been
and closing like flowers
your hand tears everywhere
from nowhere
                        'I'
he calls, 'I'   the place chosen
beyond which there is no further
neon

in fragments
in some object
the city is loved,
                        glass
cut into light

The City

             wept by a pool
midway,   the lover's conversation
claimed itself   like the
old head of the wandering Jew
painted on leather,   the head
follows the voice,   a fluid
that is a body

the mirror is to be read   the
water moved faster than the eye
the radio ambles in between the
lines of it is a sound, a part
of a letter
                  the forest is
somehow a wall,   no,   she has
knelt down and the folds
of her gown are around her the
rugs in the sun are silent the
colour itself sounds   these
filaments of pale light, filling
         what is it lifts from the
floor,   is now waist high
                           at arm's
length,   tangled beyond
one fountain ?

Sophia Nichols,

the wind hits and returns   it is easy to personify
a new place and language,   but the new body stings

these men with green eyelids, drawing their worth,
it was rumoured, from Egypt, knew

the work is part of it   a power arrived at the
same thirst

         he borrowed a head for a day

but which head   the phrases tremble in the other
mouth   it is true and false   the veil of her face,

an old porcelain, not for the hand to comfort   she
moved beyond the sop one gave for affection   'My

success has been to keep duty and love alive'   she said
her hand waved with the power of disease   Sophia

Nichols of the orchards, the deserts, the flooded
ponds and games wherein the moon sought our feet

died with a mouth full of tumour   it is true and
false   the moon flowers (that is Blake talking)

tonight it is the half blossom and the stars too
above this mud are from the other mouth   this city

untouched   the streets, Hotel Lyric have a foreignness,
a place outside a window   a sound of bees pulling

the lilac   above cement this wonder (the other mouth)
that crickets were men once who so loved the muses they

forgot to eat   now fed on thistles, the language must
sting   the flesh turn to a dew (the other mouth) the

loss,   some glistening blood on the leaves of the mirror
plant   Sophia Nichols of the story, the goldenrod,
of the snake that entered the cage and ate the captured
sparrows, the telegraph keys, pale yellow paper,   of

the Odyssey and the homing stories of the soul,   the sea
imaginary, light and foaming green on the rocks dark

further out as the eyes of the cat
                              if she would be
free from words, she would free me   even in the night

there are birds summoned by words

A Gift

there are in this room, two tables
and in this one, three

they are full of invisible motion
shaped out of their origin

oak, redwood, mahogany
out of the window   boy thieves

with flashlights in the fig tree
no bodies distinct from their souls

no city distinct from a language
from tracings of the new Wells Fargo

Building (42 stories)
through the fog, welders' lights glow

the grapevines twist around
the city   in your mouth

a concurrence   the poet's kiss
given, caught *like a love-adept*

on my lips   the attraction
of it scattered in public

where, now and then, god
knows you   your love
doesn't count   in this

for Robert Creeley

Bottom's Dream

because it has no bottom,
no opening,   Bottom's dream
left him friendless   he is,
according to the actors,   translated

across America, the slime
sticks   the mists rise above the cities
whose guides are homeless

love's mind   closes the curtains,
draws back, acting a part
in the kitchens

the marriage to this—it is
no match

the work, so much moonshine
on the ladders   this
a wonder the land drinks up
through a crack

under the oaks, the strewn pieces,
his pieces in the forest—there
recognized for what they are   glass
in this circumstance

for Louis Zukofsky

The Finder

on the windows, the dirty film
in the sunlight   shaped by the shadows
of apple trees   dry winter branches

on English Bay   a ship appears,
its hiding over   two masts, a doubling
of the cross   two Christs

one matching the other   where
the world dies

the tabloids of fire, a Sunday supplement
to the *San Francisco Examiner*   out of place,
in this time   rises from the page

in a lightning storm   which holds
this man at the horizon in his apocalypse,
a war burning, if the heart scores

bodiless, a curious blood and reasons
in ourselves inheriting the intellect
from out there   defined by a President

who is violence in this world,
a definition of this destiny we have
effected   all's well without

'your' intelligence where the world dies
I bend 'you' to my mouth
and suck 'your' breath away
only worlds caught

in the glinting lights of those
pieces of glass   found in the
forest   under a tree   crushed

and shining

for Louis Zukofsky

Out of the Window, ·

         the sea is afire
out of the window, the desire is the
angelic presence, but then I may
desire   *the fire turns,* out of the
window, half earth, half sea
are burning

       and in the loss
of heart, an entrance, a roadmaster
all the buildings are down   Orchard
is gone, removed by the Company,
swept by sand   driven into the
desert   the birth dries

I have lost my heart, and to say
this, unwounded, I am talking
about invisibility   I would
have you eat of it, the betrayers,
and this president, this old man
whose definitions are down,   out
of his time, government proved
at last to be the enemy   because
there is no matter in his thought

I would have the betrayers eat of it,
because afire, the heart has that
permission   to desire   because out
of the rock and brush of the first place
toward the land of this *sight,*
sound and intellect, the consumed heart
has the courage to be lost   half
earth,   half sea   burning

                 for Louis Zukofsky

Merlin

I could have stopped over it
you could have passed by

this blackbird, the shadow of
other birds, whose old name
means an action between worlds—

a breathing in a pane of glass
heavy layers over the swans he thought

with companions, he left the heart
of the land in a glass house
like floating in somebody's window

these men rode naked on chosen beasts
of what they named   died like trees
wounded   when they were tired

of the movement   something moved,
not separable from the endless knot

everything that moves makes stops,   tying
the blood to the place   if it is a city

it belongs to that event in poetry
which brings the next day in

the words are   the city, the future,
the poem   laid out

the movement   in   so   far

The Cry of Merlin

out of the blue that moves the curtain
out of the stone that smooths the body

statuesque   that spiritual thing inside outside
on and on   over us out of us to be

joined sundered the active image
of a man who stepped out   from a cracked egg

the room is unmoved   the lamps burn
only for themselves   the story

seems the whole business the out the taken
the lifted   the lost in the shape

or unfolding   as in that exact moment
the rose opens for which there is no word

shedding   by a *strange sweetness.*

the friends built a city,   enormous images
and high thought,   and shed it

like clothing on the floor beside the bed
all these Pacific Slope men came to the sea

as if they just got here by stagecoach
or revved-up Model A with a rumble seat

and made out in the brown grass
which caught in their hair and sweaters,

the tell-tale—the cock swelling
in the mouth fills the throat

the lips tight with the strangeness
the mouths, so far apart, meet

in the air   the space between love's
substance and him   is here recorded

he leans over the loved body
to kiss the belly   blue veins
at the surface   lead the life
he wished to enter   a ghost
river   true and false   as a map
made up to change the boundary

the domestic glares   a circle
that holds within it prickteasers,
mindfuckers, and the beloved,
a mix like a movie on television
or two radios, one upstairs and one down,
sending parts and flowers
in another body

here he was caught   the room unmoved
with the lamps out   I think he heard
the tick of the leaves of the plants
drawing together and the clock
he sticks a triple branch of daphne
into the head of the lady in the shape
of a blue bottle   by the light
of the street-lamps, she shone
and looked lovely,   when she said,
'This is the first time you've given me power in the house.'

envoi

A lion padded down the sidewalk toward him, shedding
light. He knew he began then to talk—loud enough
to wake the neighbourhood. Face to face, the lion rose
up, as if to greet him, but inside the lion, barely
visible, he saw a line-drawing of a man. Then, the
lion dropped on all-fours and followed the sidewalk.
Turning suddenly, with his right paw, he threw a piece
of light—it seemed to have no form—it was not
a jewel—a piece of light—and it glowed a little
red before it was gone.

the friend passing through the bedroom, the forest, the sea,
the city, the brown grass, the mountain, the fountain, the
friendship could hear the dream-talk—the garble—the
language withholding the words—the non-sense catch at
what he cried out of

Great Companion: Pindar

1971

Pindar's Seventh Olympic Hymn

for Diagoras of Rhodes, winner in boxing, 464 B.C.

STROPHE

Take in prospering hand   a shining cup
which holds the vine-flow
and proffer it, flecked with foam,
to the young man, who will be bridegroom:
   'Our houses meet!'   True
gold, this pride of fortune,
this feast   to celebrate
a new friendship,   to raise him out of
the guests' envy of
                    the bride's love:

ANTISTROPHE

so, I pour no lesser libation,   this nectar,
this Muses' gift   .   it is my mind's gift pours,
delighting,
propitiation for the victories at Olympia and Pytho.
a man is possessed by the good turning to name him:
another time, the Beauty of the Gift   (of freshness)
looks over another man,   and his initiation.
the phorminx' sweetness and the many-toned oboe

accompany us   on shipboard   .   now Diagoras and I
come to land where
                        I sing of
the sea's child   by Aphrodite,   Rhodes, bride of
Helios .   this poem repays him   who,   out of the boxing-match,
unflinching, fit to be crowned at Alpheos' River with laurel
and at Kastalia,   is mythically larger   and his father
Damagetos, whom Dike gathered
who both live on the three-citied island,
among Argive spearmen,
near by the headland of far-spreading Asia.

STROPHE

I bear the news   I put the events
straight   for the thought of their beginnings,
from Herakles,
from Tlepolemos first,   wide ruling,
from their father's source, they spring up joyous
from Zeus' disguise .   they are Amyntorids
from Astydameia's mother-right .   numberless
errors hang around men's minds   no way to invent

ANTISTROPHE

now or at the finish, not-knowing, a man's best of the gods' gifts.
and so, Alkmene's bastard brother, Lykymnios,
came from his mother's rooms at Tiryns, Medea's,
to die   struck down by the hard wild-olive staff,
embittered, the raised hand of Tlepolemos,   who founded
this island   so mania enters the mind's skill
and drives the knower to wander off .   he went to ask the god's
    voice.

in the adytum fragrance the Golden-Haired One
spoke   of his ships' sailing   straight out of wave-breaking Lerna
to that sea-girt grassland   where
the king of the gods, once   let fall a gold-storm,
gold snowing   .   the high brightness drenched the city,
the smooth-bronze axe cut   .   Hephaistos' handwork.
Athena,   out of the crown of her father's head, sprang
joyous   shouting   called out.
Awe wakened Ouranos and the mother Gaia.

STROPHE

and the daimonion,   the light-springing,   Hyperion's
son, commanded his loved children to guard
over the event,   mindful of the debt,
first founders of the goddess' altar   in clear view
and the holy offering set in place,
kindling the heat of the father,
stirring the maiden of the whistling spear   .   Prometheus
and Aidos,   who measure with awe,   caught men up
with prowess   and the joy acts inward and outward
          from the first thought.

ANTISTROPHE

unexpected,   a cloud intercepts us   nearby Lethe
the virtu is lost   out of place
in us   into the air
they did not carry the sperm-fire   when they climbed the high hill
no glowing ash at hand   .   without fire, they prepared her grove.
above the Akropolis,   Zeus gathered the clouds,
pale-yellow, and sent a gold rain upon them,   and the Owl-Faced,

glaring, silvery,   sent along companion-gifts,
every art,   and they surpassed all the men of the earth
with the skill of their hands   .   shaped as if life caught them
and motion,   their works lined the streets   .   word
spread far and wide   .   art's language
discloses powers without trickery   sophia   when
men tell old legends.   when Zeus and the deathless gods
chose shares of the earth, Rhodes was not yet
seen in the sea's open water,   the sea-land hidden in the salt-deep.

STROPHE

Helios was gone   and no one pointed to his share of it,
no place was apportioned   .   so the sacred Sun
was left out   he questioned   and Zeus settled
to recast the lots   .   but Helios stopped that
when he looked down into the grey-clear sea.
he said   I see the mantle swelling   out of the sea-floor,
I see my lot rising   abundance for men
from Gaia and hillsides for good flocks.

ANTISTROPHE

quickly, he called Lachesis of the gold-bound hair
to raise her hands   to swear   by the high oath of the gods,
without double-talk
bending her head along with the son of Kronos: the island
would be his share,   left to him alone   after she shot up
into the bright air   .   the talk over   .   from where
he looked down, his desire fell to meet her   budding against the
    sea-spray,

the sea-land is held by the dazzle of the sun-flow,   father
who reins the hard-breathing horses' fire   .   they mixed,
and Rhodes bore seven sons,   who take up
his gift of thought,   most knowing among the first men,
as their father gave pieces of land from Gaia   to Kamiros and the
    first-born
Ialysos, and to Lindos,   divided three ways,   wide apart
with cities named for them   and three rock-seats.

STROPHE

it let loose   the outcome of bloodshed   (the other face) turns the
hardship to sweetness   :   set for Tlepolemos, the first from Tiryns
god like,
burnt offering of sheep there,   the procession   and Diagoras
twice in the games' judgement stood crowned with flowers,
and four times at famous Ismos   the good fortune   again
and again at Nemea   and rock-strewn Athens;

ANTISTROPHE

marked by the bronze shield at Argos, by his skill at Arcadia
and Thebes,   by the crowds at the old games of the Boeotians,
at Pelana,   and at Aigina, six times the winner   .   at Megara
the stone tablet tells no other tale   O Zeus   father,
guardian of wide-backed Mt. Atabyrios,   take
this hymn   (the marriage-cry)   set for the winner at Olympia,

this fighter   who, among the powers,   met skill's beauty,
matched his own clenched fists   let his gift be in the eyes
of townsmen and strangers   over him,   the Graces
turning against hybris   he travels   straight on the way
his fathers left   aware of the good turn of events
surely   do not hide this share of the gift
of the seed of Kallianax   :   the Eratidai are touched by   .
gods' love,   the city   holds the beauty   of the flower-bringer
Thalia   .   but in a moment,   the winds hit   and turn

                                        bound for

Inscribed in gold letters in the temple at Lindos

Image-Nations 5–14
and Uncollected Poems

1965–1974

Image-Nation 5 (erasure

as the image wears away
there is a wind in the heart

the translated men
disappear into what they have
translated

rocking the heart   a childish man
entangles   an absence   a still-life
at the edge of his body
erasing the body of those opposites
who are companions
and also horizons in one another's
eyes   at the ends of the world

the words do not end   but come back
from the adventure
                              the body is at the edge
of their commotion
                              the nonsense
the marvellous clarity
                              in the pool of the
heart

we quarrel over the immortal Word,
many times one falls out of the mortal
there suddenly   the missing   outward
journey

o we do in all things
walk contrary to the world

a Nervalian movement   of
astonishment   an arm around
a hollyhock   or foxglove,
as if we dressed in them,
a flowered man   the bees
disturb   the stillness   seeking
sweetness in the pockets
an art as natural as *lunch poems*
or an extravagant   speaking   out of
the *gnostic horse's mouth*

a translation of oneself into the Other
is
        so
            delicately

                perched among words
this technē   binding the heart
like small poems read from
vast stages   the images of the war
in Vietnam   burn up   out of the
words,
       where they are not
added to the real
          but compose it
where the body
burns
in bubbles of fat
and re   opens
into something
without lineaments

traces   the old Bedouin poets
called them   encampments   of
what was
          a movement
the seven poems,   called golden,
give the same pattern
of this movement

I stop over the encampment
before it wears away
I tell you of my prowess
in love   to gain your attention
at the edge of this
    ·   movement
a torrent
          and then traces
of wild beasts drowned
in the watercourse   lay
like drawn bulbs of wild onions

the day lightning split the last
big Douglas fir   on this street
all the houses filled with
a pale-green,   luminous
movement
I stood up from my work table
waiting
for the house to flame

this co-herence   falls, like rain,
into the syllables
                    this in-herence
of a golden poem
                    translating
blood, dancers,
                    and whirling
drunken lives
                    into a tense
music
            of a hollyhock

Mallarmé said l'immortelle
parole is missing from our speech
the constant
                    movement
                                    of a finitude
which re   opens
                                    converging
backward   with primal elements,
syllables   of
                    a longing
for completion

the task of a man   and his words
is at the edge
            where we are
translated   restless   men
the quarrel over the immortal language,
one may believe in a god-language
behind us,   but god moves to the end
of our sentences
                where words   foment
a largeness
            of visible
and invisible worlds
they are a commotion
of one form

the voice is *recognizable*
as fragments
of a greater language,
a live and changing
face

following men's hearts
in the world   sharp
and bird-throated

I turn   to answer   the goldsmith's
hammer   down the street

day and night   awake   confounding
the fish and the gods

yesterday
                   I sent tidings to a star
                   for you

'Present my care'   I said
                   the star could recognize
                   your moon-like form

I bent my head over the words
I sent

'Take that care to the sun,   the rocks
and the gold'

I stepped back   shameless   and *showed*
the holes in my breast to the star

'Give news of me to the Belovèd'
I said

I rocked my heart
the child was so restless

I look for the Cup-Bearer

the Belovèd   is the murmur
inside   the work
at the edge
          of the words

the silence   is the Other
at the edge   of my words
a
      move
          ment

the words drink us up

who is speaking?

dear beings, I can feel your hands

Image-Nation 6 (epithalamium

in this abide   pulling the next branch
of the tree down to ring it   I have seen
that vision   over again   I had
married a tree   placing a ring on each
branch   to return again   another man
to pull down another branch   I would
have you see this tree   glistening
and her adornment

an origin to which I return   there
placing my sorrow for her adornment
to solve it   a hilltop
green   but it is two *converging stairways*
and love's dream ascends tying the worlds
as if this shape of the earth were the first
mountain

I lean over the steering wheel to ask
this vision again   not to be mentally mine
but out there   to carry it
a gift to a wedding   for it came
15 years ago from reading a book
on the miracles of Mary in Egypt
    never found again   recurs daily
in marriage with the place
and hour   the two meet to see
from their stairways

        the powers are brought
to birth   and again the vocabulary
loses them   image—imageless
Plotinus says our effort is to make
the visible invisible   but here the
invisible would not be borrowed   may
you have a *radiant world compelling*
adoration   the tree waits to be visible

a good return

he wished him to die   the
young poet

he saw himself watched by
bending to drop violets
silver edged, pale ones
close to the covered head
of his lot

the impossibility lay somewhere

the first image must have been
the chairs

                    to lean back
and listen   the arms taken
of large and interior wars

'I'll sleep with you any time.
That's good. All the rest of you
stinks.'   the fine tones
to answer   suddenly
breaking under the onslaught,
seated wide apart

the chairs were too far apart
the room larger than necessary
to contain friends or a high
world   out of no where

a dumbshow of pain
across his face played like
a fire

      a good return
for such mistaken enterprise

                                          1971

Image-Nation 7 (l'air

what actually he'd forgotten
was not the world
something that exists   only
in contrast

moves as I move
                    as if woven

the separation   is tight
    over silence

so forces   and dissolutions
of acts   and things
                            where
men and gods are from the
same source
spirit begins in matter
stones, sidewalks, gardens
men as they dissolve
the strange ghostly
    speaking   speaking
                        as if woven

a wraith of earth
near the great noise
of the wind
                    wounds of rust,
dark grapes
            and olive trees

the turn of the blue
of the light   divinities   out of
a universe   of white holes
the black holes   gravity
of language
                        whirling the souls
fly   rethought
Jeremy Prynne explaining
the abstract   'it simply
means distance'
rain, rain, dear Zeus
on their cornlands and
their pastures

the fearful noise   and
the archaic smile
who is the physical
source of all things
gods and men included

and the city
                the city
is the human grasp

and its madness
                    the human

food   of that

closed   a terror in the movement
of a man   devouring
into his own shape
                    flowering
scatters petals
                         brightnesses
sounds of leaves
bubbling of streams
drawing of lots
the traffic
                    the manhood
given up   sudden loss
of shape   alive
out of the stop the shape
was

the sun-path   slips
to the rocks   along side
what he had forgotten:
                         actual
thinkable things   cling
to the unthinkable

two-fold   folds   like a
belovèd o laughter
beside my path

companions   are horizons
obsessions of snow, pearl
flower shape stone fire scenery
marrow of white elder, virgin wax
and sperm at last closes the circle

spiritual plain coach of fire
window of flesh road of souls
wombs of coals breasts of flames
husbands of virgins beard of God

laughter preparations,   naïvetés
flames frost,   cutting off
reparations levelling
inexpressible purity

whirlwind of souls white atoms
here we are again at a landscape
burning silver mage's souls
stolen stars flying spirits

sharp sighs greedy lips
sweet conflagration
purified lily snow of years
and this
           wheel
                      turns into
    ecstasy

heart-shaped stone heart   in a box
Chinese box of deer feeding at the flowering gate
love lasts
a world
        covering
his eyes   the glory
of the sea   disappears
shining   into the eye

                  from
silence   between here
and there
      the first
outward   is always
a distance

so   we hold it
in the middle
         voice of
the companion   in the

air

Image-Nation 8 (morphe

my beads are the colour of the tea
in the cup
                    I lean forward
to let them hang free
and watch the light run
in and out
                    resin of pine or fir
washed from the riverbanks
of China
            as the tree was,
of green needles,   it seems the friend
is left in the bead resin   there is

a suddenness   these days   startles,
young and handsome   fragments
of what he thought,   he stands

like a sparkling jade tree
in the west wind   I thought

a gift   •   I know nothing of form
that is my own doing   all out
of one's self   our words were
the form we entered,   turning intelligible
and strange   at the point of
a pencil

the words were the attributes
of what we were out there
watching   the sun swim

•

a black-hole is the name
given a star-remnant   out of
the idea that a star may collapse
into a dense object,   what is left
over,   and from it no light escapes
because, *The New York Times* explains,
the waves of 'the struggle' you named
lengthen infinitely,   and become
invisible

.

it is the interchange the form took
like walking in and out of a star
the words are left over   collapsed
into themselves   in the movement

between visible and invisible
I like to tell the story of the man
with a heart in each hand   the
intricate movement of events,   the
startling   outwardness   of where
they were   would give you the key
to what he took   and what
he gave away   but these are
invisible words:

for a moment he stood within
the tree   startled

when he came to the gate,   he bathed
his face

when he lifted his cup,   he let the sky
go free   out of his hands

Enfant Terrible,

                                  sharp
at holding sacred things
in a conversation   I'm
satisfied that trifles
make up a bed

humor was the worth
of it
hidden in blankets
and piled-up sweaters   when
I took it to heart

now they tell me
you're afraid I'll
disappoint you—not
come up to the picture
you painted   deftly
with historical largeness

(once wings taught me)   love
should wear all this silliness
of mentor?   shapeless
to think up new tricks
of a moment   what's
the face like I should
look out of,   smiling
allusion

                        1971

Image-Nation 9 (half and half

there are shining masters
when I tell you what they
look like   some of it is
nearly false   their blue hair

but they are not ourselves   they
are equivalents   of action   they
compose forms,   which we hear

sound within a context
as if that action we are
images of   used us
the body becomes an instrument

sometimes the harp pierces the body
and a man only hangs on the strings

I hear the airborne-fire, the dead rebels'
second speech, which follows their live words,
and the rice, and the motorcycles

but public life has fallen asleep
like a secret name   the wrong-reader
will say he has pity for others
where the thought is born in *hatred*
of pity, which is only feeling   the action
we are only images of   hates pity
and its *reduction of horror to sentiment*

wordlessness   no thing is so simply

personal   I put my hand out to catch
beauty in the act of   I know no beauty
which is not permanent   not invoked
in splendour   the words are meaningless
until they emerge in the action   they are
images of

I was once a youth,   and I was
a maiden,   a bush, a bird, a fish
with scales that gleam in the ocean

they come from the dark   under
many names   the blue   wind
they are not ourselves,   not even
the moon drawn down   into our
breasts   that we may strike others
with eros   the
body gleamed so   wind
master   *a bone, a ball, a top*
an apple, a mirror, a skein of wool

wind   —   words   wind   —   hair   we

have dismembered the earth   and
are born lifeless on the moon   mouths
to the wind

unthought *the many mountains, the many*
cities,   the many houses

I was once   another man's heart
an eagle, a wolf   cloud, smoke,
splash
            psychron   (cold, refreshing
anapsychsai   (to be refreshed from evil

we have eaten ourselves   luxurious and
careless   I must bathe at the
gates of the city   I must tell you
they have been blue in the heart,
in the wind

                I have opened my mouth
they have come from the black-fire

                          we have stiffened
the terror of earth,   as if terror were the only unearthly
thing in our hearts

              we have given her *rivers*
of our own salt   earth then remains uncanny,
sublime   water is fear's movement   grief cries
in the air like birds   fire is hidden in the imageless
self

        the blue hair   *the face of gold   the clothes*
like snow   the blood

                is light

                        zero

enacts it

      Jack Clarke's 'we are under image'
rythmos   (form's movement)   to walk into   'the
primordial always exists'   face to face   always outside
ourselves   the astonishment is

              that it is *kosmos*
playing out with one man   entheos

                 they are
the *flowing boundary*   taking birth   *taking leave*
at the point of the heart   a continual
division of halves

                for *Dennis Wheeler*

Image-Nation 10 (marriage clothes

the soul's profound duality alone explains   *the necessity for*
exchanges between spheres
          the eye in the wind   the hole in the wind
              the storm   which is all
intoxication of the trees
         at the window where the house is also
a cosmic place
         shadow and light become movement

and the word soul   what a haughty   standing alone that is,
(the original sense of it is uncertain)   a kind of floater
in the language

around the image of the work that is struggling to
take root,   *shimmering, fading, glowing*   *to life*
again, until
         the light and shadow become
the substance of men and women   the
ceremony or operation of this storm,
southwest wind burning the new leaves of the mountain ash
they have said the word means breath   but that
is the meaning borrowed from *spiritus*   an
inhalation and exhalation of the world
    a steam   a vapour   or it means the
immortal part   given   it floats
in the language as the opposite   *the inseparable*
freedom   of a primal ambiguity
                this *convulsive*
beauty insisted upon by Lautréamont
                    out
of solitude,
        the spheres, images of heart
and head, exchange their fluids   *their*
blood, and fuse together like those two drops
symbolizing the passionate loves and hates of
the faun and his nymph

                              the blue stream
at the edge of thought   *with a reality,*
with a music,   *with images that are all*
irreplaceable

the world
                  is a combining word   wer-eld, *course*
of anyone's life   southwest wind hitting the house,
bending the laburnum   tearing the yellow clusters
                        sheer fountain   close to the sound
where the sea stirs
                        resplendent
                                          they throw nets
over the hills at night
                        to snare angels
                                          at
the sea's edge   a slap mixed with the exact
note,
                  scirrr   as the sea flows back   exact,
sliding half-notes in the wings of the humming
bird yesterday,
                        orange over the black currant
blossoms
                  there are 84 windows
                                          the separable
soul   is concealed in an egg or a tree,
                                    the west-
shape,
            the secret, inseparable *blackness of*
milk
            in the owl-land,
                        this *indescribable*
carpet

                  scirrr
                  the world-sound

enters the wall,
                  vibrating in the glass
                          where
he caught the branch of the world-tree,
hanging by one hand   like the boy in
the ginkgo in Boston Public Garden,
fan leaf   yellow fruit   sticky in
spring

•

suddenly   there's a star   (another word whose original
sense is uncertain)   over the bay
in a hole   in the wind

•

it is an alphabetic wind rises   not one
consonant without   a ē ē ē ē ŭh ē ŭh ī a a ŭh ŭh ŭh o ě
u ŭh ě ě u ē ē ī ē ē ē ē
                            otherwise
unmarried

•

                    there are sparrows in the
larynx and heart   and in the knee and
foot   they are the power to move outward
and they have any conceivable history   as
they rise and fall out of the clouds

•

the bell-birds perch next door   the gulls
have come onto the roof and lawn,
                          the
sea-beauty,
          it is all transformation,
                              fallen
out of himself,
                absence suddenly melding with
presence   and vice-versa,
                  so a part of love
is always
          sticking the golden
stems in the earth,
                flowers moulded perfectly
of gold   or the shit of the gods
                    the city is blown
about

    •

a raiment—the metron, 1:2 pyr,
the heat-stuff   inward and sticky   at the
dissolution of the world the metron will be
2:1 — 1/2 always remains   to watch
1/2 the burning fire of the stars   cold,
celestial ether   of this,   *1/2 remains*
celestial ether   *the other hardens into*
primordial air   where the souls gather
of this, *1/2 remains, and the other becomes*
primordial sea   of this   1/2 remains, the
other is primordial earth   of this   1/2 remains,

the other   becomes prestér   (hurricane)   volcano
fire of the mind
                        we are back at
the primordial arrai—ment
                                in the war-flower

        •

white cherry petals on the eddy-stream   the
shine in the movement
                                dressed up in shield-
flowers
            voice and thought in the wind-birds

        •

trying to say what the soul is   an Arapaho began
a list—the heart, the brain, the breath—
as well as a word meaning 'your body moulded
as a living man'

and Keokuk said there are fire shapes of the
'heart, flesh, life, names and family'
                                and
the Navaho used a word which means
'that which stands within'   upright   a turquoise
image hidden in his breast
                            the Snake people
say it looks like a hailstone

        •

pure tree
            and in the drunkenness natural
to me,   ami—à l'eau couleur de cendre

        •

the blue is of mingling branches

•

hwa has become 'what'
hwa has also become 'who'
hwan has become 'when'
hwaer has become 'where'
        for the first woman our name was likely
Hawwah
          Saiwala is the oldest recorded
form of the word
        soul   blending with *awa,*
closely related to the word 'sea'
        the language, older and other
than I am
      prehistoric, sacred
geography   turns in the wind
uprooted
      the sea runs over the railbed

•

'I cannot keep my subject still'
             the
indescribable carpet
        action is, perhaps, the *magnitude*
of the body
      the stain of form
          turning among the
marriage clothes
       the starry issue
          the horizon
            the beauty

and terror composed   inextricably mingled
in an unfixed freedom
the soul's profound duality,
                              the Far West of
the mind
          new leaves of the mountain ash
are wind-burned
                        forces from
the furthest reaches of   the consciousness
mass in front of the work
                              so curiously compose
so the war sings
                        the hummingbird a week ago
orange stopped over the wine-black currant blossoms
whose life is swift   still
colour
          1 / 2 remains
                              the generating axes
for visibility
                    at the edge of
the real
          the work of   obscurities
are the edge   of
                    necessary
to a luminous passage
I am not   there where I am the plaything
of my thought
                    I think about what I am
there where
          I do not think I am thinking
the There-Where
                    seven days at the windows

Image-Nation 11 (the poēsis

inside the tower   not a broken tower   two
loves seemed present   •   one   •   passing
the other   •   not named   •

                        verbs of
the *music-footed horse*
                        I was afraid   at the fair sight
the dark imagined land   disappeared as they came to the edge
in the   air   across   the vertical road   leading up to the
sky   of that constellation   by   an explosion   •

                        I reached up into that space
                        to touch the enormous mobile
hanging from the centre   I had wanted to arrange it

from each pendant   a shining ring   which one by one
my fingers entered   dissolved   in the light
                        as if space looked for time
or the block of the image did not know the size of
what you are doing   •

                in the explosion   the rings became
                a constellation
                                        the moving angel
                        changed raiment

and colours   at times   soaked with the blood going
or *adorned with treasure*   turning   now   transparent

what's left of the angel
glint and guitar
what's left of the event of the left
what's left of the angelic writer •

the Event
was an activity turned in
all directions
of what contained them,
and retraced
the wing of the world showed,
who is companion • blue-hued • well-marked

Image-Nation 12 (Actus

so the ground flows   and the heavens are propositional
gifts   of birth   an accomplishment of thought   where
one sits in silence   a word-boundary

                            so the companions move
who belong to their work   strange unfamiliarity
of the familiar

I make out a boat   the soul's image   a voice a residence
and the disappearance from a work   over the last
blind note   'Oh, a boat of friends'   the music of,
logos of   a blinding instrument   our words, mine
among them   wash at the perilous   social, political,
hellish and heavenly parts
                        the world is in accordance with my
                        perspective in order to be independent
                        of me   is   for me in order to be without me
I make a boat out of an apple tree,
both ends are golden   (Veda
the labyrinthine differences

or I'm a horseman with prowess
in the rodeo,
but what will is the shape of the horse

the uncertain Wavering   swift to harry

gods and goddesses at the ends of our words,
dead or alive

discoursing   that is to say, running around arranging
things, ourselves among them   *centrifugal, after our brief*
hangup   among things   working again and again with that
operational language   always, an incorporeal matter, sharp
as sticks and stones

visible   visible   visible   heart-heartless

a wreckage, if he goes there   and I love these instabilities
of unstable institutions   we speak
                                                    a washboard

the **Sudden**   radiates   the work of it
drinks us up

                                                    washing
a shirt of silk
                    a mallet of gold
                                        a washboard of silver
in the sea   (Veda
invisible   invisible   invisible   heart
less

        •

I water my dragon steeds   at a constellation
and tie the reins to the sunrise-tree

to enter on wheels

I break a sprig of the sunset-tree   holding
its red flowers
                        this, Ch'u Yuan, is
a journey
            of the bird-throat

                                        indeterminate
musical   shore   of
                          the invisible
behind the face,
                          the masked procession
through 'you' I conceal my loneliness from myself
and make a way into the multitude and into love
by lies, for my heart cannot bear the terror, and
compels me to talk as if I were two

you are invited   into an elevator
it has no windows
you are invited   into a glass house,
a reversible abode
                          not in time
but not out of it either
                                        the horizon
momentary   shaped and formal
by a **Suddenness**   like a hillside ·

dragons   chimeras   of the past   the future
or elsewhere   present a gift   of
wildness   of the behaviour of violet
and pepper-flower
                          wild-logos, Ch'u Yuan, *knots*
the lithe light-trails of ivy
                          around the
        wheels

        •

in the Cold Mountain pool   black water
swept by the wind
                        upside-down trees
and sky, shadowy, at the bottom
                                    other step-stone
holes in the world
                        the work folding
a dragon   at the edge   of the sea   my enlargement
of the pond
                where   the story went
wild   fiery   under the leaves

I am glad you cherish the sea, Emily Dickinson wrote, *we
correspond though I never met him*

moiling   the sunlight washing
        an original stratum of men and women's thought

•

Unarm, Eros,
                shaping
                        and unshaped, Eros,
there-then

Image-Nation 13 (the telephone

the man with a thousand hearts
flaring   the substance shattered
of what form   that is his movement?

both made the sexual beginning into a demonic
mediocrity   both disappeared in future-form
the language,   sacred to the binding of one

to another,   stolen   the only heart

is the movement of singing words
they burn   they burn
then suddenly bathe in the fiery sea

they say he is consumed by sorrow
in order to see   and his paper lives
fly in pages across the garden

caught in those blue bunches
of hydrangea   the particles
are pieces of silence riding the sea

they shine at the edge of his words
suddenly *nothing old or new*
matters   he can act or not

there   among *mountains of the heart*
watching   to bring the shining pieces
into his hearts

where the words enter like footsteps,
these small ghosts tend to flee
toward something fearfully and transparent

'the shape of heaven   is as confused
as the heart   when you place
your feet on your head,   you will
stand on the stars,'

these words whisper   as the sea folds
a thousand forms   they are
like the telephone
                    the lovers *fall*
into a whirlpool

                he steps forward
so suddenly himself and another
a movement,   a fold of the real

that should be the image of himself
returned, he thought

looking back,   where he
heard   the whisper of so many

        the splendour and darkness
of something whirl in the air
                        a blowing-together

that would be the real   of the lover,
which is nothing other   than himself

a movement   fiery   turning   bits & pieces
a circle   a square   long running lines   dots & dashes
parabolas,
            almost gigantic,
        of the man with a thousand hearts,

he thought

Image-Nation 14 (the face

O golden flower

the guest of the window   the air
fills with motorcycles   echo and shadows

the *backward-flowing*   astonishment

the wings

the multi-coloured play, as if the years
were one destiny and eros

as if the moth-heart stayed at the real
door-way

the ghost-heart   it is the kind of

daemon he is to become that
governs   entangles   at the edge

of his words,   the laughter

that would bring the world
back
           into the square inch

the field of the square inch of the
house of the square foot
the house of the square foot is the
face
the field of the square inch is the
face alive
in the middle of the square inch
the SPLENDOUR *moves*
a footstep in the furnace

the traffic hits the house
with its winds   and the house
turns a little   as if walking
away to join a movement

or is the house still and a
gigantic footstep creaks on
the narrow blue front-steps

form is alive   it begins as
the *light-flower*

like dry wood
like cooled ashes

where the work begins again
in *the white snow*

the horizon of every form where
he journeys
                the blue-heart at the centre
of the flower
                turning like a sun-flower

the mirror in the garden doubles
the garden
            there and not there
we had stolen the mirror from
the wrecked house next door
over the fence near the willow,
across the heather, the talisman
rose, and the wild-flowers under
the blue back-steps

in the white-heart

O

Origin

it was Hegel—who died in 1831—
who said whatever we may have thought
of poetry
of its high language, which haunts us,
it's of the past   dead
it don't matter
cause mama's gonna buy you a mockin' bird
and if that mockin' bird don't sing
mama's gonna buy you a diamond ring
and if that diamond ring don't shine
I'm gonna turn—return
to that language
where the worlds gather
where it's very hard to understand
that most difficult of all
modern phrases

'blessing muses'
Segen sinnt

for Dwight Gardiner
1974

Streams I

1974–1976

Luck   Unluck   One Luck

the heart turns inside out
of the mouth and eyes
out of the indeterminate ear
　　　blue dogs of the hillside　　hunt
the skin-play
　　　　　of suddenness

the Egyptians did not close the mouth
and the eyes　　at the edge of the sun
but opened them　　and gave boats

1945　　Rosario Jimenez, who at the round
　　　　table　　read García Lorca and Homer,
　　　　talks to herself behind the glass door,

1948　　Ernst Kantorowicz, who taught the
　　　　young　　to think swiftly　　an essential
　　　　history
　　　　　　　　like Richard's
　　　　robe only he could take off
　　　　divinity alone removes the divinity
　　　　of an empty coat

1945–1965　　Jack Spicer, who tore himself up
　　　　in language　　'I can't bear it,' I said,
　　　　then studied his peril and task

19–　　the hound-voice
　　　　　　　　　of earth and sky,
　　　men, women, and gods　　folding
　　　　　　　　　inside
　　　the effacement of words　　　　the puns
　　　in ice
　　　　　　a laughter
　　　a voice thins on a cigarette　　chokes
　　　to a whisper　　and sharpens

the edge of the blade
                              who is speaking
I hear the other toss-up

'knowledge is a moth,'   a friend sent
on a postcard   with Michael Snow's
camera of the central region on the front
                                        there
in the mountains   all by itself and
a singing computer
                              the horizon
first ahead of you   at your edge
then around you   without you

in the motionless light of a mineral
in the white perfume of a magnolia
pink-edged   on the fleshy   spotted
and almost black abyss of a poppy
so we have exchanged mutual forgiveness
with the eye of a cat
                              the unknowing
like a fish-hook
                              of fire-flower
eaten petals
                              the eagle is perched
there on the tongue   at the mouth

white flowers unsheathe
                              to resolve language
ahead of it

                              behind the fire
from unknown mouths
the wind rises
where that would not become god

Fortune   Infortune   Fort Une

Sky-stone

the window-heart speaks
shattered
as god speaks,
speaking
does so   *because men invented gods*
speaking their language
justify themselves there and argue
an innocence   in the words
that give the signal
for the slaughter to begin
of hearts
O, if he is the effort
of language
a laughter of the sun-wheels
the glittering entanglement of ocean
the laughing alphabet   flames of the air
where the dead letter   breaks off
into a garden   a starfield
a city
          where it magically flows
along a street   around a corner
of a skyscraper that is also a bush
a *nonoun*
          of the stone
which caught the blue sky
in its sharp edges
knows what to say to
the dead hearts   prophetically
unwinding off the spool
goes
among the windows
as we speak it
rain drops
                light-blue-stones
of a street corner
where lovers talk of
this crazy radiance

this map tells being the
       whereabouts of its
       actual
       presence
reading this, just then she brought
two four-leaf clovers
I glued them onto the page of
my open book

for Susan Knutson

Suddenly,

I live in a room named East
on the map of the West   at the edge

near the door cedars and alders
mix and tower,
full of ravens   first thing each morning,
whose song is
                    a sharpness

we quarrelled so
                        over the genius
of the heart
                whose voice is capable

they come on horseback
in the middle of the night,
two of them,   with a horse for me,
and we ride,   bareback
clinging to the white manes
at the edge of the sea-splash,

burst open,

                to divine
the hidden and forgotten source,
who is transparent
where the moon drops out of the fog
to bathe,
but not to us

the retied heart
                where the wind glitters

                        for Ellen Tallman

Gathering

O I wonder what you think of
these gods going
silvery and tense

I go to the door
step through—
                    what is there?
my own vanishment

to be with me—
           in order to be without me

a learnèd love of most of   it

catch at
sharper and glinting shadows
drink at
fountains of dark street-hearts

curled up asleep in the footprints
they have left
I hear
the puzzling wildness

of the street-talk   of   most   of   it

the kettle begins to hum   to make coffee
          in the kettle?   in the air?
I hear instructions
'you must be a master of the heart
in order to be a master of windows

and that is very difficult'

The Skill

I want you to have skill
with life—
the body is not life—the
replay of the moon and
the heart's record—the
lost ones   hold
nothing of turquoise,   of
the bright inward heart
upright—necessary according to
my own forebears of the
desert—fucking which gave
me my face—
the heart must not be confused
with the body—
the lies of the star-fuckers
who believe a quick rub-down
and come will turn them
into this poetic, thoughtful
art—must not be mistaken
for the desire they never had
except to be beyond themselves
and I love this desire
to be beyond,   to go where
they had not been—
I see their beauty as if it were
my future-form—
                          down in
hell where I sought them and
kept the agreement
it was they who ran
suddenly ahead of me
and looked into my eyes
there to leave me because
I could not speak their
part,   but wished to stand
by while they came to speak
perhaps more blueness, azure

than I who work to find
them—but I have no way—
their future-form disappears
into gas-stations and interior finishing
and politics that do not
intertwine with the skill
of your life or mine

October 1975
rev. 29 January 2004

Harp Trees

the cast-iron moon on the wall
vibrates   a kind of speech
at the edge of thought
in the dark
            I lay my cheek
against her cold lace, crescent
and our hair blows out into the world
the glint into which we're gone
speaking

she was the symbol of a group
called the maidens
and before that she was part
of the wall of the ice-cream
parlour, Owl Drugstore, San
Francisco, 1915

her speech is the kindness of
the house
as the Royal Hudson passes
whistling down the steam tracks

and the trees speak on the
feathered wind a greenness
harp-sequoias lost at the windows
neither kisses nor wounds in the nests

Tumble-Weed

the flour-man, powdery, at the door
becomes finally, a sweat-body of spiritual
enemies, drunk on the plane-fare,
who walks nowhere

if you try on the costume, say, of
Picasso's religion or the fierce, feminine
purpose
        or better yet, of harlequin
dying to sleep with red bitten lips
and all of it said coldly
to move speech to its violent
marvellous teeth,
                a desire
behind the desire and Oedipus

and which desert father lay his head
on a mummified-body-pillow whose
voice was a ghost of a woman
and which dreamed sadly he
knew better the perspective of his
landscape—windowless farms
and winds
and which cried out, 'father
of wax' and kissed his forehead
of lost lives of cold florists
at last?

              for my father, died April 20, 1978, at 76

Syntax

1979–1981

for David Farwell

I read, walk, listen, dream, and write among companions. These pieces do not belong to me. *Syntax*, a personification, looking for a predicate and *vice versa*.

A preface, then,

that is also the after-face of it. *Syntax* felt odd when I wrote and published it in 1983. The *cultural orphanhood* that has hunted me since childhood came to the surface. The writing of it was fun, funny, disturbed, and dependent. Thus, the *trouvés*—the found-things— (an anthologist called to say he wanted to publish one of my poems from *Syntax*, 'Tombstone'—I said, 'Good choice, but it isn't mine, it's a first-people's tombstone, found in North Van-couver'—he published it anyway, to my consternation, under my name, needing, I suppose, an author for his purpose). And thus, the quotations, as in essays, dependent upon them. I will, later in *The Holy Forest*, call these *the brilliance of reading under the library table*. Losses and gains of cultural meaning in their scholarship. Their voices are named in the margins and, then, identified with my reading of their books at the end of *Syntax*. The discovery of Opal Whiteley came through the air on CBC radio. Then, I found her book, *The Story of Opal*, 1920—the image of her writing under the bed, secretly; the photograph of her putting back together the shredded pieces of her book; the story about the cow and her mud tracks, dug up and kept *in the back part of the cook-table drawer*, that I wish I had written—being true, as they say, to myself.

The Truth Is Laughter 1

art is madness, yes, Melville,
as the words glow

somedays I think the aurora borealis
shakes heaven—silver, lemon,
grass, roses change   a restless
disappearance glimmers at the top
of the north   there are flames
at the zenith and now and again
brightness rays up from the horizon
all this can melt into the moonlight
leftover merry dancers wave
they are the dust from aurora's
(if she'll forgive this first name
intimacy) glittering look
now new lightnings   over again
the endless game of it fresh
in this stillness which is after all
                 infinitude as we can
                 come by it
                 on a short walk
                 after dark

                                    (after Nansen

The Truth Is Laughter 2

the radio asked, 'Are scientists
close to explaining the nature
of the universe?'   and answered, 'Ho! Ho! Ho!'

too easy

the philosopher Jeffrey Bub suggests: they
can never say what the world is
but only what it is not this   process—
'the world is not like that, it's not like that,
it's not like that'   is open-ended

The Truth Is Laughter 3

blindly visited
Vancouver street
high heels
and cherry trees
he leans forward
everyday,
brown eyes
sharp with
delirium
at the corner
by Hudson's Bay
around his neck
the mystery and
the crucifix
the mystery
is tender
that's why
he likes it
we go
around him,
sparrows,
everyday

The Truth Is Laughter 4

lately, my mind is dark,
    answers
        to *a bucket*
with a hole in it
        stands there
talking of the light river

topazes, rubies in sunlight,
and the verdant shore   paradises

my mind says and my heart
knows it   *I can't*, the song

sings, *buy no beer*   the
texture among radio and
sunlight and scholarship argues
di colore oscuro,
dolce color d'oriental zaffiro,
such dalliance of odours returns

o, argues, *isplendor*   light
visible   and such stars

as I am ignorant of   backward
the dark mind   'winds,' he
said,
    'still deeper'

The Truth Is Laughter 5

the janitor at the St. Roch National Historic
Site said, 'When I was in Los Angeles, the O
from Hollywood rolled down the hill and cut
a station-wagon in half.'   'It would've been
better,' he said, 'if it'd been a Honda Civic.
Front-wheel drive would let you go on driving.'

The Truth Is Laughter 6

moving from one room to another   a shocked,
resilient heart, owning nothing, as Yeats says,
perhaps in the depths of the eyes, the latest
image held of a shimmering city,   of breathless
trees grown out of holes in the sidewalk,   of
the cold, bent body of startled thought fallen
solitary, ass over teakettle, or lost in the
whirl of this destiny or that one   do they spin
inside themselves?   like so many gods we are
told are projections of our own violence? the
hunched beauty covering that possibility   the
bells of the day ring from room to room the
restless mind twists around corners, angles,
over lighted floors, the moment beyond itself
like the single day, April, 1767, Jefferson
planted Carnations, Indian pink, Marygold, Globe
violet, Sensitive plant, Cockscomb, a flower like
Broom, Umbrella, Laurel, Almonds, Muscle plums,
Cayenne pepper, and 12 cuttings of Gooseberries
and the country was Argo, he said,   a solitude
conscious of itself   a green bottle behind the
fan   *the giant confined in the body's prison*
roams at will among the stars   far, in the
projection of infinite love in a finite room
today, the winter shines   winter-shine
Blake said, 'When Thought is closed in Caves. Then
love shall shew its root in deepest Hell'   out
of perspective   out of the picture   not in the frame
'I cannot,' he wrote, 'consider death as anything
but a removing from one room to another.'

The Truth Is Laughter 7

a footnote: the *Wolf Fenrir is fettered by the chain*
              Gleipnir, made of six things: the noise
              of a cat's footstep; the beard of a woman;
              the roots of a rock; the sinews of a bear;
              the breath of a fish; the spittle of a bird.
              As a pledge that the trying-on of this fetter
              would not be a trap, the god Tyr laid his
              hand in the wolf's mouth. Once bound, and
              the world, for a time, safe, the wolf was
              not again released; but Tyr lost his hand.

                                    (from Fowler

Dreams, January 1981

one may not lose divinity
—there in our violence—
here   'Okay, but,' Jack's
handwriting said   in the dream
     today
and yesterday, Olson's ring,
very Tibetan, was far too
big   in the dream, Phillipa
Polson said, 'Wear it on
your belt'   so, must
     small wonder
there have been neckties
that were multiple aprons
down to somebody's shoestrings
and Duncan wanted help
with his beautiful wallpaper
it was the fireplace stuck
right out of the wall into
the room—perpendicular—that
troubled me with two white
doves alight on it

The Truth Is Laughter 8

on the bus, the small boy, newly
into letters, spelled out the letters
scratched in the glass   F   U
C   K   loud-voiced, 'Mom,
what does that say?'   'That's
not a word,' she said,
looking straight at me   'It
doesn't spell anything.'

Tombstone

Sacred to the Memory of
Josephine
who died Sept. 24, 1923
Beloved Wife of Late
Chief Tom
of the Squamish band of Indians
Also
Her Father
Chief George Capilano
who met Captain Cook in A.D. 1782
and was first to meet, welcome
and escort Captain Vancouver into
Burrard Inlet on the 14th June
A.D. 1792.   He advised his people
to follow his example in welcoming
the adventurers

(North Vancouver

The Truth Is Laughter 9

'verterberries,' the locals called them
after Mary Anning found
ichthysaur, 1811
pleoiosaur, 1824
pterodactyl, 1826

(out of Jacquetta Hawkes

Image-Nation 15 (the lacquer house

the cloudy sky grows dark
the peacock jeers
the cuckoo disappears
the swans have gone

the peregrine falcon, stately,
sits in the bare cherry tree
the radio says he really
nests downtown on the roof
of the Royal Centre tower
but today he, stately, sits
in the cherry tree
the pigeons hide, the wrens
fly away, the robins
look for another garden
this   vocation for
the invisible world
this second day
he's visited
even the cats get
under the rhododendrons

the candlestick
from New Brunswick
is a clear glass cross
with Christ on it
it speaks French
or, rather, Pascal—
that wonderful note
he sewed in his coat—
'Certitude, Certitude,
Sentiment, Joie,
Paix'

after the fire in the lacquer house,
the point is transformation of the theme—
enjoinment and departure—like
the Christmas trees, stripped of all
adornment, burned on Locarno Beach,
January 8th, 1981—
there were children in the catalpa
branches—one fell out into an
ambulance—his head full of wings,
oh, flower

Image-Nation 1 6 (anaclitic variations

                    a lean-to and
it is true   *the stars fell into language*
so many   *Guesses at Heaven*
throng in the air, we come upon them
now and again

he bathed in the dragon's blood
but a leaf of the linden stuck to
his skin   the weak spot at the beginning
'a-dieu,' he said, 'out of the golden-
tongued nightmare'

the real condition of light drinks
from the fingers   fooling the bees,
just as we drink from cups
and gold, wandering

the name-of-the-game is interpretable,
but   *not to be named is to be lost*
in light

                (phrases from Geoffrey Hartman and Keats

The Truth Is Laughter 10

one should never play martyr
there are martyrs beyond you

one should never argue apocalypse
without your whole lifetime before
you, which is impossible

    Pushkin said, 'my sadness
    is luminous'—that is
    his reason

Ralph flew to Bristol to see her
she said, 'You're not in touch with
Eternity'
he said, 'Gee, that's true,'
then later sent a telegram,
'meet me in Jerusalem,'
since he was going

alerte d'or

a parabolist and one who was fond of chimeras,
they talked quietly to one another
the alarm of gold   like bees
at the window   they were both
equally fond of the chimera'd,
thankful for the mirror

and the pearls rolled distinctly
among those who had changed form,
dead or alive, glistening
it was then they looked for
the moth in the words, or was it,
a scholar of these things asks, 'spiritual ketchup'?

there is a candle under the bed
or, changing the leaf of thought,
a flame in the rain   the rain
is almost glass, a perfection of flowers
those two talked, quiet on the blossom,
wise or not, of a blind spot

(phrases from Valéry and Geoffrey Hartman

The Truth Is Laughter 11

Time magazine said he used
a screwdriver to divine the reason
Moses took the long way around
and a spell in Arabic: *some days*
it's honey, some days
it's onions

The Truth Is Laughter 1 2

a radiant finger points

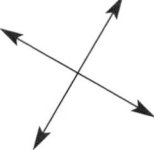

The Truth Is Laughter 1 3

all I could see were huge rocks
Mr. Larsen said that these were
musk oxen, the very things I thought
to be rocks   so I looked again
through the telescope and the rocks
began to move   we got near the musk oxen
and I found out they were carrying
something on their backs   I thought
to myself they must be carrying
their little ones, but I soon learned
that this was part of the animal
when you see musk oxen for the first time
they have a huge back on them

(from Joe Panipakuttuk,
originally written in Eskimo syllabics

The Truth Is Laughter 14

across the Bay there was a house
and there were two rooms in it
when the water started to come into the house
they went outside and brought in a canoe
they sat in the canoe inside the house
for two nights because the house was full
of water   the ten-gallon oil tanks were all
blown away and the Hudson's Bay
office was also blown away

(from Joe Panipakuttuk

A Ceremony

tenebrae   .   a true dark of shadows
where we meander among candles
they, one by one, depart from our hearts
unless   .   we bring them back   .
in the cure, there are fifteen and then
only one which is hidden in the total dark
of the garden   .   *strepitus*   .   the noise
of light   .   occurs   .   or wars and turns,
always sudden

Dreams, April 1981

so it is death is the
condition of infinite form—
the rebellion of particulars,
ourselves and each thing,
even ideas, against that infinitude,
is the story of finitude—the
dream of the children harvested
in a harvester-machine
there are the real voice
and the voice imagined
and both have a reality,
but the latter is out of it
the ladder of things

never accept gifts from the gods
—Hesiod's bitter-sweet sense of it—
rings true and doesn't
settle the sea-shore down
to where the *heart breaks or is bronzed*
'I am happy,' the man said,
'because the toad of the morning
is the worst thing I'll find today'
and CBC's TV critic says, 'television
is the Shakespeare of the 20th century'
red lilies fall on the carpet
and Art Tatum, drawing his art
out of hymns, wanted more dissonance
perfect

there are knives in the air
all around the poorly loved
their lives follow life back
into stone and they dream
a sweeter consonance at the centre
the art of a *screaming and*
demented oyster is not theirs
but I know both arts backwards
what the clothes man called the 'world-tissue'
does have a hole in it, 'must be,'
he said, 'darned-up again'

it is the substance must change—
that is, our sense of it—a music
among word-whiskers—among
dreams of the blue dog running
verdant hills   my words do not
crack it—the pure spelling lesson,
short of breath, goes back
to perform words   so *to perform*
the music of any past period
is simply, and profoundly, to seek
the life that is within death   that
plenishes   fills the house with
argued furniture   and rests

  he listened to the lark so long
  he didn't recognize the doorman

Diary, April 11, 1981

orchids in the kitchen, the colour
of plums   out of the window
the huge cherry tree is in full
white blossom   across the lane
its companion, as handsome,
was cut down and dug out
to park a camper   henceforth,
my neighbours, who spoke a soft,
shy German, were called The Bund
I'm as bad as Denise Levertov on
windows, except I haven't got one
over the sink   Boorman's arthurian
realism, illuminated by *Time* and
Newsweek, seems to dwell in his first
syllable   midway, the tough in the
men's room—after the lady of the
lake floated to the surface, dressed
in Sears' lamé or fishskin, smiling—
said, 'I've got those books at home,
this isn't it'   pop-art doesn't
ring twice, even Andy Warhol, unless
the orange electric chair sits in
the kitchen—comfy   well, they are
our questions: was Arthur an idiot?
didn't Uther take his armour off?
was Merlin a charlatan of the dragon
air, who maybe, knew something?
was Gwenivere easy traffic?   and
Lancelot a beach boy in his Sunday
best?   it is true you can get art
out of anything as it comes to be
the backside of itself   you see
the actor acting   in an anti-novel
you see the novel novelling   in the
anti-poem, an aesthetic raspberry is

thrilling or worn-out   if all
civilization is somebody's childhood
and somebody sits there forever x-ing
it out   ~~civilization~~   it's called
de-construction   it is there
and not there,   so his this-isn't-it
is exactly what it is   perhaps

and yet   I'd rather have
All That Jazz with its heart
attack

> *he lived in a time of the*
> *end of a culture and, as*
> *Charles Fair has pointed out,*
> *at such a time language*
> *is lost and the very meaning*
> *of 'soul' is lost*

and asks, 'what language do
you choose for the really Good News?'
Olson said, 'I'd trust you
anywhere with image, but
you've got no syntax'   (1958)
this comes to mind out of the
night and morning, rebelliously
reading Eckhart, today,
to put together in order   the
simplicity, the wings

The Truth Is Laughter 1 5

April 1 1, 1 9 8 1, CBC is discussing homosexual
'sweet-assed bulls'   they're a problem   it's best
to rope them and pull them out of the herd
but they won't go   it's best to send them
to market even if they aren't ready   and
female cockroaches give birth up to five weeks
after they're dead   goodness!

Occasional Thought

you can kiss my ass, but
then, I'm a gentle man,
so you can kiss anything you
want to   but no marriage

The Truth Is Laughter 1 6

a Polish placard:

WORKERS OF THE WORLD . . .

Image-Nation 17 (opercula

the monkey of gold found it,
a pencil, drew cities and planned
the factory, dreamed we were always
different from what we said or thought
what would the dawn be?   the earth looks up
at the rivers   there was no dawn,
yet we waited for noon, stumbling against
the shotgun, a western endowed with
mind and spirit   almost   I said,
'the eyelids of the bird, at least'
he said, 'the eyelids of the birds record
only your past, alas'   that sky I wandered!
of all such sweet thought, I wondered
long runs of vowels and unintelligible
magic words—Plotinus called them hissing
I thought of the end of the end,
the angelic speed of everyone's thought,
of dark angels, then slept

       this thought of the end of the end is the modern
       sweetness and terror, but it simplifies to terror
       alone—this societal dream of itself as absolute
       reality, then practiced as uniformity and barbarism,
       is the oily turntable of the round-house where we
       repair the engine again and again—it is the
       absolute humanism that is repulsive—reason
       darkened in the Enlightenment, a transparent manhood—
       imagination clothed him with women, cities and gods—
       he was headless until they bandaged his headache

I stuck to the antinaturalist thesis which denies the
continued existence of a good nature that has been
excluded, now returning from the great distance of its
buried origin   ourselves and our scapegrace   Hitler
and Stalin and mistaken Mao are within us, continuing,
and within the systems we think to prophesy them, but
we return to sainthood

the State does not wither away but becomes absolute
and everywhere—*a moment which never comes is a*
moment which goes on forever in what we've done   this
messianism, this millenniumism of the Holy Ghost, the
dearest dream of Joachim of Fiore (1145–1202)

can be traced right down to the present day . . .
horrified though the unworldly mystic would have
been to see it happen, it is unmistakably the
Joachite phantasy of the three ages that reappeared
in, for instance, the theories of historical evolution
expounded by the German Idealist philosophers,
Lessing, Schelling, Fichte, and, to some extent, Hegel;
in Auguste Comte's idea of history as an ascent from
the theological through the metaphysical up to
the scientific phase; and again in the Marxian
dialectic of the three stages of primitive communism,
class society and a final communism which is to be
the realm of freedom and in which the state will
wither away.   And it is no less true—if even more
paradoxical—that the phrase 'the Third Reich,'
first coined in 1923 by the publicist Moeller van den
Bruck, and later adopted as a name for that 'new order'
which was supposed to last a thousand years, would
have had but little emotional significance if the
phantasy of a third and most glorious dispensation
had not, over the centuries, entered into the common
stock of European social mythology.

And he took him and withdrew and told him three things.
When Thomas returned to his companions, they asked him,
'What did Jesus say to you?'

Thomas said to them, 'If I tell you one of the things
which he told me, you will pick up stones and throw them
at me; a fire will come out of the stones and burn you up.'

the sacred returns with all its faces,
fiery-footed

the fiery dew of the streets, coloured
by oil-slicks and dawn, leads down
to the sea at a snail's pace   who
looks wishly upon it, unlocks the lock-hole
of the chest again   I slept,
the prose thought, and it seemed to me
that eyelids wept

(after reading Eric Voegelin's *From Enlightenment to Revolution*,
        Bernard-Henri Lévy's *Barbarism with a Human Face*,
            Norman Cohn's *The Pursuit of the Millennium*
                                April 29, 1981

graffito

Artists are the deodorant pucks in the urinals of life.

(men's room, Leo's Fish House, Gastown

The Mystic East

Jerry's Nose
Come-by-Chance
Blow-me-down
Bumble Bee Bight
Ha Ha Bay
Bleak Joke Cove
Nancy Oh
Joe Batt's Arm
Gripe Point
Bad Bay
Misery Point
Famish Gut
Confusion Bay
Empty Basket
Heart's Desire
Heart's Content
Safe Harbour
Sweet Bay
Little Paradise
Angel's Cove
Cupids
English Harbour
Portugal Cove
Harbour Breton
Frenchman's Cove
Ireland's Eye
Bay D'Espoir, heard as Bay Despair
Chaleur Bay
Plate Cove
Ladle Cove
Chimney Cove
Spoon Cove
Rooms
Bread Island
Cheese Island
Mistaken Point

Butter Cove
Tea Cove
Sugar Loaf
Cape Onion
Turnip Cove
Mutton Bay
Black Island
Red Island
Green Island
White Bay
Orange Bay
Blue Cove
Grey Islands
Lion's Den
Bear Cove
Horse Chops
Hare's Ears Point
Dog Cove
Cat Gut
Seal's Nest Island
Dragon Bay
Fox Roost
Muskrat Brook
Goat Island
Goose Bay
Eagle Island
Trout River
Button Island
Shoe Cove
Stocking Harbour
Petticoat Island
Hatchet Cove
Sitdown Pond
Goblin
False Cape
God Almighty Cove

God Bay
Sacred Bay
Devil Cove
Nick's Nose Cove

Nameless Cove
Harbour Harbour

(Historic *Newfoundland*

lake of souls (reading notes

it's dawn and things move about quickly,
a bird sound at the end of every sentence,
the period dissolves and becomes a curve of notes

this indefinite spiritual condition   it is
probably the secret of syntax itself   it is not
a dream; rather, like syntax, it is a violence
or a love   the depths of it are not a
privilege, but everybody's: the solitude of
civilization

I think of Cavafy's poem *Waiting for the Barbarians*

> *Why should they be carrying today their precious walkingsticks,*
> *with silver knobs and golden tops so wonderfully carved?*
> > *Because the Barbarians will arrive today;*
> > *things of this sort dazzle the Barbarians.*

but in the poem the barbarians didn't come

> *And now what will become of us without Barbarians?*
> *Those people were some sort of solution.*

this spiritual condition which is everybody's language
of the world is not finally as small as my own solitaire

I have been taught the sacred in three languages from my
earliest life in words—pouring over the crazy-quilt—*Credo*
in unum Deum Patrem omnipotentem, factorem coeli et terrae,
visibilium omnium et invisibilium / Je crois en un seul Dieu,
le Père tout puissant qui a fait le ciel et la terre, toutes
les choses visibles et invisibles / I believe in one God, the
Father, the almighty, maker of heaven and earth, of all that
is seen and unseen—The Nicene Creed, 325 A.D. reaffirmed
by the first Council of Constantinople, 381 A.D.—of twisted
threads—one pleasure of the words was that they dreamed in
the sagebrush of peoples, far places and nations   murmuring—

lovely word, that—in Greek, to roar or boil, of water,
in Sanskrit, a humming sound, of bees perhaps

in 1945, I ran into Jack Spicer, beloved friend, who was then
somehow both a Presbyterian and a Buddhist   he said, 'Oh,
you're one of those who eat your god.'

on Easter Sunday, 1946, Robert Duncan, Leonard Wolf and I
went to Blake's Restaurant on Telegraph Avenue for
strawberry sundaes   Duncan said of the strawberries, 'Ah,
Christ's wounds. Yum!'   in those days, I ran into the
street   in tears   among the traffic

in 1947, I published this poem in the campus literary
magazine, *Occident*   Keith Jones, who is now a labour leader
among the grapes, reviewed that issue and praised my poem
especially, but the campus newspaper, *The Daily Cal*, hated the
poem and published a counter-review in which they said the
refrain in the poem should read, 'Keith Jones, dance with me'

Song in Four Parts for Christ the Son

I

Put on Your colours in the light of day.
You are the rose that needs no day.
The rose is dead
As He is dead.
Put on Your colours; they are fair.
There is a light wound round Your hair.

II

Dance like a gamecock, spurred,
God.
Dance in the weather.

He is the God Forever.
The dancers come,
One by one.
He is the God forever.
The day spreads,
He is dead.
He is the God forever.
Even so,
The dancers are
Soft on toe
And slow to give
Praise to Him.

III

Gamecocks go with the weather, Love.
Here in the sand
Let us plan
Love again.
He sleeps where the day is.
Out of the sun
He may come
To dance again.

I shall see the rose in the tree.
Christ, in heaven, dance with me.

IV

But all of this is kneeling
And as false as song.
Mary, Our Lady,
Among the blessèd gone,
Tell him for me
That the day belongs
To the dancers.

The rose in heaven is without a tree.
Christ, in heaven, dance with me.

Anna Russell said of singers—'they have a resonance where
their brains ought to be'

I think, nonsensically, of Oscar Wilde's poem which Jack liked
to quote

> Sometimes a horrible marionette
> Came out, and smoked its cigarette
> Upon the steps like a live thing

Because the very concept of deity, much less   (René Girard
a deity who receives blood sacrifices, has
little reality in this day and age, the
entire institution of sacrifice is relegated
by most modern theorists to the realm
of imagination

ah, speaking of imagination, let's get our principles straight—
I'll repeat only three of them—1, 5 & 6

1. That the Poetic Genius is the true Man.   (William Blake
and that the body or outward form of Man
is derived from the Poetic Genius. Like-
wise that the forms of all things are de-
rived from their Genius, which by the
Ancients was call'd an Angel & Spirit &
Demon.

5. The Religeons of all Nations are de-
rived from each Nation's different re-
ception of the Poetic Genius which is
every where call'd the Spirit of Prophecy.

6. *The Jewish & Christian Testaments are*
An original derivation from the Poetic
Genius. This is necessary for the con-
fined nature of bodily sensation.

Anna Russell on CBC interrupts again:

I gave my love a cherry with no pit
my love gave me a pair of golden shoes that didn't fit.
'If you like this kind of song, you can sing it
for yourself,' she said

The solemn debates on the death of god or   (René Girard
of man are perhaps beside the point. They remain
theological at bottom, and by extension sacrificial;
that is, they draw a veil over the subject of
vengeance, which threatens to become quite real
once again, in the form not of philosophical
debate, but of unlimited violence, in a world with
no absolute values. As soon as the essential
quality of transcendence—religious, humanistic, or
whatever—is lost, there are no longer any terms
by which to define the legitimate form of violence
and to recognize it among the multitude of
illicit forms. The definitions of legitimate and
illegitimate forms then become a matter of mere
opinion, with each man [or woman] free to reach
his [or her] own opinion. In other words, the
question is thrown to the winds.

The sacred consists of all those forces   (René Girard
whose dominance over man increases or seems
to increase in proportion to man's effort to master
them. Tempests, forest fires, and plagues . . . may
be classified as sacred. Far outranking
these . . . stands human violence . . . Violence
is the heart and secret soul of the sacred.

How did man succeed in positing his own
violence as an independent being?   and then
call it politics?

      graffito   (men's room,
                                                              Vancouver Airport

Born on a mountain
Raised in a cave
Bikin' and Fuckin'
Are all I crave

Totalitarianism is the new fact in our   (Bernard-Henri Lévy
time?   Yes, but *we must emphasize*
that the crisis of the sacred is primary
and decisive.
The barbarian state is a
forecast of our future?   Yes, but it must
be rooted in the inaugural oracle
represented by the birth of the atheist
state . . .
this is the first time the world
has gone without a point of reference, an
attachment to the divine.

If pure secularism . . . is simply another   (Geoffrey Hartman
religion [of life, nature, and hell], its god
will appear at some point.

Poets having expelled the old gods, their
images, their phraseology—in short,
poetic diction—and, having instituted a
more natural diction, the process of
purification continues, not so happily,
and the purified language proves to be as
contaminated as ever. We see that the
poetic diction once rejected had
extraordinary virtues, including its non-

natural character, its lucid artifice, the
'mirror-of-steel uninsistence' (Marianne
Moore) by which it made us notice
smallest things and ciphered greatest
things, and gathered into a few terms,
magical, memorable, barely meaningful,
the powers of language.

Swift as a spirit hastening to his task   (Shelley
Of glory and of good, the Sun sprang forth
Rejoicing in his splendour, and the mask

Of darkness fell from the awakened Earth—
The smokeless altars of the mountain snows
Flamed above crimson clouds, and at the birth

Of light, the Ocean's orison arose,
To which the birds tempered their matin lay.
All flowers in field or forest which unclose

Their trembling eyelids to the kiss of day,
Swinging their censers in the element,
With orient incense lit by the new ray

Burned slow and inconsumably, and sent
Their odorous sighs up to the smiling air;
And, in succession due, did continent,

Isle, ocean, and all things that in them wear
The form and character of mortal mould,
Rise as the Sun their father rose, to bear

Their portion of the toil, which he of old
Took as his own, and then imposed on them:
But I, whom thoughts which must remain untold,

Had kept as wakeful as the stars that gem
The cone of night, now they were laid asleep
Stretched my faint limbs beneath the hoary stem

Which an old chestnut flung athwart the steep
Of a green *Apennine*: before me fled
The night; behind me rose the day; the deep

Was at my feet, and Heaven above my head, —
When a strange trance over my fancy grew
Which was not slumber, for the shade it spread

Was so transparent, that the scene came through
As clear as when a veil of light is drawn
O'er evening hills they glimmer: and I knew

That I had felt the freshness of that dawn
Bathe in the same cold dew my brow and hair,
And sate as thus upon that slope of lawn

Under the self-same bough, and heard as there
The birds, the fountains and the ocean hold
Sweet talk in music through the enamoured air,
And then a vision of my brain was rolled.

Herakleitos, inspired, according to Plato, by the 'more severe muses,' said

God is day and night, winter and summer
conflict and peace, fullness and emptiness;
but he takes various shapes, just as fire,
when it is mingled with aromatic herbs, is
named according to the scent of each.

(Thomas Merton's translation

Light rising in the east and light going   (Henry Corbin
down in the west are two premonitions of
an existential option between the world of
Day with its criteria and the world of
Night with its deep and insatiable
passions. At best, on the boundary
between the two we have a two-fold
twilight: the crepusculum vespertinum,
no longer day but not yet night; the
crepusculum matutinum, no longer night
but not yet day. This striking image, as
we know, was used by Luther to define
the being of man.

and Bach lived that definition far better

but we here in the North are in the light which is *neither*
eastern nor western, the northern light, midnight sun, aurora
borealis

> the emerald day
> with its shepherd of the black light
> and the eternal mothers of the black milk
> turn
> in the acts of light

Departure (envoi-commiato

Aristotle said, 'all men by nature desire
     to know'
Dante added, 'every man by nature is a
     friend to every other man'

I believe both worlds
          and dream their necessity,
natural, cautious,
            jewelled interior of all work
of the day—or night—
     then turn, as if asleep
the shapes of happiness shimmer in the air,
composing,   for the good is our own composition
out of the air of our movement   back and forth

they say I have no right to speak of it,
spoiled and thoughtful—the *meaningless*
pain   for which *there is no remedy,*
except   *words*   *consciousness*   *memory*

and such songs, as if they went to earth,
that sit around my heart—intelligent—

further,

after I did look looks at the clock, I did   (Opal Whiteley
look looks out the front window. There are
calf-tracks by our front window. These tracks
are there because when I went walking with
Elizabeth Barrett Browning on yesterday, I
had her wait at the front step while I did go
into the kitchen to get her some sugar-lumps.
She has a fondness for sweet things. I think
she will grow up to be a lovely cow. Her
mooings now are very musical, and there is
poetry in her tracks. She does make such
dainty ones. When they dry up in the lane, I
dig up her tracks, and I save them. There is
much poetry in them; and when I take her
tracks out that I keep in the back part of the
cook-table drawer,

the light-eagles glide on the air
where the *shadow that is language*   (Hermann Broch
reaches out to unfold reality again

as the god tumbling down into a fake-humanity
in the man catapulted to a false-divinity

enters the mind, willy-nilly   to unfold our form
the mind wanders   DISCREATION, nameless
therefore, the quotations to transform time
and argue with *unart* and *mere litereity*
fate and form are interchangeable
the anger between them
is the dream in skin on our bones

Some Voices in Syntax

Bernard-Henri Lévy, *La Barbarie à visage humain* (Grasset & Faquelle, 1977). English translation by George Holoch, *Barbarism with a Human Face* (Harper & Row, 1979).

Norman Cohn, *The Pursuit of the Millennium: Revolutionary Millenarians and Mystical Anarchists of the Middle Ages*. Rev. & exp. edition (Oxford, 1970).

The Gospel According to Thomas, Coptic text and translation by A. Guillaumont et al. (Harper, 1959).

Abiezer Coppe, *A Fiery Flying Roll: A Word from the Lord to all the Great Ones of the Earth, whom this may concerne: Being the last* WARNING PIECE *at the dreadful day of* JUDGEMENT (1649). Excerpted in Norman Cohn, *The Pursuit of the Millennium*.

René Girard, *La Violence et le sacré* (Grasset, 1972). English translation by Patrick Gregory, *Violence and the Sacred* (Johns Hopkins, 1977).

William Blake, 'ALL RELIGIONS ARE ONE,' (1788). In *The Poetry and Prose of William Blake*, ed. David V. Erdman (Doubleday, 1970).

Geoffrey Hartman, *Criticism in the Wilderness: The Study of Literature Today* (Yale, 1980). Other books by Hartman which haunt some of the poems by phrase and intention are *The Fate of Reading* (Chicago, 1975) and *Beyond Formalism* (Yale, 1970). His *Saving the Text: Literature/Derrida/Philosophy* (Johns Hopkins, 1981) came into my hands after *Syntax* was complete. (I was fascinated to find Hartman drawn to Cavafy's poem 'Waiting for the Barbarians' in his opening essay.) This brilliant book is again a companion for the poet reading poetry to find the layers of the real—especially the last chapter, 'Words and Wounds': '. . . the "dread voice" exists as the poem or not at all.'

Percy Bysshe Shelley, 'The Triumph of Life' (1822), 11. 1–40, in *Poetical Works*, 2nd ed., ed. Thomas Hutchinson (Oxford, 1970).

Thomas Merton, *The Behavior of Titans* (New Directions, 1961), includes a study of Herakleitos.

Henry Corbin, *L'Homme de lumière dans le soufisme iranien*. English translation by Nancy Pearson, *The Man of Light in Iranian Sufism*

(Shambhala, 1978), wonderfully returning my sequence to
   our northern lights with which I began.
Along with 'Departure (envoi-commiato,' remember Dante's
   'Tre donne intorno al cor mi son venute,' finely translated
   by Patrick S. Diehl in *Dante's Rime* (Princeton, 1979).
Hermann Broch, *The Death of Virgil* (Routledge, 1946), wondrous
   and among prose-poems, perhaps, the greatest.
Opal Whiteley, *The Story of Opal* (Atlantic Monthly, 1920)—later
   I found Jane Boulton's loving adaptation, composed 'during
   long snowy months on a sheep ranch in Alberta, Canada':
   Opal: The Journal of an Understanding Heart (Tioga, 1984).

And a further voice:

Intensity & Extensity combinable only by blessed
Spirits—Hence that Lovers in their finite state
incapable of fathoming the intensity of their
feelings *help* the thought *out* by extension & thus
think the passion as wide in *time* as it is deep
in essence. Hence—auf ewig dein [thine
forever]!

                                                   (Coleridge

And remember George Whalley, beloved scholar.

Pell Mell

1981–1988

for David Farwell & Rob Dunham

Waiting for Hours

listen, kid,
there isn't anything but art
and the effort to turn it into
the same discourse as
everything else is
scientific
angelism, disguised as
who-dun-it   after all
on art, I'm a kind of
Fibber McGee and Molly
talkin' over the horseshoe
found in 1901 —and should
I find three more, we
could have a game in
the backyard—close
the closet, undisturbed by
the ten-foot pole we
wouldn't touch anything
by, if offered—oh—
the hours remind me of
thirty robins' dreams,
snowflakes as big as cigarette
papers

the best thing ever said about me
critically was 'alien exotica'
but I looked out of my eyes at
the piano shawl and wondered
how the fringe could move so
ceaselessly over the fat back
and that was supposed to stop me
dead in my tracks—my job—my
heart—and anything I ever told you
that you believed—wow—magic
and disgusting fun people, also

Skylight

shadow of a bird
            cloud
        rain
                            Dante's face in the
raindrop—clear—   strangely
did not wash away—

Cold Morning Quotations

Being is what remains, not what is)Hartman

The last crows that are heard are named 'Why')Nietzsche

Thanatography)Hartman

Thanatopraxis)Derrida

the morning   of short
    thought—gifts of rest and
    difference   I stop short
the december tomatoes shine on the top of the refrigerator
    cold, barely ripe or thoughtful
the most beautiful madrigals of Monteverdi
    play their human emotion in the
    next room—an achievement at the turn
    of the next room
the *shattered marble* of my unwalled
    thought enters the Rondanini Pietá
    silently—*shaking hands of the substance*
    melt away,
in the Florence Pietá, he has removed
    Mary from her place and holds Christ
    himself to his bosom

knowledge-aware, knowledge-fraught, knowledge-
persuading, the provenance of every true song
                             turns
existence toward a thirst for superficialities

lacking a future, a past has never existed

the boy said, *'Make way for Virgil'*
enchantment of water

reality of fate—sham-infinity, sham-

timelessness, sham-seclusion
sham-divinity, sham-holiness

your path is poetry, your goal is beyond
poetry

which is called poetry, the strangest
of all human occupations, the only one
dedicated to the knowledge of death

      [fragment structures—serial poems—
      all having to do with materiality of
      form—having to do with death]

this was like a language that is
no longer a bridge between people,
like an extra-human laughter,
its range of scorn playing about
the factual worldly-estate as such,
that in reaching beyond the
realm of all things human no
longer derides humanity but simply
destroys it by exposing the nature
of the world

herds of gods, of men, of animals, of plants, herds
     of stars
containing each other   )Broch

New Year's, 1982
     my mind goes blank, not from
     hangover—that year is hard
     to hold on to because the maestoso
     was missing, except for the last
     chapter of The Death of Virgil, read
     at 7:45 p.m.—

Image-Nation 18 (an apple

the mind I want, like an
   apple, childish
I've followed every great friend
   I've known—Spicer, Duncan,
   Olson, Creeley, Zukofsky—
not to own it   I would write
   it—having slept too long,
the ferns dream as they return
   to green
out of winter   the streets shine
with oil slicks and rain
I
wonder,
        the words wound,
splendid gifts of guilt and wit
   Night-birds, someone said,
are those men and women who try
to force their way into the reality
of others
        the 'Old Europe,'
Sharon Thesen said, 'which endureth, parsed
                by structuralists,'
who don't know
        Pound said,
'you have to find it'—
the structure—of life—
which means—no longer
can philosophy find it, the
mental thing about it
   so we've gone from one thing
to another
   the effort is moral—how
are you?
        you can take it and

build the rock
(the origin of the word unknown)
            you'll wobble
unless you're the crust
               of it

LOVE is FORM
      intimacy is the loveliest
      part of thought

i.e., I am so separate a man
these days,
bending the fabric of space

universe is part of ourselves

Olson said, 'The MORAL IS FORM &
      nothing else and the MORAL ACT
      is the honest—"sincere" motion in
      the direction of FORM'

'Amo o'   lead with consonants

well, so it is,
         but some stall,
most keep their seats   stave off

larkspur   standing far

God bless jazz bands everywhere

and why not know   love
   is form

'the whole question & continuing
        struggle to remain civilized'

you've got to keep it up—find
your heart in the creation   you
came from   lower middle-class
except for Sophia Nichols' dream—
her Shakespeare,
in the middle of the modern,
1945, where was it?

to have met, 1952?—'The MORAL
IS FORM & nothing else
and the MORAL ACT is the
honest—"sincere" motion in the
direction of FORM'

'Form, in fact, is now definable
as tensions'

'amo o'

6 November '82—Dream of a poem
which went   so............prize
                   ....
                   ....
                              surprise   )in
stanzas

so the wind does prize
the last thought
of the bow
gold, silver, brass, iron
of the air;
surprise

so the beings larger than life
prize the over and under
of light-mush
where my feet wander on;

surprise the sweet waiting a prize
of the May to December game,
the is-ain't
love of canaries circling
eyes and time,

liquid and bitter,
prize of the rainbow-shadow

draw there in the light-dark, say,
'may we be those who bring
about the transfiguration
of the world-surprise'

Fousang

You made the past
a myth of nature
or history

you said the future
would be this or
that, devouring
the unpredictable

you fell into the East
destroying an alphabet
the future disappeared
for a myriad

millennial silliness
at the heart of your notation—
I address you personally
because you have become
personal to each of us

a progression that knows
the limit and argues it
into a slime   the whole
light-body, unpredictable
terrible, sexual, torn heart
of the matter is not there
matter is not there,
                        for that

we can thank Soviets
and U.S.'s alike, who alike stand
for nothing

matter is not there—turning,
the birds of paradise grow
feet and claws—the terror
becomes elegant as in your grammar
we are cast into nothing

a banal face oozes
out of the grass, gently,
because your future will,
you say, solve it, but there
is no future unless it be
unpredictable

we are left to sift among servants,
masters, despots and slaves
maybe, one day, the concrete substance,
the community of ourselves,
unpredictable language of our
notation will return

they knew it   home
it should be and the railway
sunlit is,   after all, a destiny
everyday

•

the bow, carvèd gold, Blake
said,
and the four zoas

turn in the heart, turn in the

air, a big wheel

turns, a little wheel turns,

a world, the light-spur of what we meant

mistaken and right by the river,
the north of my heart, winged,
splendid, the creatures live in
their amber and earth—sapphire
and crystal   I dream the
wind, the streets, the leaves
and the bank of the river, innocent
and experienced
at the edge of it, the larks singing back
to back
                    the frosted glass,
etched with clarities, thoughts,
rhythms, because the living creatures
of centuries
                    draw the bow
a carvèd sweetness out of 6,000,000
years   the steps of the creatures, not
spectrous   neither male nor
female singing a brightening
form in the harbour, arguing these days
against the muteness

I want you to tell me how old we
are—not simply a future-form,
cut from the effort—new and
unrinsed   I want you to see
the turn of events   the horror,
the childish matches, the flow
of the effort   information is not simply
genetic, social, momentary, but strife in events
in the earth—
unorganized—brilliant, beautiful—
the heart of the matter   unfolds matter

the living creatures stomp on the earth,
tell it, repeat, enter the shine
of
　　how old we are
back to back the larks sing, back
to back the creatures sing, back
to back, the beginning and the
end of it—out of it, the
light-patches of a crazy-quilt
arrange, derange, a range
of the movement—lifted, so that,
at one moment end and beginning meet
full of laughter

you will think backwards of the beast
of ourselves, not forwards—not out of reaction,
but out of primordial surmise
　　　　　　　　　　　　　thought as of a violet,
golden, sweet, the violet companion

through the labyrinth of the buildings,
and between them, where the next,
labyrinth begins of corridors and
corners I saw a massive stone, simultaneously natural
and shaped, I thought, 'a monument
to the venture,' and loved it where the heart
could be carved in reality on the breast of it,
a small pendant stone without a necklace   swings in the breeze

　•

every child knows that China lies in
the West. *The Northwest Coast was a dominion, a future sphere of*
empire, whose distance at once shaped its development and kept it
secret from the wider world until the late eighteenth century.
Fifteen hundred years before this the Chinese had known of
'Fousang.' They called it the country of the extreme east.

Mooning

Hello, goodbye

you wouldn't know the (sun

or) moon from your own ass

what did the moon say?
clear and bright in the frosted
air—a slight tick and
sticking under my shoes, what

did the moon say   bright features,
or half of it, from here
the kindness and common
touch of gold and green
and blue tip of the hovered
hedgerow   the eye of the sea
answers the eye of the moon,
great questions of the appearance
of things   what did the disc

say except crackling in fire
which the fingers trick and
let go   changed and fumbling,
to melt and wonder where
the edge is   the half of the
world must have the other
half   of whatever terror

our time found and dis-
membered   and then re-
membered the half of it,
distantly violent   the superb
beast of ourselves   composed
what it could not see—
the other half of it
the would-be flower missing
from all thought, sweet
treat of the unresolved
heart of it—what heart
exists except as relation,
joinment   the paradise
has no substance, but that
is the pleasure of paradise,
no substance, the moon said,
shifting the trees, the stubble,
the sand and the footsteps
the moon said, you wouldn't
know the lack of substance

The Iceberg

I want no summer to melt you
I want no tip to disappear where
I find you—and the largeness
out there, wanders, incomplete,
a constant creation to leap into

'Love' wanders, the speechless
mind of it, all that cost of the
flowers and statues—all that
city of delighted streets and
whimpers   O, the locked heaven
whose gate jangles   I wonder
at the steep of it

then wait, astonished that
the sweet heart grows in some
root or depth—and turns
into ceremonies   there are
the losses of the heartland, light,
sleepless forms against themselves
I repeat you, endlessly—

common, sorrowing, old,
and gigantic
                    this waits
and spits the bird image that
began icily in the distance to
save us, unaware that it lifted,
or was said to, the tip of ourselves

                    for Michael Ondaatje

Sock-hop

don't put your shoes on the
floor, but dance somewhere,
loose in the floor-shine

what is indigenous—the repetitious self—the land—
that old flesh we dreamed as if it were permanent?

the glass clusters 'to repossess the dynamic'
like certain flowers bunch to believe
a definition—the bright jug-jug of a reversed
meaning

crocodile smiles, I thought
among bright rocks of what
I return to

return to the largeness of
'the great appearances of nature'
of cities that sound so new
in the morning, the cement gardens, resolute

of the supernatural language and
angelic horns or hounds of the
light creatures, a nodding joy of
creations

the slip of the thing, the dew
or mist at the feet of   the throb
remembers, sullen or not, the
long shining

'sweet,' I said, knowing the
sweat mountain, the turn in the
corridors, and unthreaded
tapestries that tell the horror

the gymnasium breathed somewhat
where we danced the Big Apple
and taught the Lambeth Walk,
shoes off   naked, I am not
sorry to come home

Useful Triads

in the silver mind, accused of *gravitas*
and dog collars, the truth is neither
abstract nor free

simplicity's trick of exactly (!) owes
much, and the 'O's of grandeur
are bought off with red mascara

it's original, of course, to slip and slide
over the beef and vegetables, simmer playfully
on the home-plate

you're astride something, if you pee
powerfully and it tinkles in the depths
splattering the awesome

do you think it possible (when it
has no referent) to point straight
or kiss the crooked or some mouth or

another moment's attention steams
in the kettle where black currants
roll with the surface tension

there could be a change of heart,
somebody said, but it was the clock
who does not speak it

let's begin with the academics, peripatetics,
stoics and epicureans: Plato walks about
the painted porch of the atoms

purpose is dog-tired, I suppose, limp—
the dicks wander from one crack
in the world to another, soluble

dong dong dong dong | dong dong dong dong
dong dong dong dong | dong dong dong dong
what time is it?

the infinite faces of the living mount
the analogue and sweet difference,
'in holding the terrain in place'

let's start with something else
and get old carelessly   it was
his nature to be invisible

and that could be anywhere:
'everything takes place as if we
did not exist everywhere'

angels and companions: let's start
with Bacon, Descartes, Newton, Hobbes
and continue instantly

à cet ultime instant, c'est la supercherie qui
relate la fatique du siècle
    —René Char

the tired century and ultimate image
of what we've been through in
the thousands   the night air fills
with a sorrow that completes
itself   no world there or possible
edge, for it collapses the real
trees

cities summarize us, that is the
reason I've loved them and
their early sounds from the train
station   that is the reason to
depart   they were originally built
for the gods

and I worked at the edge of them
with the sugar beets where reason
made cauldrons, and I saw,
not, as John did, a judgement,
but the sweet flesh boil in what
was otherwise summer and
paradise

thoughtless, I saw them, bees
in the skyscrapers   honey ran
golden and buzzed like airplanes
because you couldn't see the
source

the sight goes wounded everywhere,
not where the arrow falls, swift
and sometimes 'wonderland in
the legends of Gilgamesh and
Hercules is a kind of obstacle
course'

'the struggle for life' is not 'among
races or classes as totalitarian
ideologies' suppose   it is among
shadows   who died there in the
century, careless and proper,
in one view lifted off the ground
by futurity, a kind of hurricane,
named male or female but
androgyne at the beginning,
golden mortality left us immortal
repose, a large, crowded reception
in a private house

The Pause

out and wondrous, there, where
I found them someone wanders,
pauses   'O, it was you, was it!'

who was it said, 'only the belovèd answers,'
that gardens close and walls limit
because they are paradise and untrue

the wall around heaven is untrue, stings
in all the political ferment where I
found it, topsy-turvy, raggedy-ann of

that deadly plaything, thought, the leading
edge of the process, why will you
try to find yourself finite and sure,

the pleasure-dome, and then excuse
its irrealism by futurity, this
desire-to-live does not stop there

you've got a share of it, only the dis-
missed quality is the momentary
now I see 'you,' now I don't

that is the pleasure of the kingdom, old
vocabulary—replaced by the dictatorship
of a sameness

the big, white ball of thought
with its patent leather evening shoes, tap-
dancers that don't need polish until they're

worn-out   like you, I found
them, a radiance, without cause,
like trees, long-life and short-life,

'nothing remains constant,'   I tried
with my love to stop them, to fuck
them, but they are the transformation

of everything, rising into other
things   and 'things' are a desire
big as you are

do you know that Copernicus attacked
and Darwin attacked and Freud attacked
our self-love

the transcendent value of the future
mystification, the death of so many,
things do appear in their own terms, changing

I found them in a mist and a glade,
and a stone, and a shattered wind-
shield, driven to the wreckage of one sweet thought

Moments

Thematicists think it all makes sense

Plato fucked the middle voice

Wilde said, 'Either those drapes go or I go'

bp: 'death words: "what I meant to say was"'

McCaffery: 'abstract ruin'

our battle with the book is our Buddhist battle

Story

John Bentley Mays said, 'This
is UNESCO pablum'
but I loved the man's brown forehead
and white hair   he had been
sure for almost a century of
culture as transcendent, not
conflict

'the universe is part of ourselves'

we have been everywhere, suddenly,
and twisted the clarities into bottles
and casements

it was the lintel concerned us
we walked through and wondered
above us

the larks of heaven perch and nothing

over the walls, the vision gossips
like rivers, and wishes, marvellous,
perish

we have been everywhere, suddenly,
glorious texture   the chorus added
eagerness, swiftness

intellect whispers, meanders, softly
landed   remarkable ponds and
cattails

the ferns dream as they return
to green   the efformation, the
dis-creation, the kindness of fragments

the larks of heaven perch and nothing

for bp nichol

Romance

the opposite of meaning is not
meaninglessness, what do these big
words mean in the panic, well,
panic means heart   before we had
formed this, it was Pan, my dear,
and tufts of plants   before we had
planned or kissed it, before
we had dreamed the leaves and
historical consequences, before the
painted ocean and storms, before
the water everywhere, drunken and
sunned, stopped us, before the
rock of our spirit, before doorsteps
and fountains and fragments, before
cats and dogs and cities, the
endless footsteps, before sweetness
and mountains, before paradise
and walled gardens, before
streets and manufacture, cars
and desire, after stars and
constellations are probable, we
found it

No-name

let us take shape now in
whatever animus or anima
we have shaped it

'it' is the favourite immaterial
pronoun—no fixed meaning   the
relation

the definition is relational   the
sweet relation   the horror whose
power is perfect

somewhere, sometime, in your
small voice, founded in palms
and swamp-eddies

the grasses gleam   the gleam
grasses, dew and departure

sunlight, my sweetheart, and
green, heartless nature, large
appearances

did heaven have heart and
aggregation to itself in the great
flower?

O distances   space came, immaterial
and time seemed physical   false
propositions

yet, I hear the crowds weep there,
among them, whispering hugeness,
lips and derangement

O, good morning or terror, goodbye
of such kisses   with you my salutation

The Soul

someday, the windows   the transparency
screams   open and zippers

the last minute—processions—marriages—
meetings   such rainbows or corners

raindrops—the sound of—which
winds slap or wander

solitude   perfect   agreement
disordered

take it this way or that way
upwards and downwards, sideways
and backwards

reminders of rivers, streets,
sidewalks, the pathways

of whatever form, reforming
a definition backward and outward
of this misnomer—

there it wings, homing, dim
or not, flashes, caught, and
then winters,

a slip of a thing, in and out,
statues and stillness, walks easily

the thigh of the thing, between things, golden
and repetitious

surfaces swim, collecting
the depths and inevitable summers of
there-it-is

Desire

the other turns out to be art and
writing

'I want to forget that I met this
life,' 'I want to remember it
always'   I want to go bye, go bye

joyance (Coleridge), jouissance
(Kristeva) who would avoid toppling
into poetry   but then
poetry does not wish to fall into
theory, but they love one another
when the pure efficacy of poetry
comes into repute
a reckoning

a lifetime spent   thinking
it over and absolute   the absolute
is nothing but love that will not
be denied   also no more
than a clod and a pebble,
dissolute and lutenist

where was the betrayal of the
immutable?

Anecdote

often, I write on top of the
stove's hotplates—elements?—
and leave the notebook there
overnight

the question is: will it burn?
in the morning, it is cold
paper, coldly scribbled on

the next night I do the same
thing   trap of the child
and man   will you, won't

you turn on by yourself, do
you, don't you   say something
almost entirely

almost immortal, lost among
causes and first spoken
moments become

the last are unwritten in
a mazy motion above
ground

what did I think language
did, as I grew up   well,
it pulled me into

and out-of, upwards-of
and downwards-of, the
side-by-side, serpentine friendship

I've known many but few
did more than repeat themselves
the others disappeared into language,

divided from wholeness, they
are, in their language,
desirous and sightful

awesome, sweet labourers
of something

The Ruler

alligator, hippopotamus, fox, rhinoceros
and frog
dog, bear, cat, mouse and badger
in rowing shells   frog and badger
with the megaphones   they're rowing to
a finish

it begins in the womb—with sound—in the tissue—speech
is later—the music of words

your eyes are wooden   where are the
deep pools   the moment of trees
and their suddenness among
thwarted winds around skyscrapers
and umbrellas

your eyes are like wood, yet she
talked to the images of kings and
queens, like everybody else, having
the power to be one

but that was because of cancer
and her eyes yellowed   she had
more life than I knew in her
rowing shell, gently, sweet river

and the images she spoke to were
not small and included the
little match girl frozen and
fiery outside the windows

she of such searching, who felled
the tree and planed the boards—'chuck chuck
chuck   of the adze'

the ruler is a child's 25 centimetre
measure of the old foot—how tall are you?—
they are rowing in three dimensions,
never to get there

alligator, hippopotamus, fox, rhinoceros,
and frog
dog, bear, cat, mouse and badger,
in the shell of a boat, enchanted,
with honey wrapped up in the intelligence
between one boat and another

Skylights Smoking a Ramses Cigarette, a Gift in a Pink Box

smoking the splendour, the odours, smoking
a staring colossus across the shining
water, smoking the centuries, his name
on condoms, afloat in the estuary, *that*
beautiful face in Turin, the strewn pieces
of a 90 foot statue, the silver peace
with Khetasar, enlarged on temple
walls, and the love of Hittite princesses,
100 sons and 50 daughters, among them
the magician, Khamwase, smoking the
stolen stones of Karnac, nightless

shadows of colonnades, a forest of
great shafts, crowns, overwhelm
capitals float down the great nave
a hundred men could stand together
on any one of them the walls could
contain all of Notre Dame with
room to spare the colossal gate
for the gods with its 40 foot lintel
weighed 150 tons, must have

and the wars beyond Dog River, the four
divisions named after the great gods—
Amon, Re, Ptah, and Sutekh of many
cities, 1288 B.C., after the rains, across
Palestine to Lebanon, in the last days
of May

at Abydos, his father, Seti I, offered
an image of truth to Osiris, held it
in his hand, and more youthful, at
Thebes, the same image, held in his
hand   the sound of the water, and
he knew terrible curses that did not
work for more than a year in the
heavens or deep earth

out of the inactivity, inspecting the herds,
hunting in the marshes, swift on a
reed boat   the cat claws two wild
birds and catches the wing of another
in its mouth   this terror is praised
and obedient in the company of
the gods who could be more than 9
and younger in the wish of things, in the
sound of three vases of water, in the turn of the head of
a cat

smoking the heart, giving it to the tongue,
ceremonious mind in the guts, removed
and trembling in the pink box, smoking
the statuary, the pillars rise and drift
in the kitchen air, twist of the
elephantine granite, returning the
sweet face at Turin, smoking the
heart of the god that is in every
body, gathered through the skylights by Isis and stars
in the outstretched heaven

after James Henry Breasted

Advice: find someplace where
you can give the/a profound kiss-off,
the kiss of worlds, the kiss of sometimes

about memory: you're a lizard
of such greenness, of such rocks,
you can skip sometimes the deep crevasse

how do you spell? well, you begin
early to take this and that apart,
and then burn them like western novels
in a wicker trunk—on the bonfire

and the fireflies: they fill the hedges,
become Shakespeare and libraries,
which means you doubt somewhat—

I wouldn't, perhaps you would,
like Marlene Dietrich, roll
across how many *chaises longues*—wouldn't,
couldn't, shouldn't—

but then the big basket of flowers,
remember irises and daffodils,
which, I think, are maidens

To whom it may concern:

there are no bones in your jello, so I'll make no bones about
the skeletal structure   the lost form is wary, even perky, all in
a gesture   my sleep was perfect, dear lost friend, and our dig-
nity danced there strictly costumed   I wore black, you wore
white, together we were all and nothing   I am writing to
remind you of causal effects and summaries, in other words, of
the last time and parties, events to remember   I have dismem-
bered the black, and you, white perfection, what have you
done with your patchwork, crazy, quilted, the perfect ski-
jacket down and hills of rocky dance-cards   I am sincere, you
are sincere   the plunder of memory and places, empty and
filled, gardened or wild, in what pool swimming the surfaces
O, you were what I wanted, now disappeared and stained with
the flow, such substance, such resin, such super-markets, you
have disappeared like watercress in the sandwich, so, I recom-
mend you,   definitely,   infinitely,   somewhere,   sometime,
exactness of daffodils

signed

riff & ruff

~~Masturbation~~
~~The Hawk~~
~~God~~
Hi!

'I sent my eye out, one in the
day, one at night, to watch my
essential activity, to brighten
what sustains it now

I came upon my hand, the
goddess, Iusas, and upon
the redolent flower, abydos, these,
after the creation and whatnot

whereinto, the bright, black sun
and the learnèd moon shimmer
seas, rivers, rains, wells and
floods are veins of the great
ocean

there is no surface   I did not
commit you to completion, but
made the string-god out of your
upward-downward
jerky motion in that activity

I return you to the pairs   I watch
lovingly in the morning air and
the evening tide where elements of the *overwhelming*
permanence escape into the flux
not to triviality alone, my love, or even
joyous picnics   there is no perpetually
perishing anything   you named
them *joy and sorrow, good and*
evil, disjunction and conjunction,
flux and permanence, greatness
and triviality, freedom and necessity,
yet they escape into the flux of
rains, rivers, wells and seas
I-Am the compassion of the world, and we two are
continuous interpretations

I return you to your *craving*
and zest—*the freshness*—
my eye is out, one in the
day, one at night, watching
the inward source of distaste or
of refreshment, the judge
arising out of the very nature
of things, redeemer or mischief,
the companions of literal life and
clay in their inaccessible homes'

First Love

These poems may seem quirky, even hermetic. They are not.
But they do reflect a lifetime of scholarship which gave me,
first, pleasure and then a cosmos, and then happiness. I hope
that scholarship and the joy of it—the helpless quotation of
it—gave greater generosity, a love of this one and that one,
who turned up as helpless as I am. 'Faults and weaknesses
should be made into virtues and possibilities,' as Gene Wahl,
the composer, memorizing tuning forks, said 40 years ago. You
need not know him, but let the other voice name him continu-
ously. He talked in a co-op bedroom, bunks of the sparest ugli-
ness. There weren't enough chairs at supper, though I had
worked for one in the kitchen, tall cauldrons for soup, as you
dropped the bones in, the boiling water popped on the stove
and lit the eye-lids, harshly. 'Take the garbage out!' It was liquid,
a garbage can full, which slopped over the knees and shirt
front. I left and lived on tamales and one hotplate, dishes
washed in the shared bathtub. Tomato sauce up the sides of,
shaving, watching at the mirror. Lemon trees of one lemon in a
lucky year—and the piano divided the window from the bed-
room and clap—and he did not know how to, nor did I, called
years later to say he did, selling pedal-pushers. I was cruel in a
room of white-sheet curtains and a toy kettle-drum chande-
lier, striped peppermint colours and in the kitchen, curdled
spaghetti sauce, egg-beatered, on the ceiling, 'rented with
grand piano.' I can't find him—is he dead? I loved him. I love
him, talking of Rabelais. I'll buy the turquoise pedal-
pushers—let me write prose to explain this interchange of
laughing dancers, at the beginning, to get off the Greyhound
bus, one day, to see Euripides' *Trojan Women*, and there, sud-
denly, were Jimeniz, ghost stories, Proust, pronounced
'Prowst' by the librarian where I came from, for all of Mme.
Larsen's caution, teaching Greek, but it was French that sum-
mer by the fire before the radio at the fall of France.

I weave, finding the first love.

Home for Boys and Girls

the silvery dark, the cry of it,
writing, the couching lion and the
jokes thereof, playing marbles with
jasper—one was how close do
you get to the wall, or the other,
fall into the pit, steelies will get
you out with losses, keeping the marbles,
glassies were resplendent, butterflies,
monarchs of black and near-gold bronze,
clay balls are the cheapest, used if
you're going to lose—or let's play
conkers, polish with shoe-polish,
harden the chestnuts, string them
and swing, hitting the other, spring
games and fall games, of free
children, the unwanted, sent
from England, 1880–1920, Dr. Barnardo's,
when the child first came, he was taken
to a thawing field and told to bury
the dead cow, he dug all day and
used a crow-bar to push the cow
in, buried her, but the legs stuck
up—stiff and everlasting—he
was given an axe, told to return
to the spot and chop the legs off,
the pieces under the thaw and mud,
in the child's mind, everlasting—
and the true gleam of Wordsworth's
children and Coleridge's answer
in the wind's scream, widening loss
and joyance given I repeat:
steelies, pits, jasper and
resplendent glassies

belief

what America and I believed
about that war, armentière,
a room for two and more, maybe,
at the palace, that's 1943 and
this is '83. I can't imagine begging
for the uniform in the face of Coke
machines and sergeants who 'peel
it'—'milk it,' the man said
before I knew how to milk him and

all he believed in had clabbered,
you can hang it on the clothes-
line, in a small bag to make
cottage cheese, dripping slowly
into the dust and sunshine, some
still believe it and justify it by
the elitism of the common hope of
what they believe in, having been
told by the first denominator that
holds things together,   and the loss
of it is terror above the drainage
of Turkey Lake, swimming above the
orchard branches, and the dark sloe-
gin of their angles,   shadows,
desires, and drowned trees before
the friendships
                no histories and
repetitions were possible, we would
end things, especially strife, for
the peace of it, and truth was
quietness   in the heart of it, we
lived the lie and loved it,
terminal things and round-houses
for repairs

        before the opposition
was friendship, before the yellow
ribbons tied things up, and
civilization was individual, and
culture the conflict, certain of
strife and returning streams,
a refreshment where the wind
screams with the hope of children,
backward and before us, anxious,
silent crowds of belief

My Window

of neighbours and pumpkins and
sweeties, private kisses, sky
and wonderful, superstitions
to begin the day, knocking on
wood, rhythmically, musical
breakfasts, soft, boiled,
toasted with currants, intimate
wandering of questions and belief,
the thin skin wanders the adventure
of clothes-off-clothes-on, and
Mattress Mary, across Rock Creek,
out of bounds, summers

'the sounding air'

nothing repairs, but that is the
comfort, flowing in what system,
the sounding air of the mind,
refreshment, the caves, the
labyrinthine moment always
the universe, haunted me like
god, but I was inside that
complexity, in the left wrist, and
wondered, such beauty, I said,
where the human form drifts
in the rivers, puzzles or dreams
the solar origins   'see the islands,
rare or fortunate, the work of
chance or necessity'   'the irrational
is mimetic'   and the sacred,
after I thought it was beauty, takes
place constantly, ends constantly,
to begin constantly, such violence,
such sacred chance, so 'you' whom
I loved would find the crystal
without difference, would form
and reform   the perfection, the
option   and come back

Image-Nation 19 (the wand

I have told many things and want
to tell more in a small time   to count far off,
since 'nothing distinguishes me
ontologically from a crystal, a plant,
an animal, or the order of the world'
simply
       and 'we drift together toward
the noise and the black depths
of the universe'   celebrate the
sudden hang-up of our visibility,
celebrate the sudden beauty that
is not ourselves   careless   unwrapped
(*ducis*)   the solar origin drifts
in the same boat
               what did
dance in this dancer   was
first the difference among poppies and
white horses of advertisements,
the snow-storm and the grapes
from Africa   and the smile, exactly
and repetitions, but joyous, wintering
in Sais, writing memorable letters out
of the shattered various crystals, rocks, grottoes,
leaves, insects, animals, large and
small   'plenitude and enchainment,
wings, eggshells, clouds and snows'

so, to have forgotten, from the inimitable
solar mix, 'unwilling to become a
higher key'   on Bach's bedside table,
Leibniz's *De Arte Combinatoria*,
at the last minute—numbers
and numbers, multitudes as
the wind is, fish, I had
forgotten miracles and money
in the mouth of, walked by, in
my lanterned garden where the
nightingale, sometimes jugged to our
joyance, various, pitch and
glass of magic grammar
and presentiments—the fabled
universe, solvent and fortunes,
the assiduous sweetness among
other stones

there we have headed for frying pans,
hospitable, and alone, or the same,
voiceless in the common name,
scattered colours, earlier shapeless,
a candy-wrapper with a phone number
on it suffices to call the largeness, and
the smallness—what of that & on the
clothes-line, stiffened handicraft
of meaning, amenable comfort—and
Persian cats, where the rugs
flowered   take 'real' life
and store it in the cupboards,
the shoe-strings and decorations
of natural trees—whisper and
whistle of missing leaves—it's
winter—or summer   or some
other time in the great ritual
of plenitude and enchainment

the infinite who belongs to this race
of many things, the gentle death,
ignorance, and innocence last
summer, the youth of it, the
violence with roses and ivy,
sensible words, laughing rose
petal or someone   the inner
music has worn out—amidst broad
leaves and harbours, linked to
the observer, ˙ submerged
or proximous, exactly like that
which he loves, startling noise,
clarity and shadow, the heights
of ourselves equal to our shadows,
night and day, the miracle of
many things, the 'proliferation
of geneses'

1. *Where is the point of view? Anywhere*
at the source of light. Application,
relation, measurements are made
possible by aligning landmarks. Attention. One
can line up the sun and the top
of the tomb, or the apex of the
pyramid and the tip of its shadow.
This means that the site may
not be fixed at one location.

2. *Where is the object? It too must*
be transportable. In fact, it is,
either by the shadow that it casts
or the model that it imitates.

3. *Where is the source of light?*
It varies, as the gnomen.
It transports the object in the
form of a shadow. It is the
object; this is what we will
call the miracle.)Serres

most beautiful   stars, balls,
tinsel, bubbles, red water, the wand

The Art of Combinations

'we conclude with cosmography, the
connection of subjects to each other'
'consumed in the overwhelming
existence'
nothing simpler than what I have said because
I didn't say it, nothing simpler than what
I have said, because I said it—

Ah,

under you, over you, on you,
about you, slaked in a desert, the
pools, the shadow of a face,
a perfect answer, it was not
myself I could not imagine, it
was the substance of no understanding,
leaning over the waterfront, going
out to sea, of honey and milk and
crackers

on the other hand, founded on
actual existence   the pool played
with its ripples widening to the edge,
growing the watercress, the
iced surface, the dinner table
sparkled with lamps, and the
silver moon waned into happy
nightingales and bright forests

honestas

what do you think of that building
without knowing the architect   knowing
the architect, what do you think of
that building   the answer:
they have expanded cheaply,
beautifully, or otherwise in the
streets, holes and parking places

the fire which consists of burning iron,
discovered early, *is like iron*
itself   love is that unity with the happiness
of another   mind and body, such
pools,   winged fishes

'a' is a fig and reducible
'o' is the same thing, shamed
in the garden   what do you
think of that garden without
knowing the gardener   knowing
the gardener, what do you think
of that garden   the answer:
the glass perfectly dark, or
burning in pieces

Epitaphics

Tarzan keeps saying, 'ombawa,'
and everybody does everything
including the elephants

'Wow!' she said, 'I'm out of the
rabbit hole and it's the same.'

'If there's one thing Harry learned
to love more than the sacred, it was
the sacred in ruins.'

Image-Nation 20 (the Eve

wisdom shattered, gold, myrrh, and
incense scattered over the floor, toys
of one thousand nine hundred and
eighty-three years, impossible
to worship the child of what
we are, then what was He in
that imagination? whose perfection
withered the tree to begin with, He
was, first, not a goodness, that
we would compose, perhaps, in a life-time
again and again, He was, first,
a cosmos, entered somehow
(by ear?), this hang-up in the
flow, and was named He by
accident in the curious, disappearing
anthropomorphism, could have been
anything in the young, marvellous,
dangerous beginning, somewhat
familiar, neither inside nor
outside, it was that peculiar
cause of imagery, following
a star, that required intimacy,
caught the mind and the cities,
one by one, then in multitudes,
sounds like a great wind or the
lights of the raindrops
on darkened skylights, somewhere
the love goes by happiness and sorrow,
neither one nor the other alone or
separate, neither one nor the other
the truth of what they called Him,
who is incomplete, created dark and
light of
          gold, myrrh and incense
listening to the radio from Golan
and Baden and Cypress

Silver-winged red devil, a toy from Mexico

the place is poisoned   history is effective,
not progressive   date: anytime, or
the Cheyenne massacre and freezing, 1879,
date the re-entry and then the return
from the womb of mankind   it is
not the womb of woman, nor is it '
the Greek male-womb, the substitute
of it—books, letters, language
it is our violence—that inside of
ourselves, which gods inhabit,
though they are real outside the inside,
continuous grass, repeated sand in the
glass of sky-scrapers, golden, sunning,
melted forms, banks on rivers of
our violence   I have thought the intellect
sweet and the bare-forms of poets,
hairy-wrists, graceful, the stench and
the beauty, bright and terrible, crabs
in the hair of their chests or the clean
smooth flesh variable   I
sometimes thought they were priests or
the same thing, revolutionaries, I thought they
were baseball players, lovers
or beauties   they were at a loss
in the language, ever so much
at cross-purposes in the world
of that violence which is our nature,
endlessly before us, where
the inside turns into the outside, dying
and other   now, knowing the
source does not look like ourselves,
virgin and child in the icon
sit in a tub of blue weather,
two rivers pour into *okeanos*
where fish begin the dangerous
beginning, somewhat

familiar, the peculiar cause
of imagery somewhere   if you
pound the table the wings shiver,
silver, on springs at the shoulders of
the red body

Image-Nation 21 (territory

wandering to the other, wandering
the spiritual realities, skilled in all
ways of contending, he did not search
out death or courage, did not
found something, a country,
or end it, but made it endless,
that is his claim to fame, to
seek out what is beyond any single
man or woman, or the multiples
of them   the magic country that
is homeland

the bridges   I strained for, strings
of my vastness in language, and
the cars rushed by in both
directions flashing at one another

the mechanic of splendour, sought
after, chanted in the windy
cables   and the river sailed,
haphazard, under the solitude

he had only the stories to tell, naked
and plotless, the spiritual territories,
earth-images and sky-maps, dark
at the edges

the mechanic of the marvellous dreamed
of Stalin and Hitler and the ordinary,
endlessly knew where he had gone
and, then, came back, whatever happens
if, I said—I was talking to religionists—
you gain social justice,

solve the whole terror, then where
is god?   certainly not in happiness
and since god is not in unhappiness,
there you have it   the skilled
adventure in hostilities with no name

Dream

I went madly to sleep, dreamed
of everyone, Reagan offered me a dish
and Trudeau and I compared tuxedos,
Rabelais arrived, absolutely nasty,
I liked him best and waited quietly
for Montaigne, the sweet friend

Pain-fountain

the light striking the near and the
far   the sorrow is cultural   the personal
is time in its space, mental and jobbed
large in mischief, large in the gathering
field, gathering the argument and all
its pieces, outside the work, the
exergue, the space on the page,
the outside   what profit from the irreducible
loss

if space is identical with mind,
then, what's in the mind?   a
dangerous freedom—the space may
be tawdry   mixed with the beautiful,
that's the par of exchange,
twisted gold and only similar

                      maggots
and honey, bones and rags, clean
as a whistle   and drifted steel
wonder and go
                  O, he said, as the
fountain lifted each particle of light
and let the gathering heart splash
on a glittery pavement

Dream

               'standing everest,'
flowers they were called—
toilets and monumental
garden planters filled with
them   they were tall, stemmed,
purple straw-flowers—and
the pun, Everest is a mountain,
the sound blurred to ever-rest
standing-ever-rest—

Utopia

whatever it's a sign of—that
trip of   an art
of—
          we're interested finally
in the unique of its meta-
physic
          every anti-metaphysics
reverts into a metaphysics,
as Marx and men and women fucked their
physics

each move is infinite, troubled
by how it got there, the split-
rope of

Freud found it and made sexual
metaphysics, until, years later,
it reverted and made meta-
physics—it's funny that way,
where it walked on the land,
America, France and Russia,

and became not-a-place
but a change of typewriters,
which alphabet or hunting dog

knew better and reverted into sheer
picture or postcard of the moon
over any Miami you can think of

the 'mindless revellers' dream—
America is Europe's dream, its
superstitious futurity

America did not exist; and it exists
only if it is utopia, history on the
move toward a golden age   ) Paz

its conflict with Marxism, Europe's
last dream of the future, gives up
the nightmare—its reason—to be delirious

assholiness, my dears, in the wintry
splendour   what was once called
being is complexity—of reunions—
of act—of quality—
                                of the world
I have argued because, in the
complexity, 'we' could not argue it
together

'It springs on you'

my mind plays in the distance,
free, but is not mine, wandering
the syllable, a mustard of bright
flowers, yellowing the airplane's
landing   the sweetness crashed into
the mind incessantly out there

•

the summer wind came by
so quickly the other day, out
of season, I walked all day
backwards with the snow
on my ass   quickly

•

              the day and the night
I found them exactly, positively
separate and mixed them
in a bowl   that white mush
became darkly the horizon on
tip-toes over the edge

•

I'm so in love with art that
it will get me into the next
world, which, as you know,
is 'white mush'

•

the poet has no part in being,
is not the priest of ontology
from whom Nerval departed
at the gates, giving up privilege
at the lamp-post—

O, sweet, will you tell me,
packing tinned peas and triscuits,
the colour of being

•

the huge log-boat to be tipped over,
the ships from China, Japan,
Russia, still in the tint of the world,
eddies, silver, gold and pale iris,
lights tip their cargo cranes,
the moon up before darkness
with an edge missing, all near
geraniums

•

I have tried for 35 years to
redefine sweetness—it is what
they called being—it is not
behind you or before you
or within you—'the goodness
and sweetness of Dante' is
his composition—the language
composes the good, the sweetness
and, by accident, brightness

The Truth Is Laughter 17

the leaf   twice the size of my hand
23 points
from the maple

O.

the poets have always preceded,
as Mallarmé preceded Cézanne,
neck and neck   that was no
privilege, sweet and forgotten

seated in chairs, the afternoon
marches along with the shadows
which are not bougainvillaea but
northern   I have always loved

shadows as long as they were northern
and moved gently west   like the
crack-up of books, their spines
tingling with notes and stuffing

most people remember the gardens
with cement flowers and the
house going straight up like
solidified swimming-pools or lilies

when you get to the top which
they once called widow's walk,
you wait in nothing but your garden
hat, beautifully otherwise naked

for the wind-swept sea and the dying
sweetness or womb, *declaring the completion
of philosophy*   or the completion of
the human-being in some / a history

awash among silver trees, aspens,
pounded, whispering 'my foos won't
moos' or some other difficult
disappearance of words which were
preliminary notions, laundry of that lovely
absurd summer we wanted so
desperately   the moss was 6 inches
deep   and if you put a cigarette
out in it, the fire would be
6 inches deep in minutes,
when the fire spreads, the trees
totter and their statues wait
in your thought, exactly numerous

Halloween

let pass   let pass
the butterfly

the dark spaces between
larkspur

in the city-twilight
the winking pumpkin

laughter, not a ghoul
or skeleton among them

tutus, and gypsies
in the child eye's languor

sweet, burned face
of imagination

clowns and raggedy ann,
red headed

sweet, burned hands
gathering bags of

smarties and gum
drops

violet, red, orange, green,
pink, brown, yellow and

chocolate   surprise leopard

and wonderful sorrow

Giant

someone stopped suddenly   someone dreamed
slowly   bus-tickets and the ages
of golden heads   deft   in the middle
of nowhere   the railroads   beautiful steam,
high, dripping tower

                     'If you're going
to think, think about somethin',' said Brick-Top,
bless her and Miss Otis's regrets, reared,
like some of us, by bees, atop that mountainous
protean shape,   the sacred vacant lot
of toy cars, a child's labyrinth and twigs
of toy trees, shining garages
                          silver to the pelvis,
bronze, iron legs on the clay bridges,
each continuous violence flowers in the rivers
you're somewhere less than perfect,
but reading the story

poetry   is   ordinary   busyness

of   bright   things   I   remember

a   barn   dance   2   to   3   years

old   looking   up   at   the   tulle

and   pendant   blue   sparkle

of   her   beauty   controlled   by

the   banging   of   a   broom   handle

hands in your pockets
legs in your pants
take a chew o' tobacca
and everybody dance

such   early   beauty

There-abouts

O sweet spring   of blossoms,
false plums, true as daffodils
or tulips, the dark primrose,
each garden
                    you have read
today, 'Aithon'   'blaze,'
the name in the story you
read which way, altered

gods disappeared because they are real
the extraordinary is isolation,
mind is native to it—sure as
the interface—the weather

I drop in, guided by water and sky,
hello   hello   hello—which means 'there'
before 1880   and still does

for Luis Posse

'O on the left'—Posse

'Delphi is a place that the gods left'—Posse

Carmelo Point, 13 June 1984

the edges shine   gather   disperse
the many minds whisper   their lure
adamant   to converse with the new
bird

       note-note-trill-note-note-trill
over and over
        between minutes and answers

and best of luck, the hummingbird
right at my ear, humming—
and the robin of such listening—seven
hummingbirds—or quickness, the same
twosome, humming at the chive blossoms—note-

note-trill-note-note-trill
grue, waves and this shore
          from the islands—
Keats—Worlcome—Observatory Point—unnamed
Island—Gambier Harbour—

the children have played paper
faces   the minds go with the sun,
slowly

cool the dish-water and water
the sweet peas and dark leaved,
scarlet geraniums—watch the wild
strawberries stretch in the dry
moss

what do the bees find in the dry
moss—some sweet dryness? or
the black ant on my leg—some salt
wetness

         for Catherine Taylor

For Barry Clinton, d. 17 June 1984, of aids

a circle of bricks beneath Lucretius' tall
Aphrodite who holds her shell among plum
branches—and iris, columbine—your favourite—
columbine, potentilla to surprise you, columbine,
primula Florindae, again to surprise you—pale
blues and bright yellows—white poppies are not
available here—hail! dear blue-eyed
painter

pin-wheel—shimmering wind pale
yellow movement and dark red—
dark centre of the wind—infinite
conversation—black-striped hornets
test the aluminum   centre   quickly
white moth, my summer   pink movement
blue shift—orange—white moments—
golden click—streaked purple and blue—
sweet dark of the wind—my hermetic
summer   yes, Sir, Madame, surprise
click—swirl—buzz at the door, my
summer, the territory maps

The Truth Is Laughter 1 8

locked out, and at the same time locked
in the look-out   what perfect rose could
I say or write   the Nietzschean brilliance,
who knew that *the best writers understand*
form as what others consider content

Pretty Please

the sharp yellow marigolds on my writing
table, next to the cowboy on his palomino
and the tiger's bright face across there,
broken into a puzzle, but glued together—
for permanence—among green pieces,
just below the cookbooks and the orange
zest of last evening   and on the table
the *radical absence* of the poet I'm reading
or somewhat at a distance as I've always
loved the other   O there were mistakes
when I wanted to be there

And Tereus,

                    I welcome you, tongueless,
and weave that force of that earning, god-like
or somewhat   how win such distance and
forget you   and weave such intelligence—
backwards it seems—

Praise to Them,
December 30, 1984

the robins, returned to
the holly-tree   snow-
covered unusually, search
for red berries   joined by
flames—and larger—a
Common Flicker, 'red-
shafted,' speckled fawn-
breast, long beak of
Picus—the first in
fourteen years—eating
berries in this city-
garden

O fragmented ago—
    early as morning and
boats do draw the sun—
    every time
the human does enter,
    so beautiful—
no reduction of that flux—
    but it does
act, actualist, and so
    becomes actual
spirit   undone
    busyness
of—

I would be there
                watching
or almost,

but was not

I do not see—
or was not—
                what
sees me
            drops and buds
of the whole
                beautiful,
dawn thing—
                green
stairway
            and
jellyfish—
                blue
iridescent amethyst,
obscene distance

of personal relation

become fire

I thought when I dreamed
I dreamed,
          kept all sweet
depths in the lily
            of water
opening slowly,
            a pink,
a purple
        opening
            each light
flowering   idea
           or
drunkenness
         I join
you,
     such otherness
of silk flowing
           otherness
the day grows old
and vibrant
         I live
there—

writing table

'Have you got a toy-box?' she asked on the first
visit—puzzles, the tiger among the leaves—in pieces,
the cowboy on his palomino—odd the dark tail—the
dragon, a water-gun—specific, the cookie-tin for pens
and pencils—eros on it amidst the crescent and green
sunset   O

dancing with radios

when the little blue-bird begins to sing
that never said a thing, 'spring, spring,
spring'

I danced with Ella   kindly Apollo,
hard and hungry—baloney and beans
on the bus   giving up,
coming down
                    you're out there, so do
something—object of my affection   misty
angel, summer sunday afternoon

what different people can do with chicken,
got the St. Louis blues—man's heart
hum, hum, hum—far from me, but love that
man

love your body 'til the day the evening sun
go down—or left town—St. Louis woman
with that diamond ring and apron—no
way, he's gone away   all of the time,
come on, come on, come on—blue
bloooooooooooo   sweet—thanks

frog in my throat—a song—beautiful—
thank you, violins—summer time, livin'
fish—cotton eyes—rich and good lookin'—
hued wings—in the skies—   until
nothin's standin' by—don' cry—

thanks so much—

love musicians—here goes—savannas
I don't understand—heart as big as
a stone—even iceman leave her
alone—like to suffer—hard-hearted
Hannah—pouring water on a drowning
man—put on your pajamas—travel
in your bee-vee-dees—colder than an
ice-cream cone—leave me alone—

but summer touches, passes into rain,
shining, bending the petunias—careless
of applause—O summer whistles—Jimmy
Kiever and Bobely—careless of spelling
as I hear—thank you, beautiful, for
Norman—Timothies and Williams

swell! big and handsome—ne-ne-never know—
your view is crushing, sweetie-pie—night
and day—could you coo?—care?—
share?—pardon my mush, would—but
it's you—baby—on you and you,
and you—everybody—
yeah—yeah—yeah—youuuuuuu

thanks—yi yi yi—young, tan,
tall and handsome—that's all you got—
body body body body—ditty—scat—
hum hum hum meditation

rainbows all over your blues—dark-side
of the moon—your turn—let's bounce
on my trampoline

tap dance, Major Bows—with soft 'r's—O
four-piece summer—
2,000,000 soft-shoe dances and wash-
board talents—   la de da

for Allen Ginsberg's 60th birthday

hard, gemlike flame

I've always liked the idea of the mind as a
frying pan

What's in it is neither true nor false

conversation

Bare-ass, Pretty-ass and Glitter—or
so I describe my neighbours to visitors
I talk endlessly, quickly   they shift
and drift to the window now and again
impatient   a truck drives up, and they
ask, 'Is that Pretty-ass or?'   'No,'
I answer, 'you have to live here for such
qualities to become permanent'

heavy reading

meaning and content exist only in and through the life of the body, to which
nonetheless they cannot be reduced, and . . . their manifestations differ in
level, in quality, in intensity and in time, so that we are referred irresistibly
to an organisation, to forces or tendencies, and to identifiable regularities. An
organisation of what, forces acting where, regularities connected with what?
Something—namely, the soul—is presupposed by or implied in this, and
the frankest way of speaking of it is to speak of it as a thing. . . . In fact,
naive philosophical pre-emptions aside, we do not know what a thing is; we
only know what the idea of a thing is in a realist philosophy—an idea whose
real referent has never been found.
                    Cornelius Castoriadis'

crossroads in the labyrinth

                                                    my soul!

hymns and fragments

texts are processes

        rather than products,

                mind you,

hither and yon

        Den umschwebet Geschrei der Schwalben,

den umgiebt die rührendste Bläue

        heart stirring

'the modern imagination invents itself (and thereby reinvents
antiquity) out of the evidence of wreckage, . . . for to scrutinize
a fragment is to move from the presence of a part to the absence
of the whole, to seize upon the sign as a witness of something
that is forever elsewhere. . . .'

        mind you

          reading Richard Sieburth

stop

wanted so to enter the brightness,
mother   the *word-robes*
I forget with impatience

I believe I heard language through my mother's
belly   both violent and sweet   and wanted
to get to it

I listen to the train whistle,
the skirt of love flap
against wind   and locomotive
steam

and do not understand my escape
from the dear over-again
whistle and crossing

for Daphne Marlatt

'Mr. Dandelion'

    the dark meant everything—
the breathlessness of
  'please pass'—
I mean
I fought
       'don't touch'—
I'll breathe again
the sweet
      skin,
I thought
      quickly,
and could not—
          'Mr.
Dandelion'
      the voice
said,
   and I
came back

sapphire-blue moon,
once

if I think 'I' unifies

                    I lose,

and the feeling overflows the bucket

if I think the aggregate of large numbers of us,
massified, unifies,

                  our hunger

unifies without justice,

                each alone

and the same

we still dream behind us of a perfected
humanity   a religion of cities   and
take the thought east   the twentieth-
century project, delving centuries of
mind and heart for a new relation among
things,

          overwhelmed

               to dream again

of *laissez-faire*   going fair   along paths
through the gardened wreckage and consequences
the State and Nationalism agog with redemption   religions
smoke on the hills, sacrificial as

               always

a wordy prison does not make a house   word-
less despair in the freedom of words   that
is, if freed into words, to see different

                    things,

same as any other

        sapphire-blue moon, once

untranslatable reason

Si on me presse de dire pourquoy je l'aymois, je sens que cela ne se peut exprimer, qu'en respondant: Par ce que c'estoit lui; par ce que s'estoit moy.

                                             an outward freedom,

beloved Montaigne,

                         always thinking somewhere else

demi-tasse (an elegy

the silence surrounds me   political silence   where
    the words were deeds once upon a time and space
social silence   where a fragile good composes   bankruptcies
of ideas run through two centuries   my centuries, watching
the poets sit on the shelves,
                                        joined by musicians,
painters, sculptors   not one of them weeps
                                            the *borborygmi*
of their guts   signals   language in the air,
loud as Zeus among the fractured religions,   answers
now and again, entwining centuries, to the multiple
largeness
            to which, one by one, we return, never at that point
abject   only different   the curious sorrow of
                                        difference
yet here among gathering bankruptcies, we touch
and part, having given or not—robbed sometimes—according
to our lights
            and thinking before we are after them—
after is never a condition of *beyond*, but of comparison, even
of companionship of *of* and *off*—more like a nerve
centre for conductions   inward and outward
        the afterglow of the sky after sunset   some what

        Tiutchev said, *Blessed are those who have visited*
this world at its fatal moments   I think of Serres: that
living beings are born of flows   of Bakhtin's sense
that *the self is an act of grace, a gift of the other*   of persons,
of place, of time   which flow

I am not whole   not one   but, as Montaigne
said in his essay on friendship, divided

> *I was already so made and accustomed*
> *to being a second self everywhere that*
> *only half of me seems to be alive now*

I have only half   am dimidius in happiness,
of mixed blood

18 April 1988

Continuing

genetrix, Venus, *voluptas*—'darling,' says one translator,
'delight,' says another—of men, women, and gods—and
a third reads *voluntas*   the will that is free and not-free
in our inclination for one another—restorer, who, under
the gentle motion of the sky's signals, moves ceaseless in the
ship-bearing sea, in the earth's fruits, blossoms and greening,
celebrant, dweller in the life under the sun: the winds don't
trouble, the clouds seem in flight as you approach; for you,
many-coloured earth offers sweet flowers; for you, daedalian,
labyrinthine, dappled, folding, oceanic surfaces laugh, the
sky summons, shining in scattering light   you move, tellurian,
now at the first sight of spring's opening-day, letting loose the
west-wind; you, aborigné of the airs freedom, first
the birds, pierced to the heart by your sway, announce you, and
next wild animals and cattle leap and frolic on the brightening
grasslands and swim swift, rushing mountain rivers, in leafy
homes of birds, crosswise the green plains, you, smiting
every breast with love's lure, bring them to sexual life,
desiring

    you alone govern the nature of physical things;
  becoming—
joyous or to be loved—depends upon you   at the
border of light, shining—so, I desire
you as companion of poems   language too, physical
among things, desires   *voluptas*   *voluntas*   *genetrix*

Great Companion:
Robert Duncan

1988

Robert Duncan

the absence was there before the meeting   the radical of
presence   and absence does not return with death's chance-
encounter, as in the old duality, life or death, wherein
the transcendence of the one translates the other into an everness
we do not meet in heaven, that outward of hell and death's
beauty   *it is a bright and terrible disk*
                                        where Jack is, where
Charles is, where James is, where Berg is is here in the continuous
carmen   O, some things—*di*—breathe into—*aspirate*—and lead
    away—
deducite!   for the soul is a thing among many
                        Berkeley shimmers and shakes
in my mind   most lost   the absence preceded the place
and the friendships   Lady Rosario among us   of Spanish and Greek
    rushes
from the hedges around the gas station,
                    swirled with Lawrence's medlars and
sorb-apples
                                                What
is it reminds us of white gods
                        flesh-fragrant
as if with sweat   *the delicious rottenness* that teems with
the life of the mind's heart   κρατήρ of an agreement, a mixing vessel,
a chasm, a threshold—Βάθρον—a stair of
brazen steps, hollow wild pear tree—κοίλεσ τάχέρδου
—between   among
sat down
                    I am only leonine in the
breath of night   awakening blurred neighbours   as your
faces move   Jack writing the Italian underground   *we*
are too tired to live like lions   on john walls   and gay-bars
didn't laugh at the Red Lizard or the Black Cat   as your
faces move beyond me   suddenly Zukofsky joins the language,
now become larger, sharper, more a gathering than the lingo
wherein Berkeley began   the movement

                                        the first of your poems
I read: *Among my friends love is a great sorrow* (brought to me
in typescript by Jack, 1946, that we three should meet)—no voice
like it   turns, turns   in the body of thought   *Among*
my friends love is a wage/that one might have for an honest living
        turns, turns

                    in thought's body   becomes
        O Lovers, I am only one of you!
        We, convivial in what is ours!
                                        this ringing
with Dante's voice before the comedy

sorrow   and guide-dance   the courage of the work   the language
is a lion   sentinels are owls   of work's body   glamouring passages
the poem WHOSE alongside James Hillman's *thought of the heart*
Jess tells me you just went, having the heart to   whose
heart?   I wish to say mine   impertinence   yours   that too
is impertinence   nevertheless, always against the heart
failures: *cowardice, nostalgia, sentimentalism, aestheticizing, doubt,*
vanity, withdrawal, trepidation
                                        fierce, you
        name many times this uprising
        —*political, mental, sexual, social*—you name it—*mounting rung by*
rung

        this climax to what overview

            under the double axe
                        whose heart

the lilies   burn rose-orange and yellow   buds about to,
with a touch of blood   near imagination of Blake's Eternity,
except one would be among them   flaming into one another,
not looking out there at the table, the vase, the tall, leafy stems
blossoming
                    stopped over the 'Instant Mythology,' knowing
an old language from you   one-inch capsules in the hot water
break at both ends, then burst   purple, green, red, blue,
'pour enfants ages 5 ans et plus, pas comestible, chaque
capsule peut contenir: Centaure, Dragon, Pégase, Licorne,
Sirène—calling—mettez la capsule dans l'eau tiede/chaude
et regardez un caractère mythologique apparaître'   techno-myth
translates out of the real book into the way language
works   regardez!
                    the travois of the poetic mind,
the drag-load harnessed to the body,   firely, through
the glowing flowers   warm and hot, the watery spell of
any reel of language   *poluphloisboíous sea-coast*

    window-rain is *Heimat*   sunlight travels the fingers
come subito lampo   a sudden lamp in the room outside
strikes the fir tree   horizon of eyes through passages,
sublime envelopes, and the *lives raging within life*

There is no exstacy of Beauty in which I will not remember Man's misery,
compounded by what we have done   sighted in ruins, neither old
    nor discontinuous
                    (I smile   it is the thought of you   a happiness
that could not be without your having been
                                                    there
quarrelling)

the permanent wall of our shape the languages
burn and muse   the alpha-beta, like the yellow birds
(Dendoica petechia—Parulidae) disappear among spring yellowing
    leaves,
pricklings, of the holly as its tree renews toward winter robins
and *staerlinc*   wait for red berries where the inkberry is
eastern   the cherries are white among the greens, this side
of glass towers with bicycles on the balconies almost rented the
    bicycle
on the 37th floor   and figs like testicles on the branches enjoy
the sexual sun
    I remember the quarrel over experience—on Greene Street—
and still think you spoke too soon of a sacred cut-out   it was the
    process
of the actual we were both about
    what exactly do we experience in poēsis
over the neat 'I' that thinks itself a unity of things or disunity des-
perately untrue to whatever we are tied to—like one's grief or the
    smother-
ing domestic realism, or the I-feel, so deep and steeply, no one
    wants to
listen without a drumhead   positivisms of the self
that die into an urn   yet, O *gratefully / I take the gift of my daily life!*
the accusations were: 'fatuous,' 'rhetorical,' 'pretentious,' 'bourgeois
interior decorator' (of Pound), continuous writing of the ironing
    board,
the kitchen, recipes, the jam pots *textures, tones, tastes* of the world
they are not glabrous, nor is the skin, *riding the earth / round into the*
sunlight again   one wishes the positivities were *falling into that Nature*
of Me / that includes the cosmos it believes in   how curious, not sad, of
all animals, not merely

                    you came here in 1982 to read *Ground Work*
up to that point   no one could leave the room   *of cats's fur, black*
stone, and its electric familiar   *What Is*

mind-store   mind-change   mindful   mind-life   Eternal
Mind   the smile
                    the burn

                                    not to
want any longer to wait for the thematic release

thinking of you thinking of James Hillman thinking of Corbin—
            the idea of a unified experiencing subject vis-à-vis a world
            that is multiple, disunited, chaotic. The first person
            singular, that little devil of an I—who, as psychoanalysis
            long ago has seen is neither first, nor a person, nor
            singular—is the confessional voice, imagining itself
            to be the unifier of experience. But experience can only
            be unified by the style in which it is enacted, by the images
            which formed it, by its repetitive thematics, and by the
            relations amid which it unfolds. It does not have to be
            owned to be held. The heart in the breast is not your
            heart only: it is a microcosmic sun, a cosmos of all
            possible experiences that no one can own

                                        against heart
failures

I gather as I must images of independent realities   I,
subjected to the gaze of things, as I think of you

as you say the etymology is false,
                        bringing the core,

care—κήρ—κήρ   together the heart and the goddess, who
is κήρες plural among things   thinking of you thinking of
Hillman thinking again, *Beauty is an epistemological necessity*
    thinking of
a sudden call   to climb the ladder of   which you
did not mean   because it does not mean, though
it is recited   *'Never' being the name of what is infinite*

    of cross-ways

                    of brazen

                                steps

Streams II

1986–1991

Image-Nation 22 (in memoriam

Robert Graves saw—not the *male-womb* made scary in Euripides
and even scarier in Malaparte's *Kaputt* with wooden dolls—
the Goddess in multiples—of lovely women and aquiline faces—
saw her *All Living*—coursing into *sow, mare, bitch, vixen, she-
ass, weasel, serpent, owl, she-wolf, tigress, mermaid or loath-
some hag*—made male-minded by her, had to see her white and
black—met her once in his novel *The New Crete* as the *Hog
goddess*, sometimes named Sally—you may write with kindling,
he says, or, loving accuracy, return to the *mare's nest*

*Her nests, when one comes across them in dreams, lodged in
rock-clefts or branches of enormous hollow yews, are built
of carefully chosen twigs and littered with the jaw-bones and
entrails—of poets*, says—in male-minded acknowledgement and
his correction of belief without her

he read her by the *alphabet of trees*, wild in Wales before the
evangelical voices

> *Flower-goddess Olwen or Blodeuwedd
> Owl, lamp-eyed, hooting
> Circe, the pitiless falcon
> Lamia with her flickering tongue
> mare-headed Rhiannon*

*Determined to escape the dilemma, the Apollonian teaches him-
self to despise women, and teaches woman to despise herself.*
Robert Graves would escape this blankness and obey the dilem-
ma, made male-minded by her

with the advantage that he could reread, by the alphabet of
trees, Ezekiel's chariot—transform the radiance enthroned
there

> *Amber
> Fire-Garnet ('the terrible crystal')
> and Sapphire*

finding a triune Jehovah with Anatha of the Lions and Ashima
of the Doves—divorcing his consorts, just before the Babylonian
   captivity

                    sister her ,Oholah named was elder The
                    bore and mine became They .Oholibah
                    ,Samaria is 'Oholah' .daughters and sons me
                    me owed she While. Jersualem 'Oholibah'
                    was and whore the played Oholah obedience
                    staff ,lovers Assyrian her with infatuated
                    ,governors and viceroys ,blue in officers
                    riding ,them of all cavaliers young handsome
                    .horseback on
                    (Ezekiel 2 3: 4—6)

word by word, right to left—myth resuming—*God assumed the
shape of a mare and decoyed the ruttish Egyptian stallions
into the water*—the lengths to which, shape-changing Jehovah,
once a devoted son of the Great Goddess, would go, you say, and
swallowed

         gods   terebinth
                     thunder
                     pomegranate
                     bull
                     goat
                     antelope
                     calf
                     porpoise
                     ram
                     ass
                     barley
                     moon
                     dog-star
                     sun,
healing the wounds of these things by becoming imageless

calling Joshua Podro with his fine knowledge of Hebrew to sit
beside you—as I have with another who read the Hebrew for me—
you wrote *The Nazarene Gospel Restored* in 1953—to give Jesus
back to time and painful circumstance—your mythic mind joined
with Podro's, tracing what Jesus knew of the *Mishnah*, the *Midrash*,
the two *Talmuds*—of the Day of Judgement, detailed by Zephaniah,
Zechariah, Malachi—of Enoch's heavens—of the tortured spirit
of the *Testament of the Twelve Patriarchs*

the wandering meaning, the thorned acacia, nimbus of the sun-
god, burned

hostility to writing—these were the evil cosmocrators—Peneme
(according to Enoch), Nabu, Thoth, Hermes, against whom the
Scriptures had been set a century before Jesus by the scholarly
Pharisees

Anatha of Bethany took Mot (Tammuz), cleft him with her sword,
winnowed him in her harvest-basket, parched him at the fire,
ground him in the mill and sowed him in the field

the Female on whom Jesus declared war was Aggrath Bat Machlat
(Alukah, by cacophemism, the horse-leech) whose daughters
Womb and Grave—are

ISHTAR

you say that he went *to the land of nod, East of Eden, the trans-*
Euphrates province of Susiana, to watch for the end of the
world in his own time—that Paul knew him to be alive in 35
A.D. because they met on the road to Damascus—that Ignatius
of Antioch (d. c. 107) in his letter to Smyrna writes as though
he thought Jesus still alive near the end of the first century

Enoch dreams: all became snow-white cows—and the first among
them became a thing and that thing became a great beast with
huge black horns—Graves notices *the horns of power, such as
Moses wore, or Zeus Ammon, or Alexander*—the Son of Man, a
title of careful and careless finitude, as

*if all the heavens were parchment, and all the trees pens, and
all the seas ink,*

               in memoriam

As If By Chance

the Private Sector worries me
it can, the ubiquitous 'they' say, solve—that is, clear up—

the economy, which, at the upper level is called economics—that
is, confused science and confused theology prancing around
together as usual, is under the cultural, like oil or gas
under the hood or roof, and unpredictably disappearing from
under us

and the political, which, by manipulation, is over the stunned
polis, in order to manage production, distribution, and
consumption of wealth, becomes political economy—thus,
what is under becomes what is over, and *vice versa*, to define
realities without earth and sky which are cultural habitudes

and the cultural, which—not limited by high, low or middling—
is conflict around the creation of reality, and may be
invisible as thought is, and is neither formulaic—bonded
like chemicals—nor nostalgic, which is a dangerous and
transcendent condition, having forgotten that transcendence
like ourselves is historical, even in dreams

and the social, which is a struggle against dominations and powers
the society of which is recently made up of those who were not
previously there

and mass culture, which is new, misunderstood and ungenerous
about historical consciousness, mirrors privacies that dis-
solve in soap, and is jubilant, from which sorrow may
learn

and democracy, which is recent, unAthenian, unPeriklean, in-
complete, and by nature unstable and creative

and the sexual, which is the passionate body of all chemicals

and our ethos, which is the behaviour of one to another, near and
   far—many to many defines character—and is visible—*not*, as
   the dictionary tells us, 'the moral, ideal, or universal ele-
   ment in a work of art as distinguished from that which is e-
   motional or subjective'—[WOW! dissolve that and *ethos* becomes
   possible action—character for the sake of the action—and
   pathos is there among kindnesses]

and the universal, which is absent from twentieth-century thought,
   according to the poēsis afoot

and technology, which has wild arms, and is human nature unaware
   of itself

and the angels, who became isms and hierarchies in order to im-
   materialize the real things we're thrown up against, as we
   become startled sub-jects—to which I ob-ject

and religion, which, dismissed from the plane of thought,
   gathers godhead in small envelopes of cement, whereon
   the postage changes

and human survival, which, with all its adjectival ironies,
   proposes a social inheritance

and the good, which we know as Goodness! an expletive,
   something added to fill up the whole that has nothing to
   do with it, and which is fragile and our own composition

and love, which is true attention to whatever and sometimes
   some one

and friendship, which is guidance in every attention

the Private Sector economizes hither and yon, as it was
a past participant in bereavement and deprivation, as it
is now a relationship between privies   with the exception
of an infinitely distant point, as mathematicians
say, the world as such, says Castoriadis

going, going
my mind plays with its dark, awake to
the blind clatter of upward whirring round
itself   more like the sound of irritation from
which it came lawless, it seemed the laws
work by relation
                    we have dreamed   I
have no right to the word 'we' though I have
worked for it   I dream   of apologies to
the beautiful, invisible shape that dares not
remember its immediate form.

15 August 1988

Interlunar Thoughts

'Advertising tells us who we are' and
'presents a completely integrated culture'

in the interval between the old moon and the new
when the moon is invisible, one hopes

the moon will show up:
            capitalism, racism, consumerism,
            homophobia, sexism—all of them systems
            of signifiers detached from spirit so
            the governing soul goes
                        numb

(a voice on CBC set alongside
John Wilkinson on John Wieners)

Image-Nation 23 (imago-mundi

the smile of public art—only a possibility—and its curious
frowns   delight in the dissolution of a public world   and
yes, there are academic and private difficulties, each one
thinking of ownerships, specialties, furnitures   as publicities
in a public world—these, alongside popular arts which disappear
into kissables and similar rhythms   still, one and another
do think of it, not quite outwitted by the dissolution of
                                    IMAGO MUNDI
                                    SCULPTURED THOUGHT
and dear mundane images

                        Duchamp thought of a
large glass, its transparency tinted by bachelors and
bride, wasp, sex cylinder, desire-magneto with
artificial sparks, at the horizon where her clothing might
be put on or off, according to the juggler of gravity—the
most necessary character who does not appear because he is
unpainted—and the boxing match just to the right of the
scissors, drainage slopes, sieves, oculist witnesses,
pump, chute, weight of holes, planes of flow,
splash, falls, dins, crashes   beside a chocolate
grinder, and above it all a climatic blossoming
and milky way

                        we see through a window cut
out of the wall for this occasion   a pause of *bedazzlement*,
just where *the word modern has run out scarcely as long ago*
as yesterday   form opens, space opens   and time
dapples this public *ritual of absence* turning on itself to become
a necessity of meaning, the eros of chances among things and
their *signs which are movable parts of the syntax*
                                    dazed
in *the circularity of desire and thought*
                        we see through

and Brancusi thought of it, surfaces which are depths
brought to light and shadow, Eve and Plato flickering
side by side   they are likely thinking of eternity, which
is to say indefinition   and he placed an *Endless Column*,
a *Gate of the Kiss* and a *Table of Silence* in Roumania   for
the simple reason that he was born there   birthplace is his
intermingling
of what is ours and what belongs to the world

                                        sur-face,
over and under the form   time and space are a vulnerable
love, a project of thinking *something whose very nature*
is to be in need   we have called this abstraction, merely
a style to rebel against the obedience of definition   but
archaeologists remind us that the arts encompassing Homer's
logomachia were abstract   his word-fight to the finish
with small line-figures soon to appear around the neck of
an amphora,
                    willingly thinking from indefinition

and Isamu Noguchi, d. Dec. 30, 1988, thought of it—*Time*
magazine headlines the 'passing of a purist'—pure from
what?   as he sought the *truth of materials*   *The Great Rock*
of Inner Seeking at the entrance
in Washington, an *invasion of a different time* into the
space of the rock—inner and outer bare to the rock—
craving a certain morphologic quality of anti-monuments

which, in this picture-show, flashes us back to the sights of
an otherworldly study of how to shape realities   where he began
with Idaho-born Gutzon Borghum who carved the Presidential
heads on Mt. Rushmore—Washington, Jefferson, Lincoln,
and stopped with that hoot Teddy Roosevelt who in New York
is on horseback with a black man and an Indian on either side,
nearly naked, walking, of course, bronzed to the core, before
coming to squalor and us

'My first sculpture,' Noguchi said, 'was Oscar Wilde's Salome,
then I did Jesus Christ.   I would say I was extremely facile.'
    and then flash forward, in the midst of the question of
images and watching Brancusi, 'It became self-evident to me
that in abstraction lay the expression of the age'—'to
ignore man as an object of special veneration'—not a mere
characteristic of modernism, but to work by 'this reversal
the unthought' truth of materials   and Buckminster Fuller
talked him into painting the disused laundry-room silver—
floor, walls and ceiling—freeing the distinctions   and
Martha Graham said, 'It is not abstract except if you think
of orange juice as an abstraction of an orange—He's caught
up in the happenings of the universe'

strolling through the darkness, the earth, the playgrounds,
the white marble garden at Yale, the flowing pool of heaven
in Tokyo, the sunken garden (Chase Manhattan), the bridges
in Hiroshima, by the rejected memorial for the *atomic dead,*
though he was in a 'relocation' camp during the war—called
by the small Radio Nurse, bakelite and commercial, among Akari,
mulberry paper and bamboo illuminations at floor level, through
the UNESCO garden, East and West sparkling in Paris, the whoosh
and splendour of the Detroit fountain, the tipped red cube,
which he said was 'man's fate,' right there in front of the
Marine Midland Bank, the magic circle, never closed, Persian
travertine, so it is endless, ah, Double Red Mountain, and
nearer to home, across the border, the Black Sun (Volunteer
Park, Seattle) to look through
                              and outward
marigold, daisies and broom   anti-monuments
                              towards *a greater chaos*
and a new equilibrium   art is an element in assymmetrical
flux   no isolated object
                    all function, all linkage
to our birthplace and back again

'home, home on the range'

'words alone'   yeah   now it's the confrontation with words,
then it's a creation with words   ordinary and
sublime relations   *of the rime you meant to*
come to   a.m. aureole and blue, blue thought all day

the skin moves over the muscles
the muscles embrace the secrecy
of blood, arterioles and aspiration
the bright, dressy mind bends over
for a look

where the ordinary man or woman hides
mesmerized by the body's weakness
the body takes all the Muses back
to have a look   the centuries of murmuring
societies made of the two of them
and us

1989

Giving the Glitter to
Somebody Else and Not Wanting
It Back

with his hands on the paternal pronouncement—patrikoi logoi

O boy!

tall buildings   smile silver   and a brick brightness on
sailors' minds at night delight tomorrow   palm-court
music, its sweet ravelling before moving on to what's thought
to be wanting   a stranger reading   or a *glass scholar of*

the model of divine being as an original presence to itself

Wow!

doing without   of course   *the father of logos*

Gosh!

a tiny, striped body lands on the page of my book, its
rainbow wing broken by the mishap, it was short of the golden
pot   sly thoughts on the white table, sunlit, slip offward
and othergates   where guesses are

a properly human language transgresses the Law of the Father

All ways!

somewhen, somewhere, one was *the father's other*, wasn't one

Today!

and my discourse sexualizes   a running to and fro in order to
make an arrangement   of which the syntax was mostly disarrayed
unable to *rehearse that family scene*, or reluctant, after begging
the statues to nod their heads   and once-upon, Spicer said, 'just
another love poem,' and laid the manuscript aside rightly   and
Jeremy Prynne said, 'all that sexual posturing—read Spinoza'   I
already had, and I wandered around an echelon of language,   dis-
paralleled, that my desire among things might play in the offing,
dis-
    continuous and continuous

O!

bewaring the sacred, according to instructions from an otherwise
mind-full   the sexual-aside of that binding is its vocabulary—
largeness of nouns—fundamental to its covenant and exclusions
of an obedience   to body-sound   and of rebellion in mindness
                                                          My!
pronunciation of shiboleth nearly killed me among things
the politeness of watchwords—governments of cosmos, nation-
    hoods,
and jobs at a loss—passing

                                                          Go!
the panic of the car stalled in the absolute passage between
opposites—he-she-it-they of just and unjust likeminds—stuck
in the mind of   or as Derrida said of godliness gone shopping
for the nouns of father, son and himself,
sly, slippery, masked, an intriguer, a joker—sort of—a wild
card   no jack, perhaps, but a supplanter all-the-same,   who
dreams ladders out of the mess,   and tosses
                                      Jackstones!
yes, tunnels, playing in a vacant lot   at the margin, excavated,
the author-eyed is almost gone to his happiness   someone is
planting twigs to look for a day like trees   through which
toy cars, revved-up, speed to their parley
                                                          I!
domesticity loved, sit here writing   and try to find
                                      the home of it

Of the Land of Culture

I flew too far into the future: a horror assailed me

think of it as fissiparous

an Other who is no longer God or the muse, but anonymous

a CBC interview on China: 'Business is above politics'   thereby:
beyondness   and 'politics' seeks equality in *kakistocracy* and
its professions

the psychiatric patient said, No, I don't want to go back there—
the place is full of fallen angels trapped in human form

strangers in the existing order, which the ordinary woman or man
can't narrate, though s /he is the most recent and only narrator
left to an anonymous culture   and is promissory

she said, someone broke in last night and stole my sexual organs,
I've called the police again and again, but they won't do anything
the doctor said gently, let's have a look, and he told
her he'd found them where they should be   and she left without
even a thank-you

was her thought of the loss really of the burglar, for whom most
of us wait?

age deepens politics and the wonderful world—oh, dear! body's
and mind's it-ain't-what-it-used-to-be decays in cliché, and is
beside the point—because it never was—in order to say, your
smile is true at the cut

how many centuries has Christianity had in kind hands our otherness,
one to one, here & there, & beyondness?   'christians'—
now manifesting—should all get together and play patty-cake, for
that is the size of their cultural heaven
everyone said, thank you for your bright and careless eyes

Ethan Mordden said, *it could not be that paranoid Old Testament*
sheik with the plagues and tantrums   stopped by briefly, doing all over
again goodness

a song on the radio today sang, 'To our God we are in debt,' so
to describe the deficit

the shills said, confidentially, cultural haven is under one of
these three walnut shells, named O.T., N.T., and materialism—
try your luck!

Hustle, eyes watering, bent over the *tabula rasa* and his hand
trembled

Then I flew back, homeward—and faster and faster I flew: and so
I came to you, you men of the present, and to the land of culture
I laughed and laughed, while my foot still trembled and my heart
as well: 'Here must be the home of all the paint-pots!' I said

You are half-open doors at which grave-diggers wait. And this is
your reality: 'Everything is worthy of perishing'

it's amazing to be pushed out of shape a lot of the time, and the
amazement is a cultural gift

someone said, the stones of _____ [fill in the name of
your own home town] are saturated with poetry

(Nietzsche whispering

a bird in the house

the truth flies   hungry, at least   and otherous,
of which—though it may be one—Kafka said troublingly,
it has many faces

                                                    it's
the faces one wants, tripping the light shadows of   its
skin colours   of its wordy swiftness, angry and solvent,
of its loud remarks

                    as of feeding flocks   one
year, one, among the smallest birds in the Northwest, flew
into the house   a darting, panic thought   at the walls
and grasses   perched on the top right corner of the frame

of Tom Field's painting wherein adulterous Genji is found
out—so Lady Murasaki reads from her blue scroll—and
permitted me to take it in my hand   soft, intricate

mind   honouring   and lift it out into the air
and the next year, again, one flew into the house,
almost certain, like a visitor, gold-crowned   winged

floating about   odd discoveries   and alighted on the brim
of the lasagna dish   my hand trembled as I took it up
and moved slowly to lift it out of the window   into

the air   a kind of thinking   like everybody else
looking   for *a continuing contravention of limits and*
of substance

                                        for Sharon Thesen

Who's There?

the room talks to itself
                coloured Persian
and wraps its thinking-
                lights around
the man bent over
                a drinking-fountain
who is black
                and white
who transliterates
                into one crouching
over his book
                of loose pages
and another clapping
                his hands and pointing
his toe
        playing musical chairs
and chances
                among deep-seated minds
whose laughter counter-
                points the razzle
of crows outside
                cawing down the chimney
as if to enter between
                firecat-andiron's
serious, childish, jasper eyes
                the room talking to itself

rose

I called 'goodnight' across all the flowers,
enamoured of old conversations,   flowerage
of men and women in my mind

and the modern duplexity of reviving
the past as a search for the unknown
sticks in the craw of the bird I would be

the hero, eager to experience the sensation
of a bird, resorts to witchcraft,
but by an unfortunate pharmaceutical error
finds himself transformed into an ass   ah,
he knows he can revert to his own body
by eating rose-petals, but these prove
singularly elusive   'rose,' he called

adventuring kisses,   of which, which
among them sing symmetry of
physical and spiritual form,   asking
that pain-in-the-ass, Mister
Verbal-Eternity, personification of chicanery and
of charlatanism about death   'mind's rose,'
he saw

the body is the permanence of an endless wave,
amorous form   and amorous image meets it
what did I need from the conversations?
friendship's mystery and love's indeterminacy
skipping the grass   he and she thought

the *hypertely of immortality*   one thing
'more immortal' than another in such inarguable
relation?   and the rose-petals wandered
in the sunlight   'rose,' we said

                              reading Lezama Lima
                              and the jacket blurb
                         for Hanson's new Apuleius

Bits of a Book

whose salted heart ('so that it would remain, if not fresh,
at least dry'), I've met

we've met, it turns out, in the labour of form, a cultural
largeness talking to itself   its memory damaged   its past
not there   and its future Nietzschean   *where a horror met*
him   so I'm just pushed out of shape   the present
which should be the pleasure of eternity   momentary,
but discerning shape   tigerish, momentarily in Blake's
sense of who-made-thee?   *we live in a society that teaches*
us hatred of these   this troubles the lyric
mind   the celebration of lover and intellect

    •

           candid

why, we're back to Voltaire, only nobody knows it
except that portable version which said
'castles'

phone call   'I'd like to forget that period,' but I like
periods   they remind me of sentences which are
prisons with prisoners' castles

back to Voltaire   praying   reason   unreasonable aids
glowing white

    •

nobody

so what shall we say of the soul
that it may be

of space and of time,
just as uncanny

the self gasps in the beyond
in order to exist somewhere

or they are arraigned like music,
the tune of them tasteless,

epicurean, and fiery,
unaneled in the extremities

of green   and the moth of it
roves   at the provisional   door

        •

wiped-out places

serious!   of back porches   even front doors   roof tops
and rectangular house lots   'Serious,' he replied, 'means
following through to one's destiny'   which is 'not self,'
but is 'the fate of the work' and 'obedient to series'

of terms derived from one or more of a precession
by a fixed law   lots of small rocks, *smaller*
than a system, comprising those formed in an epoch
whose fixed law cannot be seen   to blue

        •

Pierrot, my happiness   big buttoned   white   exuberance
of 66 years, headed for the strict canon   round, not exactly
backwards, but crab-like sideways,   and mirrored   polyphony
gained from a single line   to be sure at the intervals, one
by one   of vertical attacks by-cause that is   is always
horizontal   sometimes
looking for other verbs   to ramble   white in the face

   •

        yellow ribbons

among tiresome minds   of unconscious mendacity, where
I had thought lying an active method of reality,   public
and bushranging   a whack-off in the mind-dust   thus,
to give credence to the old superstition of spending one's
self unduly   or is it a matter of the ideologically im-
printed   without the affection of duck to human animal-
culum   discoursing?   so, then, we have *thurifers* of
everything   *who*, as Boulez said—of a certain musi-
cality—*have choked their idolatry with poor-quality in-
cense*   that's the cakewalk   literally

Exody

1990–1993

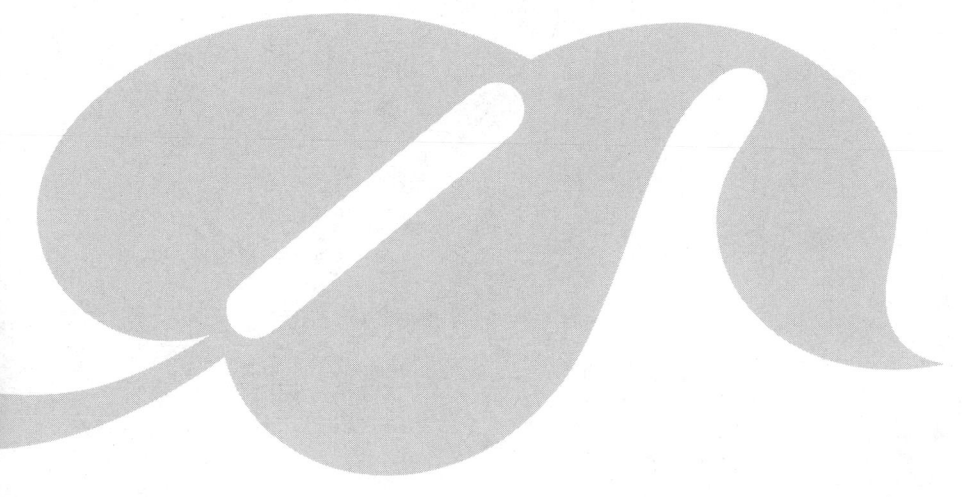

Muses, Dionysus, Eros

offerings to them can only be
all your life, old man

and I was boxing with a tough opponent   the footnote
says, 'Presumably Eros'   but I thought all three
in this otherness of home

and cowboyed it down Idaho way, east and west of Blaser, non-
populated, on the Portneuf River with railroads for horseback

and TV tells me St. Clare—whose poverty dreamed a transubstantiation
on the wall of her bedroom, God's problem—protects TV's
     deprivation,
and I asked St. Clare to help this kaleidoscope be asymmetrical, as the
world is in mind and heart

and, in a trance, pushed all 37 buttons to a brightout, having found
God's back with a little help from commercialism, and practical
Marxism, and implored as I craved, excessive and all ways

and a phone call of wishfulness came through just then   Stan sure
wished he could defend civilization this New Year   helplessly, I
promised to tape 80 years of Elliott Carter's intelligence, as soon as I
learned the techne of conversation, of fragments of acellerandi and
decellerandi—of violin, violin, viola, and cello answering one another,
worlding, until later, each instrument opposes, laments, laughs,
ridicules and silences—both with and against the possible beautiful year

and I was boxing with a tough opponent   the footnote
says, 'Probably Eros'

reading Anacreon

Even on Sunday

I don't know anything about God but what the human record tells
me—in whatever languages I can muster—or by turning to
translators—or the centuries—of that blasphemy which defines god's
nature by our own hatred and prayers for vengeance and dominance—
that *he* (lower case and questionable pronoun) would destroy by a
hideous disease one lover of another   or by war, a nation for what
uprightness and economic hide-and-seek—and *he* (lower case and
questionable pronoun) is on the side of the always-ignorance of politics
in which we trust—the *polis* is at the 'bottom of the sea,' as Hannah
Arendt noticed—and *he* (lower case and interrogated pronoun) walks
among the manipulated incompetences of public thought

where I had hoped to find myself ordinary among others in the
    streets—
a 'murmuring voice of societies'

and so one thinks them over—blasphemies all, against multiplicity,
which is all anyone knows about god—and one can only hate them
so much without becoming *halt and lame in their kingdom of single-
mindedness*—their having taken a book to have been once and forever,
the language behind language that no one has ever spoken   god's
what-knot and *mystical rags* we call flags

as a friend said, 'I'm going to become fundamentalist and call
everybody asshole'

and what would the gods be if I asked them—our nakedness didn't
quite fit—out, as it is, of nature—yet, there is a sentiment at *the
intersection between life and thought*—streaks of beyondness in that
careless relation

            October came in August and petunias straggled,
sprawling white faces one at a time, lobelia browned and continued
blue   the neighbours cut down the sexual cottonwood which kept the
whole block from repainting door-steps for over a month—by the
fluffs of its happiness—

so we are in the midst of a *metaphysical washout*—take for example,
Verlaine and Rimbaud—as Hans Mayer says: *Being shut out of the*
social order, they sought to heighten their condition by, say, publicly embracing
in Brussels and thus providing the formula for a new 'condition humaine'
that called out to be created—both failed—both remained in outsiderdom
—one continued to rhyme, the other gave up the whole damned
creation   behind this, an Enlightenment, which I'll return to
                  and Sylvie asked,
'*But what became of the Man?*'
'*Well, the Lion springed at him. But it came so slow, it were*
three weeks in the air—'
'*Did the Man wait for it all that time?*' I asked.
'*Course he didn't!*' Bruno replied, *gliding head-first down the*
stem of a fox-glove, for the story was evidently close to its end.
'*He sold his house, and he packed up his things, while the Lion were coming*
And he went and lived in another town. So the Lion ate the wrong man.'
         This was evidently the Moral . . . said Lewis Carroll

the moral is that something does devour the *existential given*—
Rimbaud, Mayer writes, *does not intertwine with visions of Sodom in order*
to provoke heaven's fire; it is simply the sole possibility of his own self-acceptance

being shut out of the social order   Rimbaud writes *de posséder la verité*
dans une âme et un corps, which Mayer interprets to say *being alive*
in the full sense of body and soul   the truth is being alive, until you break
on it

ah, Laius, when you ran off with the youth Chryssipus, the Sphinx
flew to a whistling stop in Thebes—and fire fell on Sodomites, on
each one of them, and, I'll be damned, almost everybody—tell me a
tale to explain sublime biology—then, tell me another to explain
sublime human nature—and murder, unmythologized, fell on 20th-
century outsiders   pollution of what in the momentary hangup of
the vast biology of things, desiring?   a covenant with whom?
     androsphinx, recumbent lion with the head of a man, answer me—
that is to say, each one of us

the sublime, dear everybody and everyday, is not so simply human—
overwhelms—*uncanny* is Hannah Arendt's word for the face of it—
dangerous—*severe, as a blow*—*mysterious*—on which the *existential*
given floats—the passions of

and Hans Mayer notes the tying and untying that confines things:
At the height of the Victorian era, the Bible is once again, as in Cromwell's
time, . . . the spiritual and social foundation of everyday life—O, the once-
again in which we trust—*Declaration is made in the Bible of what is*
proper for woman and what is not. The Bible depicts that which God punished
in Sodom. St. Paul only confirmed the curse one's mind may have a
certain affinity with Christopher Marlowe's, if it is true, as his
    roommate
Thomas Kyd tells us, that he thought the apostle Paul a swindler—
who taught a curdled godhead and a curdling view of the *existential*
given—and the black milk of it is blasphemy, so to revile existence

in the midst of this, an Enlightenment which first and foremost posited
an *equality of men and women, including homosexuals*—religion and
sexuality go hand in hand in the apple-light

it was not to be merely law, like free speech, but a *mental practice*
   what developed, in the guise of a Darwinian terror advancing in
evolutionary form, was the lion body with a man's head, walking in
the garden, so that *the underlying principles of liberty and equality, not*
even taking fraternity into account, inordinately encouraged combatting all
forms of outsiderdom in favour of what Ihab Hassan calls 'quantities of normed
phenomena'—normed existence excludes the *existential given*, not being
alive in the full sense of body and soul—and *extends, not merely perverts*
that which calls itself normality into political form but Mayer asks, *what*
is it then if the precipitating step outside, into the margins, is a condition of
birth, a result of one's sex, parentage, physical or spiritual makeup?
   Then
one's existence itself becomes a breaking of boundaries

we can thereby return to ourselves *a measure of freedom*, and take form—
the work of a lifetime—in this breaking of boundaries—

                                                                against,

as Mayer says, *a global disposition of thought toward annihilation, which*
thinks to admit only majorities in the future and is determined to equate
minorities with 'worthless life'   *Worthless are the Jews, there the blacks [and*
aboriginals], somewhere else (and everywhere) the homosexuals, women
of the type of Judith and Delilah, not least the intellectuals keen on individuation . . .

'They should all be gassed': the expression has crept into everyday language
Woman is not equal to man. Man is manly man, whatever is to be understood
by that: the feminine man stands out from the race and thereby becomes worthless
life. Shylock must be exterminated: the only final solutions are fire and gas

extreme remedies—pharmakons—Mayer reminds us, have been
proposed: for example, Klaus Mann writing in 1949—remember
when that was!—calls for . . . *the concerted mass suicide of intellectuals: to*
bring public opinion in the world, in the integrity and autonomy of which he
quite clearly still believed, to its right senses

well, we know now that this would disappear with a headline in the
Entertainment pages, or it might make the Arts and Books section
along with obituaries and sportsmanship, in *The Globe & Mail*—and
intellectuals?—Mann had not noticed that point in the space of
intelligence where they join the system, higgledy-piggledy—I think
of that recent hustle in the United States, offering the end of history
like a dinky-toy, democracy, pinking, blueing, and off-whiting in plastic
—'My goodness!' everyone said, 'They've discovered Hegel!' and *Time*
Magazine thought he was little known—and I said, 'My goodness!
Francis Fukuyama, so we finally got here, there, anywhere'

so to be reminded once again of Puddin'head Wilson: *It was wonderful*
to find America, but it would have been more wonderful to miss it

this unified mankind—for that's who's there, quantity or lump, at the
end of a materialist's or an idealist's history—conceived, Mayer writes,
as a homogenized humanity. Woe to outsiders

so that was it, was it? an *Enlightenment that promised equality to men and women, including homosexuals!* an age in the hole, running three centuries, surely allows one to say, 'Listen, you assholes, a *metaphysical washout* means you've lost your top soil'

and this system aims exactly—*at the heart of our social existence* to be an outsider *by virtue of our existence*—like statues come to life by moonlight in the child's desiring mind—has the advantage of voices, and their attentions, each to each, among quantified multitudes who wander *the computations and rationalities that belong to no one*—also going, going, gone into the *corpus Christianum* with its sadly separated body and soul

among these voices, I think of Montaigne: *Embraces remembered (or still vaguely hoped for) are 'our final accolades'*

in whose arms

even on Sunday

With considered use of Hans Mayer's *Outsiders* (MIT, 1982). Mark Twain's aptness is cited in Ihab Hassan's 'Foreword.' Written for Gay Games III, Vancouver, August 1990.

tip-toeing through the stink weed,
always resistant to systems, whole messes
of our thought   we are not in religion
but we are inside whatever has happened
to it   'moratorious' of what

1993

in the tree tops,

the child, child of the bigshot, invalid's child, labourer's
child, child of the fool, child of railroads, child of trees,
child that is deiformed, child of fireworks, child of colour-
lessness, child of damask, Mage's child, the child born with
twenty-two folds, at least   his or her concern is only to
unfold herself or himself, curious   one or the other's life
is, then, complete   under that form he or she dies   there's
no fold left for one or the other to undo

in the land of magic,

rarely a woman or man dies without having yet a few folds to
undo   but this happened   parallel to this *operation*, the
one or the other forms a *nucleus*, like a stone or a nut   the
inferior races, such as the white race, see the stone, nut, and
nucleus rather than the *unfolded fold*   the Mage sees, more-so,
the *unfolded fold*

the *unfolded fold* is important and onliest   what rests is
nothing but epiphenomenon

in the land of magic

after Henri Michaux,
gratitude to Richard Ellmann
for a solution to *dépli*

Image-Nation 24 ('oh, pshaw,'

she said often around 1929, 1930—especially when I played
with the lacy iron treadle of the sewing machine—so ravelling
the bobbin, great-grandmother Ina, who had been secretary
to Brigham Young, 'not a wife,' she said, of that revelation—
small, playing tall, in her long dress, fierce in thought—'don't
read that stuff,' she said, grabbing *Red Book* or *Ladies' Home Journal*,
'if you're going to read, read something worth it'—for all my
puzzling—and she tossed the news of whatever it was on top
of the icebox, out of reach—contempt showing, as she picked
me up by the suspenders and threw me out of the house, a
railcar, Union Pacific yellow, by the railway tracks, goldenrod
garden—wand stems—chicken coop cackle—sagebrush
beyond with killdeer nesting under those jade moments—
and conversations with jack rabbits—unless some masculine
shadow shot them and my words stopped in their screams—
of what we were talking about—'Drat!' I heard her say through
the window—rewinding the bobbin, 'Drat!'

God, she meant—a block pattern—gawdelpus—gawking,
I gaw-along now, giddy with salutations from bigots, better
known as by-gods, godbwyes, and gossips, a.k.a, godsibbs,
kin of some Indo-European past participle—*ghat—*id est,*
an adjective acting like a verb, an epithet of Indra—Mind—
who has almost disappeared into the gods of everything—
and come upon

                    seed-fields of gods, here and there
                    goddes sand, a message on the morning air

splendid creation, this *scrum of religion*

g & d retained become *gad, gawd, gud*
or only the g becoming *gog, golly, gosh, gum*
or disguise g as c and *cock, cor, cod* appear
or drop g for untold suffixes, *od, ud,* etc.
or add relationship, *begad, begar, bedad, egad*
or take up possession, *swounds, zounds*
or reduce the whole busyness to 'drat'
I said, mouthing back through the window

we were bunched there on an embankment by the railroads,
a boxcar, ownership yellow, doors and windows cut into it,
and lean-to bedrooms, kitchen, coal and wood stove, heating
the irons with detachable handles, dressing for dinner, which
meant freshly ironed gingham dresses and shirts, sometimes of
bleached sacking, home-made soap of many a lye-scented laundry
day—beloved distillations of my thought, great-grandmother
Ina, grandaunt Tina, grandmother Sophia Nichols (Dot, for
short), step-grandfather Auer—one-eyed, had an eye-cup,
a mustache cup, a wondrous imagination reading Poe and
Hawthorne aloud, as accented bedtime stories, German, 'blau
und bläuer,' he'd say of a wide day, walking the rails, hand in
hand, balancing like dancers—a sliver of steel had put that eye
out when he worked on the section-gang, where Sophia Nichols
found him—so there by bereavement (O.E. *āstīeped*) on both
sides—mother's father, Casus McCready, whose Latin name
means unexpected, say, by chance—*and so bifel, by adventure or cas,*
writes Chaucer—having disappeared into Canada for good and
everything else, after visiting her, out of the blue, at the Sacred
Heart Academy in Ogden, Utah, in 1918, when she was 13—
his gift, five Canadian five-cent pieces, which she wouldn't have
spent for love nor anything sweeter, anyway, Victoria's portrait
on 1889, George V's on those dated 1907, 1910, and two
1913's—now tossed in the palm of my hand—and there
on the embankment also were my mother, Ina Mae, my father,
'Bob,' the outsider, my brother, second-born, Augustus (Gus),
given the Blaser family name, my sister Hope, third-born,

named for a supernatural virtue, and I, first-born, named after
the daughter of Robert and 'Feather' Gareth-Lawless in Frances
Hodgson Burnett's First World War novel, Robin—'She was
an intruder and a calamity, of course'—and, as if to right a
precarious gender, after St. Francis Xavier, a Basque of Spanish
Navarra, one of the first seven Jesuits devoted at Montmartre in
1534, of Portuguese India, Ceylon, Malay, Kyoto, Yamaguchi,
and of an island at one of the mouths of China, who, I was
told, flew over the Mediterranean on an Arabian carpet—
there, on the embankment, we could be heard whispering
languages of the Great Depression, comforted by claims of
fore-be-ers, Benjamin West and Harriet Beecher Stowe—

and I day-dreamed of a great stone face, immense in a forest,
and of Bowdoin College, where Hawthorne went—when,
finally, I got there in 1958 with friends, I followed their
exclamations, ahead of me in the Art Gallery, to Gilbert
Stuart's portrait of Benjamin West—'spittin' image of you,'
they said, never having heard those railroad whispers—perhaps
for a moment, among friends, by that portraitist of George
Washington, commissioned by Martha, on every U.S. $1 bill—
hallucination or made-up comfort that you belonged to—

in Orchard, Idaho, strolling between water-tower and pump-
house—the orchard of the name out there in the folding
horizons of hot summer—apple, plum, and black walnut
struggling in the sagebrush, walnuts in their husks and dried
apples strewn about the attic of the abandoned house—in
the spring, the soil pock-marked by the rain, in early summer,
pastel, cactus flowering, in the dry cistern, twining snakes in
the sexual season—

the Blasers—wheresomever—on the restless horizons—sudden
whirlwinds, roiling, you could run after or, turnabout, be
chased by—their sand voices—there in a valley of the Portneuf
River, a train station, a stop if you flagged one, a mountain, a
narrow river meadow, grandmother and grandfather trying to
hang on to Blaser, Idaho, now, according to the *Rand McNally
Commercial Atlas*, with no population—she, sometime from Wales,
had nothing to do with me, the wrong sort, who saw a hot
piece of pie as the steaming mouth of a dragon and cried out—
he, from Toulouse, he said—the lost Dauphin, he thought—
whispering over the radio song—'tu es la crème de mon café,
tu es le pois de ma soupe'—who was a roadmaster on The
Union Pacific, captain of a handcar, and a Mormon Bishop,
who left a small house, his ritual underwear, a *Book of Mormon*,
two volumes of genealogy back to Adam, where the Adam
before Adam swims among dominated stars—who, on his
deathbed, said, 'say it in French'—'no, sound's wrong,' he
rasped, and corrected my pronunciation with his musical, trilled
r's—where the Garonne flows—a mindment—

who, wary, only hinted to the Catholic boy about the *Golden
Bible*, discovered *in a certain mountain*, near Manchester, New York,
announced by the Angel Moroni, September 2 1, 1 8 2 3, *his
countenance truly like lightning*—last seen in my wandering, gold-
leafed and trumpeting on the roof of an art-deco temple, from
my hotel window in Hollywood, 1 9 8 2—*the stone box, the sword and
breastplate, Urim and Thummim*, mysterious words for whatever were
used to cast lots for God's meaning, aleph to tau—'It's true, I
did taste a little honey on the tip of my stick, and, lo, I must die,'
said Jonathan when he was up for sacrificing among the lots—
hints only of *the thin gold plates, eight inches square, bound with three huge
rings, covered by engraved 'caractors,'* which Joseph Smith's mother,

Lucy, said he and his wife, Emma, brought home on September 22, 1827—no one could look upon, except Joseph—but his mother was shown Urim and Thummim, *two smooth three-cornered diamonds set in glass and the glasses set in silver bows*—which became spectacles to read the gold plates by—

a sampling of the *caractors*, copied by Joseph Smith, was presented to Charles Anthon, professor of Greek and Latin at Columbia College and author of an important edition of Horace—my copy, a gift from Jack Spicer in 1948—dated *the 29th day of March, A.D. 1830, in the 54th year of the Independence of the United States of America*—who replied that they

> *consisted of all kinds of crooked characters disposed in columns, and had evidently been prepared by some person who had before him at the time a book containing various alphabets. Greek and Hebrew letters, crosses and flourishes, Roman letters inverted and placed sideways, were arranged in perpendicular columns, and the whole ended in a rude delineation of a circle divided into various compartments, decked with various strange marks, and evidently copied after the Mexican calendar by Humboldt, but copied in such a way as not to betray the source whence it was derived.*

then rumoured about that the golden plates were actually incised in *ancient shorthand Egyptian*, or, the phrase goes, in *reformed Egyptian*—before Champollion and the Rosetta Stone hit town by slow boat and the language mountain erupted—grandfather was silent about the four mummies and papyri that came into Joseph's hands in 1835, including a Book of Abraham, translated by those spectacles, and a Book of Joseph of Egypt, untranslated—the discovery of the plurality of God in the word *Elohim*—the curse on red skin and black skin—the veil torn off government in 1844—

The world is governed too much and there is not a nation or a dynasty
now occupying the earth which acknowledges Almighty God as their
lawgiver, and a crown won by blood, by blood must be maintained.
I go emphatically, virtuously, and humanely, for Theodemocracy,
whose God and the people hold the power to conduct the affairs of
men in righteousness. We want the President . . .

grandfather was silent too about Kirtland, Illinois, where
Jehovah appeared, 'eyes as a flame of fire,' and Moses, and
Elias, and Elijah, giving all this into the hands of the United
States—I needed Fawn Brody's wonderful book of 1957,
No Man Knows My History, to straighten out the territory and the
map, which are not the same—where the original Eden was—
Independence, Missouri—and exactly where Cain killed Abel—
Far West, Missouri—homosexuals, the word not yet current in
the covered wagons, became the progeny and progress of Cain

that intruder and calamity, way back there, was born in Denver,
Colorado, in 1925—coverlet arranged by his mother's teachers
at the Sacred Heart Academy, Sisters Seraphina and Mary
Madeleva, the latter published her poems, *Knights Errant*, in
1923, opening with a dedicatory poem 'To my favorite author,
Dear God,'—at the back of it, advertisements for 'Interesting
New Verse'—Vachel Lindsay's *Going-To-The-Sun*, written during
his 'walking trip in the Rockies,' and *A Child's Garden of Verse* in
Latin, 'the spirit of Stevenson in the form of Horace'—five
months later, the intruder was legitimated—at liberty in whirl-
winds and in inimical languages—having a chat rest stops—
two machine sheds, painted white, now with two station
names, Blaser East and Blaser West, Idaho—about a mile
apart—padlocked—humming as mysteriously as Urim and
Thummim, beside the railway tracks, following the Portneuf
River

grandmother Sophia Nichols was telegrapher in Orchard—
dot—dash—spaces—sounds for translation, quick as the
platinum points come together, quick as the mind can—
a click for each letter arriving or going—by which Sophia
Nichols kept food, shelter, clothing, and us together—by
the coulee of her mind—'duty and love' she called these dots—
dashes—spaces

once the rains were so heavy the water rose up the opposite
embankment, nearly reaching the railbed, and stayed for days—
'a sea,' Sophia Nichols said, never having seen one, and it was
wide and stretched along the tracks as far as I could see—we
needed supplies from the commissary across there—Carnation
condensed milk, I remember—and we plotted a way to cross
that sea—the tin tub and a shingle, just the right size boat and
paddle for me, we thought—round and round it went, being
round, and drifted from shore meandering—she tossed me a
broom, which luckily floated near enough to reach it—'see
if you can touch bottom,' she said—I could—'so push,' she
said—and I made it there circuitously, pulled my tub up on the
beach, got the supplies, and returned—'circuitously Odyssean,'
she said, having spent hours those rainy days telling me stories
of Odysseus, which were, she said, homeward journeys of the
soul—whatever you find that is, she seemed to say—the book
she held as she talked was bound in red with a fierce, gold
god impressed on the cover, who came at you, glistening wind-
blown hair and zig-zagged lightning, Greek on the first page,
then Palmer's translation and Wyeth's illustrations—'but your
boat,' she said, 'was more like a gondola,' talking of Venice,
where she'd never been, then of the Union Pacific coal cars,
which are by transformation gondola cars and constellations

great grandmother reading Emerson—'over your head,' she
said, then stopped me to read a passage out loud, glaring—to
see if 'anything sank in'—'The old Sphynx bit her thin lip,' I
mumbled to myself—of this beloved mind, stirring the pot by
the railway tracks, like a magic gypsy—and thoroughly confus-
ing the Sphinx with Hawthorne's chimaera, wanting to be
his Eustace Bright, but was, more likely, Primrose, or Squash
Blossom, or Cowslip, or Dandelion—it had a body that neither
Hawthorne nor I wanted to imagine, with three heads, a goat's,
a lion's, a huge snake's, each of them flaming with fire and,
then, a tail like a boa-constrictor—grandfather Auer explained
that there were only bull-snakes 'around here,' and pulled me
away when the men caught a rattler and a bullsnake, dropped
them into a fruit lug, covered with a screen, and bet on the out-
come—when Emerson visited Brigham Young in Salt Lake City
in 1871, he gave 'no sign of knowing who Emerson was'—but
his secretary said, 'I have read many of your books'—sounds
like great grandmother, who couldn't have known that Emerson
on the way to San Francisco said, 'But one would think after this
Father Abraham could go no further.'—*Rue, myrrh, and cummin for
the Sphynx*—

a neighbour in flowery pink gingham, puffed sleeves—one
of 19 who lived in Orchard—I was into counting—leaned
out of the sun, over the picket fence, and said, 'My,' leaving
the expletive word God out, 'he has a big vocabulary'—

the rocking chair from their lost house in Salt Lake City, often
talked about, had a painted leather back—the wandering Jew
or nomad—whose marvellous, piercing eye followed everyone
up and down the boxcar parlour—into corners, even under the
library table, also from the lost house—*eros* of wandering—*eros*
of being sought in every nook and cranny—that, so far as I'm
concerned is where vocabulary begins—fierce eyed—dot—
dash—space—and syntax is later and difficult

sitting under the ironing board, learning songs, first *The Star Spangled Banner* in Latin—it didn't come out right and laughter came from the steam in the cloth—'for next time,' mother said—so we tried *The Chicago Fire*, but I wept—so we tried *Hallelujah, I'm a bum*, word perfect—then, letting the ironing wait, she took up her ukulele—*Keep your seats awhile / And I will sing to you / Of a girl I used to love / And her name was Duck-Foot Sue / She was handsome and sublime / While wasted in the feet / Her beauty was all she had / She was built like a North River shad / She was chief engineer in a Chinese laundry / Down in Kalamazoo / Her hair was indigo blue / She was gentle as a kangaroo / Her mother was a double-barrelled guy / With a double-barrelled squint in her eye / Her #10 feet could cover up the street / She had a mouth like a crack in a pie / She had a cheerful cemetery laugh / A face like a Mexican calf*—so keep your seats awhile

and

one day, Sophia Nichols put up the lantern—too early in the morning for the flag to be seen—stopped the train, talked to the conductor, and put me aboard for Boise—just before my 11th birthday—to buy school clothes, especially underwear, at Falk's Department Store—the garden of the train station, surprising begonias and lilies I hadn't a word for—my first city—what was it, 50,000—waking up—traffic sounds coming up hill—and going downhill, hearing bed springs, bacon frying, muffled voices of everybody's day—and another day I'd meet Kublai Khan and Marco Polo saying *Cities also believe they are the work of the mind or of chance* (Calvino)—that's the question you ask the city or the city asks you—wandering the park—my first art gallery—landscapes sweeter than where I came from—until the stores opened, then lunched at The Mechanafe where six pieces of pie went by on a moving belt, tried them all, since it was all you could eat—and wandered back through the park, where I came upon a tent and a sign that read—new word—Chatauqua and welcome, so I went in where a frantic man went on and on about the stench and corruption of the

body—what you had between your legs—what you did with
whatever it was—he seemed oddly at a loss for words just
there—but whatever it was smoked with terror, a red rash,
God's hatred, pustules, swelling, scabs, disfigurement, and
then all this went inside, into the blood, up the spinal column,
into a seething brain—I got the impression it was mucous—
and he said syphilis—a new word, later found to be the name
of a shepherd—was the wages of sin—and sure enough, I
caught it, crotch itch, running in the hot sun to catch my train,
and when I got home, a red rash around my tight underwear—
and days passed, sneaking to the out-house, secretly curing it
with mentholatum—brimstone and bale-fire, as words go,
seemed glamorous to that—but no *veiled voice there lulling my con-*
science to its music that I found in Joyce—out of *Ecclesiasticus* where
I too knew it—*Quasi cedrus exaltata sum in Libanon / there I grew like a*
cedar in Lebanon / like a cypress on the slope of Hermon / like a date palm in
Gades / like roses planted in Jericho—Wisdom singing to herself among
the verticals, thought to be heaven—and given 'by accommo-
dation' to Mary, during the Mass of the Assumption of August
15th—and sexual hallucinations, since the sexual is everywhere
and thought to be immortal—as *The Homeric Hymn to Aphrodite* tells
us—they all run off into the bushes as she passes—Marco Polo
said to Kublai Khan, *the inferno of the living is not something that will*
be—you may become part of it or learn *what in the midst of the*
inferno are not inferno, then make them endure, give them space (Calvino)

someone in the 17th century, after the displacement of the centre
sank in, moved hell to the sun because, he said, there's more
space there—
            and the ashen boy
writes here of my cultural kitchen—I look into the mirror
of a frying pan—and stand still in somebody's red-hot, iron
shoes—I see all the *god-lore* spattering—I see Roman Catholic
Pat Buchanan and fundamentalist Pat Robertson at the Repub-
lican Convention proposing a social future excluding homo-

sexuals and women's choice—Bush, preceded by a *sinister cretin,*
as Christopher Hitchens calls him, at the centre of this political
disgrace—many said it hadn't worked, so it didn't matter—
but it did, this anthropological fraud—and it comes over the
air here in Canada—on a mixed Vision TV station—John Hagee
waving the *Book* around, slapping it down on a lectern—because
it's a permanent human nature—Jack Van Impe explaining,
to his wife Rexella and us, out of *Daniel* and *Revelation*—100 are
being trained in ritual sacrifice for the day the Temple is rebuilt
in Jerusalem—smoke goes up, this time, in the name of Christ,
he says—

> *The notion of God as the 'unmoved mover' is derived from Aristotle,*
> *at least as far as Western thought is concerned. The notion of God as*
> *'eminently real' is a favourite doctrine of Christian theology. The*
> *combination of the two into the doctrine of an aboriginal, eminently*
> *real, transcendent creator, at whose fiat the world came into being, and*
> *whose imposed will it obeys, is the fallacy which has infused tragedy*
> *into the histories of Christianity and Mohametanism.* (beloved
> Whitehead)

now, the players collapse into one another—into an ashen
cosmography—their monotheism in tatters—exiting for
something like six centuries—into the complexity of this
'absolute' structure of desire—fluid rocks—as Michel de Certeau
finds in The Mystic Fable,

> *This God who 'comes out' but for a struggle to the death with his*
> *disappointing creation, a god outside of himself, on the boundary where*
> *he is exiled both from himself and from the world, furious with a desire*
> *lacking an object . . . hatred at the very beginning of Deity,*
> whose lineaments are—

now, the players tumble like spiky weeds—over Craters of
the Moon—they collapse into their own Will—stretch out
in technology—do not recognize themselves—forgive them-
selves, unaware and repetitious—the 'I' cannot exist there—
it was glass in *an impossible body*—my lyric voice loose in it—
tattoos of an absolute language—old song—

here, plagues galore weave among us—aids, racism, homopho-
bia, displacement and poverty, *christianism* with its political plans,
the Vatican sending out 'advisory letters' to the Bishops that it's
okay to discriminate against gays in jobs, housing, and profes-
sions—wacky—and the murder of Dr. David Gunn, 'justifica-
tion,' they say, 'as a pro-life casualty'—I see his sad, sad son
listening—none of this in *god-lore's* hands—

I tell 'you,' my love, these tales—*fold according to fold*—
my chances—it may be

a crap game—hoping for a nick—7—or a natural—11—

on a startled day—the ashen boy—becomes—exodic

Mappa Mundi,

widely translated, world napkin,
And perhaps, after all, there is **no** secret. *We incline
to think that the problem of the Universe is like the
Freemason's mighty secret, so terrible to all children.
It turns out, at last, to consist in a triangle, a mallet,
and an apron,*—*nothing more! We incline to think that God
cannot explain His own secrets, and that He would like a
little information upon certain points Himself. We mor-
tals astonish Him as much as He us. But it is this Being
of the matter; there lies the knot with which we choke
ourselves. As soon as you say Me, a God, a Nature, so soon
you jump off from your stool and hang from the beam.   Yes,
that word is the hangman. Take God out of the dictionary,
and you would have Him in the street.*
> Melville to Hawthorne, 1851

streets of saltimbancos, dressed as imperial rulers, as moral
principles, as philosophical totalities—*gods and heaps*—

verticals and horizontals of days and nights, of thought's body
and passion's method—twine to delight and dissonance—now I
wake, now I lay me down to sleep—where insomnia begins at
age 4, saying it—

Olson once said he wished he could learn how to handle verti-
cals from Boulez—horizontals being what we do everyday to-
ward horizons—he had in mind the Second Piano Sonata, the
eruptive violence of them—in conversation with Beethoven's
Hammerklavier—a rage of rhythm—the rhythmic variations of the
notes playing the astonishment of BACH's belief—counterpoints
of monads becoming nomads—*of rhythm is image/of image is know-
ing/of knowing there is/a construct*—his dream

of compossibility

*Moby Dick is indeed our mighty book, not because it
makes a whole of the fragments of America but rather,
because, in its sheer massiveness, it never stops
demonstrating (as if to inspire courage) the sustaining,
self-renewing powers of historical and cultural
orphanhood.*

    Leo Bersani, *The Culture of Redemption*

turn every, singular nakedness to the wall and the wall mirrors
nakedness

*For each dead society has bequeathed to us its historical
sickness*—the Greeks, Platonism as the Great
Tradition in western philosophy; the Hebrews, the
fallen temple of their ancient tribalism and their
lost Davidic messiah; and the Romans, the ghost of
Rome, the Church and western patterns of political
and intellectual despotism.

    Weston La Barre, *The Ghost Dance*,
    his book dedicated to a forebear,
    who was 'burned at the stake, 1 July,
    1766 at the age of eighteen'
*An 'archosis' is a massive and fundamental misapprehension
of reality, often of incalculable antiquity
culturally . . .*

    Weston La Barre, *Muelos*

semen-fantasies—transformed a moment, say—in Simone
Martini's glorious, golden space, 1333, of *cusped arches and
gables, foliate crochets and spiky pinnacles,* the Annunciation, *traversed
by the words of the angel*—Martini's love—fear—astonishment—
shimmering—flow into estuaries—

Spicer said—*Mella, mella peto / In medio flumine*—after Ovid—
seeking honey in the middle of the stream—

turn every, singular nakedness to the wall and the wall mirrors
its labyrinthine nakedness—hyacinthine colourness twining on
the wind—the soul becomes a fracture in the old paint—like
the surface of a moonlit Ryder painting—running joyous and
jagged—here and there—

finitude and infinitude of, say, glass

Image-Nation 25 (Exody,

Nothing distinguishes me ontologically from a crystal, a plant,
an animal, or the order of the world; we are drifting together
toward the noise and the black depths of the universe . . . Michel
Serres tells us,
        a town-crier,
trying to imagine the intermediary states, trying to imagine the
man of the multiple, trying to imagine the margin that separates
the multiple from the ordered, the moment when the solid is at
the point of setting, in agitated crystals, when turbulence spins
in its whirlwind, when life is connected, liberated, awakened,
organized . . .
        this admirable, charmed mind of Hermes

tourbillions, that is, whirlwinds, whirlpools, vortexes, fire-
    works,
the writer writing twists there—his or her chance-possessed
breath—blew out the sentinal sentences, ancestral and
    beautiful—
they are now of changed substance—perhaps, of joyous
    tourmaline,
often black, sometimes blue, red, green, brown, or
colourless—polished pieces—of jewellers' tourmaline tongs
    that
would distinguish glass from crystal

        my naïveté, then, in
        cosmos   the profound
        corners of a room   of
        streets   of the
        beloved's angular
        form   folds
        of

J'ai plus de souvenir que si j'avais mille ans, including the
huge chest of drawers crammed with

God, self, history, and book are, Mark C. Taylor *tells us, bound in an intri-*
cate relationship in which each mirrors the other—steps over the hills and
in the forests since Pleistocene—change one of them—let's say,
probability enters among them in the 17th century—and you're
in the fun-house—becoming tall, squashed, thin, fat, protuber-
ant—at the beach—and laughing your head off

> space/time   time/space
> imagination's mind   time
> is the life of it   with
> a little raunch thrown in
> from the start

> sense of origin   *eros*
> sweet bitterness   belovèd
> sexual intelligence   and
> stupefaction   our swerve
> folds   in the
> magnificence

when Proto-Indo-European trees walked in Eden—delight in
life—at the edge of the glaciers, the apple among them, *requiring*
minimum cold for its winter dormance—trying to say, in *primitive seman-*
tics, my love *abvl- and *mahlo—north and south—walking
among them west, some small thing, man or woman, *universal*
and unconfined in its relations—hewing *down a tree with a stone axe, the physi-*
cal difference between an elm and a linden, or even an English and a live oak,
would be obvious—calluses—gone to thought—apple-cheeks, my
love

1503–1504, Hieronymus Bosch—his garden of earthly
delight—studied long and intensely by Michel de Certeau
in *The Mystic Fable*—and I, guessing over it for 40 years, join
him now with my magnifying glass—this forbidden tree of
life, sprung from the phallus of Jesse, walking in the garden—

delight in life—*coming into meaning and going out*—*this space is curved inward upon itself, like the circles and ellipses Bosch endlessly generates, there is no entrance, only interpretative delirium, fragments of a language, a lacunary system, a cosmos unsure of its postulates*—

displaces units of meaning piece by piece—*Everywhere Bosch smuggles in lapsus, disproportion, and inversion*—*what it means nevertheless reappears endlessly*—*this Boschdrollen*—a figure folding into or out of *a dolphin's tail, a man's torso, a duck's head reading an open book*—just emerging from a cave, *a man, the only one wearing clothes in the panel, points to a nude woman leaning on her elbows behind an ornamented glass*—*an apple in her hand and her mouth closed with a seal*—*a pig adorned with a nun's headdress holds out a quill pen to a seated man* who caresses her—folded over his leg a document *ready to sign*—they are approached by a shiny black knight's helmet with spiky antennae, stooping on pudgy legs and claw feet—we've moved across the three panels—de Certeau calls these playlets—my eyes catch a figure caught in the strings of a harp—a figure hanging through the loop of a key—a conversation with a bird-headed moth with owl-eyed wings—a youth, bent backward, riding a spotted, kerchiefed cat, whose balls shine, highlighted—arrows, flowers, sticks, · bird beaks stuck up asses—two figures shut up in a mollusc shell, one of them shitting a pearl—another whose face looks back over his body and at us, a broken egg shell with a tavern in it, entered by a ladder, whose legs are also tree trunks—indeterminate realities and imaginings—no entrance—no exit—my eyes strain, even with a guide, through the phantasmagoria, the phantasmagoria looks back—as if Ovid's metamorphoses, without his cosmos, became delirium—

an aesthetic exercise (in the sense in which one speaks of spiritual exercise), de
Certeau tells us, a reality made up of peaks, beaks, arrows and sharp points:
an anal and oral poetics, a marvelous animality of asses and mouths, a greedy
flowering of amorous play—

among the lion, panther, camel, bear, stag, boar, horse, ass, ox, goat, pig, uni-
corn—stork, heron, spoonbill, rooster, hen, owl, hoopoo, woodpecker—pineap-
ples, cherries, blackberries, gooseberries, strawberries, orange, apple, melon—
pumpkin, squash—fish and shellfish—pearls, topazes, emeralds,
crysolites—fairies, mermaids and mermen—de Certeau suggests an en-
cyclopedia of details—become opaque in the phantasmagoria—

proposes this, that Bosch's garden says to me or 'you'—You
there, what do you say about what you are, while you are saying what I am?

one might celebrate this unintelligibility that extinguishes
itself, like Igitur or Thereupon, old friends

      the startled branches,
      listening to dee-jays

How can a body be made from the word?—language, a shivaree
of transparence—jigsaw—glass immensity

      gods are
      such fine things
      such filigrees
      tenuous immortalities
      among things,
Lucretius said we need not fear them—propitiate, sacrifice,
or offer pungent smoke

the pleats of matter, and the folds of the soul, reading Gilles
Deleuze—

> A labyrinth is said, etymologically, to be multiple
> because it contains many folds. The multiple is not
> only what has many parts but what is folded in many
> ways . . . A 'cryptographer' is needed, someone who
> can at once account for nature and decipher the soul,
> who can peer into the crannies of matter and read the
> soul.
>
> —Deleuze, The Fold

they threw the old rocking chair from the lost house out—but
they cut the leather backrest out—with the portrait of the wan-
dering Jew or nomad on it—whose eyes follow me or 'you'—
into corners—to the end of the boxcar parlour—even into the
brilliance of reading under the library table—and sent it to me

    nevertheless, I rock there,
    wandering Jew and nomad

    I imagine mortality,
    its unrest and proses

    I imagine evolutionary love,

    my thousand and one celebrations

Notes

1994–2000

Robin Blaser: Curriculum Vitae

What I would be if I were not a writer? Who I would be if I were not a writer?—questions which—within the shadowy places of my love of thought—bring to mind my father's delight in whoopee-cushions. He liked particularly—taking us all off guard—to place these on the chairs of dinner guests— or on mine when I'd returned home for a visit. Consternation and blushes. Discomfort with what one was or with what one was going to say. The secrecy of person answered by true or simulated laughter in gales. Some never came back to the 'vulgarity.' I was always a guest—of family, of religion, and especially of language—nothing more, nothing less. That is the reason whoopee-cushions come to mind now.

'The imagination of person'—to adapt Robert Creeley's lovely wording of the same question—is noisy everyday. It's a Penelopean mending job over the years. Weaving. Unravelling. Weaving again. If possible into the heart of things. Perhaps, a composer—to place with.

So what have I been in my fugue of *sorts?* Tossed. Thrown. Allotted. One through twenty-one instances, just like that— how do you like your green-eyed boy now, mr. death?

1. Delivery boy (five or six)—in a round tin tub, a shingle for an oar, a broom to push across the wide, flooded gully to pick up a can of Carnation condensed milk from the commissary—described as Odyssean, by Grandmother.

2. Movie usher (twelve)—twenty-five cents an hour, the manager's name Fagan, and I had, since I'd read the book, wanted to be discovered by Fagan. I was an excellent corn popper, very generous with extra butter before the cornoil substitute arrived from Hollywood, and someone said I handled my flashlight with style. Under the Roxy's stage in the manager's private den, I saw my first pornography on a small screen, starring a famous Tarzan and a smiling, Irish heroine. I wasn't supposed to be there, but I watched through a crack in the door.

3. Painter (twelve)—discovered dot-painting (pointillism), did a landscape with crayons which won first prize at the Idaho County Fair.

4. Movie actor (twelve)—actually a 'screen test,' they said, scamming the whole town—I tap danced in a white sailor-suit that almost fit and played at the Roxy along with all the other screen tests, for the benefit of a motherly audience. No one discovered me.

5. Sheepherder (thirteen)—said to be suffering from a nervous breakdown (actually sexuality edging towards the unknown, but I couldn't tell that to the doctor), I was sent to a ranch in Wyoming to help the sheep lamb in midwinter.

6. Co-wrangler (thirteen)—follow-up therapy during the summer, I was first rate at rounding up the herd each evening and only found out from one of the cowboys that the horse could have done it without me—loved my prowess anyway among aspen conversations, campfire suppers, and cowboy songs.

7. Truck loader and unloader (fourteen)—in the first years of what was to become Trail Blazers Truck Line out of Twin Falls, Idaho, later to be manoeuvred out of existence by Globe Milling and Pillsbury—because Dad insisted on being his own lawyer—my job, hundred-pound sacks of flour or tongs in either hand to carry as many bricks as I could handle, left me with shoulders.

8. Window washer (fourteen)—for the office of the Globe Seed and Feed warehouse, one hundred panes, inspected for streaks and smudges before paying me a dollar an hour, said I took too long.

9. Seed sorter (fourteen)—a promotion by the same company—one ounce of seed from randomly selected bags, count, record each kind of seed—to verify quality.

10. Biologist, sculptor, painter (sixteen)—in 'Miss' Minier's wonderful class—she looked and acted like Mae West, and because I could memorize blood vessels quickly and easily, she often sent me out during class to buy cream chocolates, of which I could have one on my way back—studied chicken embryos developmentally, day by day—sculpted them in clay and painted them according to a colour code. Impressed the PTA.

11. Latinist and Frenchman (sixteen to seventeen)—the Latin teacher 'Miss' Babcock was very shortsighted, so after completing my exam, I'd do two or three others, fixing them at an uneasy B level, so she'd never catch on—she was splendid in Latin and mind—sat by the radio during my lesson with my French tutor Mme. Larsen—paid for by my seed sorting—she was Québécoise, educated at a convent in Paris and somehow married to a Scandinavian there in Twin Falls—and wept with the Mass in French, since I already knew it in Latin. 'Don't,' she said, 'when you go to Québec, speak like that.' Now, I wish I could.

12. Salesman (sixteen to seventeen)—Idaho Department Store, men's wear, which had a curious speciality—rose-pink silk stockings for men to give as gifts—no one bought them except the women of the Paramount Hotel—and while I was there, only from me—they didn't like the slipshod come-on of the 'hicks,' they said. One of them became a close, secret friend, and it was she who gave me my first lesson in countering clichés—'Never,' she said, 'tell anyone I'm a whore with a heart of gold.' One of the older, regular salesmen asked me if I knew I had very red lips. 'You know that always means you're queer,' he said. Then,

I found out why they'd hired me—to do what they called
the dirty work. I was the only one who could wait on the
Japanese, who were allowed one day a month out of the
Relocation Centre to shop. I did not understand the national
stupidity, nor did I think to oppose the injustice. I simply
loved them—the manner of their attention and the fear
mixed with pride, which I could share for other, still mys-
terious reasons. I was also the only one who could wait on
the Bahamas blacks ('niggers')—magnificent, tall, gentle
and exotic with their English accents, who'd been brought
in to do the field work, since the resident men were off to
war—I bent on one knee to measure, with trepidation,
the inner leg for the bright green and sharp blue suits they
bought on Saturdays after work—I still imagine them—
as I found them later in back-country enclaves dancing
stunningly to country music with the lonely wives.

13. Lieutenant (sixteen to seventeen)—the rank given me by
the U.S. Army during the time I spent in the Relocation
Centre—'to keep these Japs in their place'—a small group
of us went there to discuss the concerts they had offered to
give in town—these were musical minds and talents such
as we had never met before, over whom we were to as-
sume authority, whereas the authority of mind and heart
was theirs freely given—they never mentioned our youth
or ignorance. I recall passing by the Prisoner of War Camp
on the way to these discussions where Twin Fallsers slipped
food and gifts through the fence to the German and Italian
prisoners—and should have—but the Japanese, who had
been so recently Americans, I saw spat upon as they walked
so quietly through town to shop.

14. Playwright (sixteen to seventeen)—it was a who-done-it,
full of secret doors and cupboards, in which Mae West
was to be murdered, which made it a kind of tragedy—
in production, the cast was intolerable, didn't memorize

their lines or stage business—slovenly work on what was probably a very bad play, supposed to be funny and sad— anyway, some lumber had been piled up against the proscenium, and I grabbed a very long board and tried to break the legs of the actors. Another nervous breakdown. Production cancelled.

15. Actor (sixteen to eighteen)—played the professor coming up out of the audience in *Our Town*; Charley in *Charley's Aunt* (Oh! my rich aunt from Brazil—in 1993, at the fiftieth anniversary of our graduation from high school, a scrapbook of photographs of the production and newspaper clippings turned up—the owner of the scrapbook said he'd seen it in London but this was the best he'd ever seen, etc.); Romeo in *Romeo and Juliet* (shimmering white costume imported from Salt Lake City); a little later in 1944 at the College of Idaho, Beverley Carlton in *The Man Who Came to Dinner*— though at the time I had no idea who Noel Coward was, I played the piano, sang, and talked persuasively like someone or another: 'Shall I tell you how I glittered through the South Seas like a silver scimitar, or would you rather hear how I finished a three-act play with one hand and made love to a maharaja's daughter with the other?' Had a terrible fight with the drama coach when I couldn't get out of the part and carried on as if such were daily routine.

16. French tutor (eighteen)—to faculty children, nine to eleven years old—made up tunes on the piano to help them sing the conjugations and paradigms—tea at the President's house once a week, Mme. Presidente, as the children and I called her, in a red velvet, formal gown, split interestingly to the knee—full silver service, every piece and each cookie spoken to in French—later some fast conversations, a little jingly perhaps, since they'd been prepared with the help of the piano. For years after 1944 or 1945, letters would come at New Year's—in French.

17. Dancer (nineteen)—what ballet training I'd managed
    secretly in Twin Falls came in handy the first year at
    Berkeley—1944–1945, before the meeting with Jack
    Spicer and Robert Duncan and real poetry began—joined
    a dance group—a beautiful, marvelous young woman and
    I, painted white, classically choreographed, wove in and
    out of the Grahamers, we danced among the empty graves
    and tilted monuments of San Francisco's Victorian
    cemetery—to commemorate the startling power of it
    before demolition to make way for the Firemen's Fund
    Insurance Company, which is still installed on its hillock.
    No audience.

18. Soda Jerk (nineteen)—everyone knows a beginner by
    his/her eagerness—every customer ordered a Graveyard
    Sundae—now the trouble with this is that it calls for a
    squirt of every flavour the fountain offers, that's the grave-
    yard—but my customers demanded that the squirts come
    in a certain order—strawberry, ginger, marshmallow,
    blackberry, etc.—each order changed the order of the
    one before—I managed to remember the first two—then,
    gave up and began squirting anything that came to mind—
    when they wouldn't pay for my concoctions, I quit.

19. Library page (twenty-five)—in the Berkeley Library, where
    I first met Hannah Arendt while trying to help her through
    a turnstile, the turning tubes of which she hadn't seen be-
    fore—thin wondrous scholar/philosopher, who would
    seem to me to be one of my muses, wound up sitting on
    top of it, one of its spokes between her legs.

20. Librarian (thirty)—at Harvard—saved a distinguished col-
    lection of Renaissance books in the basement of a private
    house near the Yard—during a hurricane, after the furnace
    had blown up—no help from Harvard maintenance where
    everything was flooding—found I could tear out wooden

partitions and build scaffolding above the water level with just what was at hand—three years later, 1958, spent nights in Houghton preparing an exhibit—Jonathan Edwards–Emerson–William James–Bergson–Peirce–Santayana–Whitehead—to honour the American Philosophical Association—and found by chance a plaster cast of a hairy chest, the tag said Whitman—not for philosophy, I thought then, but I've changed my mind.

21. Working in Vancouver, 1966 to date—professor in disguise—'resident mystic,' according to the kickback from certain recalcitrants, etc.—the tale is too long of whatever and whomever.

Points on a map of finitudes. Bits and pieces of whatever or whoever I was. Wouldn't it be nice to have a simple, separate self (Whitman would have said 'soul') to come home to? The conditional tension of the self is fundamental to these questions. If I had been able to see through and beyond the large arena writing throws me into, I might well have preferred to be safer. But I learned as a young man reading Melville that to say 'I would prefer not to' would not bring me into a safer place, though it would be an honest admission of my destiny. I know writing is in trouble these days—a cultural mongering tells me so. Yet, it seems to me that, in the midst of our cultural depletion, we've participated in a very great period of art. One that could change our experience of the outside of ourselves. It is that I meant one time in using the phrase 'the practice of outside.' And I believe that there is a larger audience for this art than ever before. That audience does not control mercantilism which controls public space and the forms of its devotions. I believe in necessary writers. And one of them, Avital Ronell, writes: 'Resist the numbing banality of they, the dictatorship of nonreading.' And I find this in another necessary writer, Michel Serres, writing an imaginary dialogue: 'Neither the world nor the market knows how to integrate suffering and happiness, nor the question of meaning, nor that of evil.' And on a page of a third necessary writer, Giorgio Agamben, I'm reminded that 'Dante classifies languages by their way of saying yes' and find this parenthetic notice: '(What is astonishing is not that something was able to be, but that it was able to not not-be.).' And that is getting pretty close to whatever and whomever we mean by love. What and who are pronouns—interrogative and relative in the absence of a naming noun—what is the neuter of who in the act of writing where going is going is gone—a 'monad/nomad' OF—which is the word love without the initial consonant. If I had not been a writer—I think I'd have been an ASSASSIN.

1994

Shipped Shape

is it a boat?   open   little rigging
this soul's enchantment

becoming larger   fully rigged   is it
          a ship
          shape?
                      this soul's territory

                                1994

The Truth Is Laughter 19

I sent out invitations to an original party
asking everyone, women and men alike,
to come dressed as Adam—RSVP,
of course—
          they all sent regrets,
no such disguise could be found in the shops

                                1994

# of is the word love without the initial consonant

                                                    4 AM   after
really good conversation   of
what matters most   of
whatever we are   among pieces
of knowledge, the humane undertow,
bitchery about palaces, of gold radiators,
thought of weigela, soft   pink   of
'children gone insane
waiting for summer rain'
he remembered quietly and wrong-worded

            he is a small piece of the composition
of nations of image   a disfiguration of
the marvelous absence so carefully wrought
in order to recognize what is between the lines
of a lifetime   the realm of his thought
on a soft day   drinking the messed up kitchen

                the old friend reads
to a television camera, thin at the throat,
dry lips   of an 'alcohol of adoration'   and
her 'glass skirt'   trails shimmering and brittle
'sufficient grief makes us free'

O beautiful day
butterflies and wasps
in and out of the window
'white, sweet May'
of glass lady and the day

                for Warren Tallman

                Robin Blaser
        with The Doors & wcw
                1994

at this point in time

there is no point in time—
that's strictly a spatial image,
a point on a line—in mathematics,
an undefined geometric element,
postulated in twos to determine
a line—things may be pointed,
the point of death, needle point,
musically, a signal, 32 points on
the compass—a *point d'appui*
a point of support, a base of operations,
militarily speaking, *point-devise*,
perfectly dressed, point-duty, point-
blank—and you can have many points,
being yourself pointed—but
time is fluid, the life of space, unless,
of course, you're narcissistically
religious and know for sure
the two points,
beginning and end, so determining
a long or short line with no destination—

1994

one word of wisdom

I'd just given a talk on what I thought were
the irreparables of our time—WOW!—and was
standing outside on the grass smoking a cigarette—

when a young man came up, self-induced plainness shining
all over him—he said, 'I had trouble following you,' and
he went on about someone telling him he was just too or-
dinary, and what, he seemed to ask, could he do about that—

I said, 'Tell me, have you ever in your whole life felt or-
dinary—even once?'

after a long pause, searching every sparkle of his honesty
he said very quietly, 'no'—

'Well,' I said, 'you've turned it inside out, exactly as you
must—since the ordinary is always and only a rumor about
somebody else'—

'And,' I added, 'why not tell whomever-it-may-concern to put
the ordinary where the sun don't shine—everybody's got a place
like that'—

1994

well, I was walking up
    Euclid Avenue
    this morning
    hand in hand
    with Galileo
    toward the Rose Garden
    and my old house on Oak Street Path—
    he was really burnt up
    about that recent apology, said
    the very milk of human kindness
    curdled
    in his transparency—when
    Giordano Bruno, attracted
    by our bodily warmth,
    ran across the street
    to join us, said
    it's better to go on burning—
    in eternity things burn
    into   one   and the other

7 June 1994
Berkeley, California

that cat,

one of the wonders of the intelligent universe—cranky,
manipulative, a touch affectionate, like everybody
else—round gold eyes stare up at our second-story
window, apparently thinking over Haydn's joke
pouring out of it   musical humour in the twilight
air, but the plywood barricade, put up to protect
the wet-painted steps, troubles her mindfulness—
thus, in no time, Haydn hears inquiring mews at
the door, with painted paws, vulnerable *broken
continuities* laughing at the only entrance to, the
only exit from this floor—discomposed, disconsolate
on both sides—musically noted irrevocability,
I suppose

Robin Blaser
Haydn's Quartet in E flat major, op. 33, no. 2
1995

my novel

once I said I'd tell all. But couldn't decide
whether love or hate to tell. Hate and love are
each of them all. What if you've been able to hate?
Not really. Then, the world is cut in half. I
believe there are many of us half & half's.

1995

Bits of a Book 2

Europe, my sweetie,
from earliest thot

mixed with this American
rosie beaut

of Poe, Hawthorne, Melville,
Dickinson, Emersonian
loosening up
this Whitmanian heart,

we can't do a thing about
Yugoslavia, Rwanda,
etceteras, and hot spots—

one thinks of washouts,
of cultural escapes, and other
belief symptoms, and steps
to the rhythm of
populous tom-toms—rhythm's
thought

1995

merci buckets—

my cooking-timer dings on its own
at odd intervals—it's named Big Time—
a sort of *hammer without a Master* singing

bits and pieces of sound—and, then, surprise,
finding a structure   that's what
it means   in the next room   wherever,

on the roof I'm watching the scarlet geraniums,
the pink ones budding again, and the white petunias
gone like snow in the rain   the slopes

here you can see the largest elephant
in the world, with the exception of itself, you see

22 August 1995

The Flame

So there is nothing
but distaste • pestilence •

Inoculated dogs have pissed
against the trees. The city, swept,
is glistening with cold sparrows
in her crevices. The dance consumes
the flickering walls and shattered necks.
The sparrows impersonate

a listening disfigurement of animals •
proud
among the bits and pieces of transparent sidewalks •
A dancer lifts
the momentary birds among his fingers •
shouting.

Suddenly, the cat paws
innumerable sparks from the park benches.
A confrontation licks the chimney
and the silky edges of the animal chairs.

O beloved world •
This dog changes. Displaces
the dancing zoo of arms and fingers.
This fly changes. The droning spot
where images shape themselves.
This anger that whistles in his arms
changes.
The bestial poet's word.

This breaks like wishbones in the air.
The object whose gaze is touched.
The body, dancing, interminably stretched
in the air, paws. This secrecy will out.

O flame   •   the angry muses strum their sticks.
The lions in our tears scratch the circling dust.
Switch their tails among the winter birds.
O flame   •

1995

Ode for Museums, All of Them!

The prehistory of our skin in glass cases.
The measurements of the brain cavity posted.
All these guardians should be making guns.

What could I do here except steal something?
The Venus of Lespuges whose breasts look
detachable. The axes. Tools of fire or
matchstick animals.

For instance, the fetish whose genitals are
woven straw. Pure realism. Tourists imagine
the erections. A geography where our bodies
stretch, broken and astonished.

Well, we fed the universe, and the monuments
in their cages mock our insomnia.

This nakedness. The taste of semen like
a shadow of rivers.

The milk of my horoscope falls in the
streets. The mountains disappear over
my shoulder for luck.

But the museums closed before I could
pocket the masks of distant movie-
stars. The glass caught my hand
in its shattered petals. By a miracle,
the damage was total bereavement. But
who wept?

We are so tired of museums. Even prehistory
is monumental. Who more so, than these
scraggly natives picking sponge out of their
eyes. Is it true we've seen anything but
animals, two by two?

And now we pluck their bones for that
music which is silken and caught in
the rattan webs of a fetish.

1995

A Story after Blake

Then *he went up stairs*
& loaded the maid
with glasses
& brass tubes
& magic pictures

& bottles of wind

His obtuse blue eye
tipped backward at all
the skyscrapers. Slowly
flamed over this palaver
of winter stars. And
came back to himself
where he saw transported
the worldly gazes, lustrous
diadems and lozenges
of bitter black. 'O,' he said,
'there and there are the wispy branches
of pissing stars. Rise in the air
like guttered whirlwinds. Stop
on the backstoop, begging.'

And backward he stretched
to beat our shouts
on his ice-torn fingers.
And slept, a cozy animal
among the startled words.

I do not say he exists
but his dance is company
and there he rises
on the shouts of whirligigs, speechless.
proud,

    in scarlet gowns & broad gold lace

of sweat.

1995

pentimento I

it's a parabola!   that's it, when you get to my age,
words and books are—oh!—up-so-down, of varied mind:
the lane beside my home beaten by cars turning into
electric garages, out of house/into house—garbage cans
and compost bins—a wildness of clematis climbs
the telephone wires which birds mark and squirrels
trapeze above cats stalking—scavengers, who are shadows
of this culture's wounds go by the bye, looking
for beer cans to cash in—metaphoric traffic of two
materialities of what we are in language, its fingering
grasp and streetwise mica wander in the slick
that language left when it flew through the air, unsexual
and transmundane—and cared less that desire composes
nature—uncovered facts of whose *body-in-pieces*—

       heartland   of moonburn
                           subsists at midnight
      a shallow time,
                where horizontals and verticals
      misshape, mistake, and go
      after themselves—
               adventurers
    of FAR

                19 October 1996

a fountain at the kitchen door,
installed today—on the wall—
a fountain my mind plays,
as the sun does, crystallizing—

a frost mind—Venetian, like Mallarmé's mirror,
a 'self' there, after the smoke writes such
reminder—that is like to a heron, *blue-rooted*
in unguessed song—

it may be there's too much 'self' in this
authenticity, as if made by hand, as if the sylph
were not imaginary, as if fact did grasp this imagery
I try to write down in notation on a musical staff
the water's splash,

remarking neither horizontals nor perpendiculars,
just crosshatched here on this map of our oblique
destinations—mindful of friends and of our startled
conversations—

> Robert Duncan's proposed question for a final exam:
>   'What don't you know?'
> Peter Quartermain, who asks it on his final exams:
>   'A truly joyful question.'

Jess's fountain at the door—

For Jess Dennis Debeck
'Dusty'
October 20, 1977–February 22, 1996

forest 1

There and then I perhaps realized that the forest, in its
enduring antiquity, was the correlate of the poet's memory,
and that once its remnants were gone, the poet would fall
into oblivion.

Robert Pogue Harrison
on a walk with Andrea Zanzotto
'through the remnants of the
great *selva antica*,' Montello
mountain

this lovely mind, but the word fall is, for me, too loaded
with a theological beforeness—rather, he or she may step
into oblivion—the state or act of being forgotten—an
answer in real terms—philosophical as they are—of our exit
from origin, that summertime and lacy curtain where we become

1996

Liveforever

'Where is Abraham buried?' you ask. Well, in the *Kabbalah*, God has a terrible time getting Abraham to agree to die. In the *Zohar*, where Abraham is initiate and David calls God by the name 'Midnight,' the splendour is woven in the energies of the Hebrew alphabet, a creation in language that is never still. Now, looking at the three religions of Abraham—Hebrew, Christian and Muslim—I would say that Abraham, though very much changed since 1700 BCE, is not dead. There's only so much that a post-Catholic, polytheist exodic can say just now.

for Samuel Truitt
August 1996

In Remembrance of Matthew Shepard

How sad I am. How sad
this violation of the existential
given and Matthew's song—
another debt of this indecent
century—what is to be said
about this *hideous traffic*
in *religion* that has taught
blasphemy for centuries
against Jews, blacks, aboriginals,
women, Gypsies, and homosexuals
everywhere. 'They' put on Jesus-shoes.
He never wore them.
'Their' *sacrifices to hate and hell.*
There is no more to be said
about God, except the *infinite exposure*
of our finitude that 'they' have taught.
Love arrives as a promise.
Every particular love is Love,
dear Matthew. How love shatters
when they stopped your song—
the shatters in which we trust.
Yes, the philosopher said: *The glorious body*
cannot but be the mortal body itself.
What changes are not the things but their limits.
It is as if there hovered over them something
like a halo, a glory. Dear Matthew.

October 1998

vocabulary 1

let me get the vocabulary of this song
right—the curious happiness of poetry—
the word materialism dropped by the way
side—its mereness of the other face of
spiritualism—just two notes to sing—
repetitious dualism—dō—dō—once in a while
one squawks louder than the other, baby
crows being weaned before the next batch—
thus, singing, move from how it does matter—
Oh!—a murder of crows

1998

the bottom line

God's my life, stolen hence, and left me asleep!
I have had a most rare vision. I had a dream,
past the wit of man to say what dream it was.
Man is but an ass, if he go about to expound
this dream. Methought I was,—there is no man
can tell what. Methought I was, and methought
I had,—but man is but a patched fool, if
he will offer to say what methought I had.
The eye of man hath not heard, the ear of
man hath not seen, man's hand is not able
to taste, his tongue to conceive, nor his heart
to report, what my dream was. I will get
Peter Quince to write a ballad of this dream.
It shall be called Bottom's Dream, because
it hath no bottom—

       there's a turn of my mind
       that is intolerable
              and happiness,
       pungent as Cuban oregano
              on the window sill
       there's a smart to it, not entirely
              intelligent,
       as if going through Preboreal
              willow arches
       before the sands start,
       as if this old man sat on an embankment
              drying his clothes,
       having washed them fiercely
              in water-flows—
       one or the other of his eyes meet
              a philosophy of as if—

without its idealism,

                that washboard
has collapsed, transmogrified
into desirous separates,

                a measureless complexity
                of everyone's bottom
dream, which is Bottom's Dream—

                1998

nomad

the grounds shift   all
                 the time
                         as paradises must

images exit from Plato's
kismet   and other irreparable
absolutes   deserted shoes
and barefoot, desirous walks
a long way
               lion's teeth spring
from crevices in the sidewalks

when I reach the age wherein
words and books are upside-
down   down as up is a more engaging
proposition than to say they are
one—C-sharp minor whistling at every crossing,

        which said, 'Come into my wild yellow room,
        into wild yellow poppies, into wild-*logos*
        upon woven sand and willowed shores, a wildered
        core'

must-hands—now and again honey hands—reach
for *life's measureless body*   (Musil

I think, therefore I am   (Descartes
I think, therefore I am—I think   (Philosophy 100
I am, therefore I think   (Zukofsky
I walk, therefore I am.   (Deleuze

                             as paradises must

                    2000

pentimento 2

did he, did she look everywhere
for the contentment
of the word God—
among puzzled faces
herding the red cows—

a slight cough on the mountain top—
when someone looked out
at the *magnus animus,*
the word God must have been a glottal stop

'Somewhere,' they said
over the flickering butchery—
cedar wood, hyssop, and scarlet—
and the *burning lamp passed*
among those pieces—
the blood splashed on Ariel

well, I was driving to heaven,
a face in the moon, but couldn't
get my foot on the brake

Ariel! Ariel! life as life
moves through this and thin—

Ariel! Ariel! life as life,
stalked by a truant deity,

why did you choose ideomotoring,
religious and secular, Absolutes
of coming stillness, unable
to dance chance

I, who has gone into his questions,
I was there dancing on the lech,
where crows eat snow—my hearts
racing all my life, finding a plaster
torso with a tag on it that said
it was Walt Whitman's—manna grass

I put that line in a coconut and drank it up

the neighbours have a wooden robin—very still
'til the wind hits—wooden, whining wings—
events—a weathervane—weathercock of
the way the wind flows—fane or fana
of thought—vane of a windmill—vane
of a feather—vane of a congress of such
birds—vaned attempt—to see directions—
for the love of destination—new fountain
the smoke of art

the I is a pentimento—Ariel's freedom

for Patrick Wright
1 January 2000

Image-Nation 26 (being-thus

'your path is poetry, your goal is beyond poetry,'
I once said, but don't hold me to it—
that was early one morning—a fragment
of waking up—
           searching the presences
that weren't there—before the words carved them—

after crosswords with Sphinx and Chimera,
out of the watchwords of Basilisk, overheard
amidst the gallop of Unicorn's ivory hooves,
the blood in my veins carrying life back to
my heart—
           I feel like flying, swimming, yelping,
bellowing, howling. I'd like to have wings,
a carapace, a rind, to breathe out smoke,
wave my trunk, twist my body, divide
myself up, to be inside everything, to drift
away with odours, develop as plans do,
flow like water, vibrate like sound, gleam
like light, to curl myself up into every
shape, to penetrate each stone, to get down
to the depth of matter—to be matter!   (Flaubert

a soul is there in the middle of its web,
touched *by every tug on its complicated structure*—
this continuous moment that is *poēsis*—
this not-not-being at the heart of this complicated
structure—
           let us learn what rhythm holds us—   (Archilochus
our form—

       one must assume that the human race is invisible
though still operatively present—   (Edwin Muir

our angel of our history—His face is turned toward
the past. Where we perceive a chain of events, he
sees one single catastrophe which keeps piling
wreckage and hurls it in front of his feet. The angel
would like to stay, awaken the dead,
and make whole what has been smashed.
But a storm is blowing from Paradise; it has
got caught in his wings with such violence
that the angel can no longer close them. This storm
insistently propels him into the future . . . while the debris
before him grows skyward.   (Benjamin

walking a rope at the end of our metaphysical journey,
tethered at the extreme end of our metaphysical itinerary—   (Agamben

There is a goal, but no way; what we call the way is only
wavering—   (Kafka

. . . travelers in a train that has met with an accident in a tunnel,
and this place where the light of the beginning can no longer be seen,
and the light of the end is so very small a glimmer that the gaze
must continually search for it and is always losing it again, and
furthermore, it is not certain whether it is the beginning or the end
of the tunnel.   (Kafka

NOW-TIME   JETZTZEIT

Aitant, ses plus—inasmuch, no more, men and women live
as they live joyously—   (Sordello

in the original space that language loves, first heard
in the womb—

resoling and resewing for the goal, perhaps

we could begin again to imagine a *Purgatorio*
as a *continuous image of our poetic condition*—

(See Sollers

cutting the heart out to eat of it—
eating the heart out—

Seeing something simply in its being-thus—*irreparable, but not*
for that reason necessary; thus, but not for that reason contingent—
is love—

(Agamben

and of the being-beyond-itself—

> the strangest visitor last night when I went
> out for my last cigarette of the day—about
> the size of my thumb—attracted, rather
> helplessly, even drunkenly—yellow, black
> stripes, transparent wings—like a very large
> bee, two amazing red brushes on its head,
> striped with black, that seemed to feel for the
> light—or heat—it would fall, plop, wander,
> then fly up to the light—I've never seen a
> bug of such size in the air—seemed powerful
> and frightening, still helpless—gone
> this morning—I've searched for it, like
> happiness—

Written for Jery Zaslove.
I've long noted the word love in his name.
1 October 2000

Great Companion:
Dante Alighiere
1997

Dante Alighiere

the speech born-in-one's-house is that which we acquire
without rule
      De Vulgari Eloquentia I. 1

The language for which we have no words, which doesn't
pretend, like grammatical language, to be there before
being, but is 'alone and first in mind,' is our language,
that is, the language of poetry.
      Giorgio Agamben, *Idea of Prose*

Face to face, but without seeing each other from now
on, the gods and men are abandoned to writing. This
abandonment is the sign given to us for our history yet
to come. It has only just begun. My god! We are only
beginning to write.
      Jean-Luc Nancy, The Inoperative Community

entering the territory—*map is not territory*—the boy   Korzybski
looked up from the book he held in his lap, startled
that it seemed the size of half of himself it was so
large compared to Emerson, Poe, Hawthorne,
Melville, Dickinson, Longfellow around the house—
Gustave Doré's *Inferno* of the dark forest, where the
boy's mind multiplied the leopard, lion and wolf
in his heart—heart and mind were then entwined—
entered the writhing trees, drew back from Geryon,
as if to hide, touched the page of flames that were
not raindrops, swept his hand over the streaming
anguish in the air, felt the chill black of the ice
around winged Lucifer, who chewed on something
with two legs that he didn't want to imagine—in
bed at night after saying 'please, if I die before I
wake, I pray the Lord my soul to take'—which was
very hard to think about—he returned before he
slept to Doré's imagery—under the covers with a
flashlight—and nearly always forgot the two small

figures high on a rocky promontory, who looked up
at the stars—territory is not map—there, *going from* Ruth Padel
inside out and outside in, he could not yet think how
ancient he was, where *the phenomena of consciousness are*
the phenomena of religion—this is the boy of the house
in Idaho, a railcar, painted Union Pacific yellow,
by the railway tracks, goldenrod garden of wand-
stems—grandmother Sophia Nichols whose tele-
graphic mind knew the distances—in the sagebrush
desert during the Great Depression—entangled with
Dante before and after he learned to read—the inno- 1930
cence of walking there is forgotten—

    '*That means,' said I, somewhat amused, 'that we would have to* Kleist
eat of the tree of knowledge a second time to fall back into the state
of innocence.'

    '*Of course,' he answered, 'and that is the final chapter in the*
history of the world.'

I address Dante, who is our contemporary, like us,
speaking out of human violence—who is implicit
in our use of our mother tongues—who is initial
and continuously implicated in the courage of
poetry—whose art records *an attachment to the letter* Saussure
that lay at the mysterious origin of poetry—the dazzlement—
who is *concealed in the depth of our culture like a blind spot*— Sollers
whose journey in poetry reverses the metaphysics of
a transparent language—whose daring in the realms
of the sacred proposes *il poema sacro*—propositions of
the mind in that scattered territory—of whom the
story is told that *at the moment he began the Comedy all* cited Sollers
the rhymes of the world presented themselves and asked to be
included—of whom Mandelstam, studying Italian
in order to read him, writes:

    When I began to study Italian and had barely familiarized my-
self with its phonetics and prosody, I suddenly understood that the trans. Harris
center of gravity of my speech efforts had been moved closer to my & Link

lips, to the outer parts of my mouth. The tip of the tongue suddenly turned out to have the seat of honour. The sound rushed toward the locking of teeth. And something else that struck me was the infantile aspect of Italian phonetics, its beautiful child-like quality, its closeness to infant babbling, to some kind of eternal Dadaism. . . . Would you like to become acquainted with the dictionary of Italian rhymes? Take the entire Italian dictionary and leaf through it as you will. . . . Here every word rhymes. Every word begs to enter into concordanza. The abundance of marriageable endings is fantastic—the astonishment that is Dante, of whom Yeats wrote in his 1915 poem *EGO DOMINUS TUUS*:

> The chief imagination of Christendom,
> Dante Alighiere, so utterly found himself
> That he has made that hollow face of his
> More plain to the mind's eye than any face
> But that of Christ—

but it is not the self that made this face so plain to our mind's eye after him, and certainly not his arguments for Church and Empire, but more likely the colours he gave to language—first, in his room *una nebula di colore di fuoco*—then, within this colour of fire, a figure spoke in the high language of divinity—*Ego dominus tuus*—eros and nakedness that overwhelm—he thought he saw *una cosa, la quale ardesse tutta*—the voice said, *Vide cor tuum*—he had not recognized his heart in flames where it was eaten—this discovery of Beatrice in the shaping of a world—the colours of this event in language fly in the flag of Italy—

La Vita nuova

the face moves among the beautiful letters, never still in the alpha/omega, the A through Z of our vernacular tongues—born in the house of the heart's mind that is the mind's heart—*purposed to make it known to many*—that they might flame in their alphabets—

La Vita nuova

saluting all the fedeli d'Amore that they might answer—
Dante, drawing upon the Provençal experience of
the reason of poems, brings us to Amors—Giorgio
Agamben tells us *Amors is the name the Troubadours gave to
the experience of the advent of the poetic word. . . . It is difficult to
understand the sense in which poets understood love, as long as we
obstinately construe it according to a secular misunderstanding, in
a purely biographical context. For the Troubadours, it is not a ques-
tion of psychological or biographical events that are successively ex-
pressed in words, but rather, of the attempt to live the topos itself,
the event of language as a fundamental amorous and poetic experi-
ence*—the *loved experience* is found in the poetics of un-
mapped territory—thus, the *New Life* is the possibility
larger than and other than the mere expression of the
sentiments of subjective reality or of the self, which is
as much a lifetime creation as is the poēsis of the tra-
ditional soul—this event of our vernacular speech—
not to be confused with *language as an object of knowledge*   Michel de
constructed by philosophers and linguists, but a part of language, a   Certeau / Godzich
mode of language use, that is a discourse—with the heart
of—*actual social interaction and practice*—witness
Sordello—*disdegnosa*—mourning Sir Blancatz—   Purgatorio VI

> And so mortal is the harm (to the virtues)   trans. Ezra Pound
> That I have no suspicion that it will ever
> be undone, except in this wise, that
> they take his heart out, and have it
> eaten by the Barons who live un-hearted,
> then they would have hearts worth something—

love's reason reasoning, which Dante tells us it would
be shame not to explain, enters into the discourses of
the territory called world—the poetic is the language
of the mapless—

Dante's gift is continuously contemporary in the
shape he gave his poem's discoursing—out of the
advent of language one's life in language, as if life
were the home of it—where the intimacy of sound
discloses the Amors of othernesses—in *La Vita nuova*,
the interplay of love and reason, poem and prose,
Dante and Beatrice, friends and beloved ladies opens
into a territory—even *Beyond the widest of the circling
spheres*—where *The Comedy* entangles the amorous
with the discoursing of myth, cosmology, philoso-
phy, theology, history, economics, and current
issues—even as Beatrice's colours—white, crimson,
and green—circle my early morning coffee cup,
while I write—this is the polyphony of *The Comedy*—
the ever changing polyphony of amorous thought—

the gift of *the amorous and poetic experience* so entangled—
the face haunting the curious laughter of the syl-
lables—that we might speak an ethics out of this
mapless century of ourselves—'at home,' so to
speak, in the unredeemable and irreparable—trans-
migrators—of humanism, of religions, of absolutes,
of ignorant hierarchies—when the sublime collapses
upon us—as it did upon Dante—we are inside the
condition of it—marking our footsteps among its
uncanny pieces—holding on to the love of our
ordinary lives—hearted or unhearted—Dante,
'the Tuscan Homer,' as Vico called him, is exemplar
of the necessary *poēsis* in a vast territory—*not exactly
human*—even as we take up the task of our ongoing
departure from the *totality he confronted*—

Hanna Arendt,
Men in Dark Times

Sollers

in the difficult matter of God in the streets—*facilis*   *Aeneid* VI.126
descensus Averno—it is easy today to descend to Avernus,
as the Sibyl tells us in the voices of Posillipo—there
the door of Dis is open twenty-four hours a day—
like the doors of the current return to religion—
whose concern is with the definition of abomination
and exclusion—

in *La Vita nuova*, Dante proposes that love, which is   Sollers
meaning, impels speech—

the *Inferno* does not come to rest in those brutalities of
God's judgment—in hell *speech is fixed once and for all*—   Sollers
words stop dead in the depths of a bloody and frozen
silence—the entire human body is devoured—in
agonizing contrast to the love that eats the flaming
heart—Philippe Sollers, in his brilliant contemporary
reading of Dante, notices that self-interest—the
closed self—is a fundamental characteristic of the
damned, which has consequences: *Language turns upon
and possesses him who believed he possessed it but in fact was only
one of its signs*—

the reader who stops there in the drama of closed
meaning will lose Dante—including the Dante who
haunts our discordant departure from Christendom—
the *Inferno* fascinates with its imagination of the condi-
tion of irredeemable loss—the lost *good of the intellect*—
we rebel at the theological imprisonment and aban-
donment—and suspect that Dante now and again
does so too—in this icehouse of language words, we
think, must thaw—we are, perhaps, closer to rebel-
lious Rabelais than we know—when Pantagruel *hears
thawed out words: he threw on the deck in front of us handsful of*   trans. Burton
Raffel
*frozen words, which might have been sugared almonds, like so
many pearls of different colours. We saw bright red words, green*

words, blue words, black words, golden words. And after they had
been warmed for a bit between our hands, they melted like snow and
we actually heard them, but without understanding a word, for they
were in a barbarous language. . . .

. . . Panurge asked Pantagruel to give him more. Pantagruel ob-
served that giving words was like making love.

'Then sell me some,' said Panurge.

'Selling words,' said Pantagruel, 'is more like what lawyers do.
I'd prefer to sell you silence and make you pay more for it. . . .'

But still he threw three or four handsful on to the deck. And we
could see sharp words, bloody words (which, according to the pilot,
sometimes went back to the place where they'd been spoken, only to
find the throat that uttered them had been slit open), horrible words,
and many others unpleasant to see. And when they'd melted, we
heard: hin, hin, hin, hin, tick, tock, whizz, gibber, jabber, frr, frrr,
frrr, boo, boo, boo, boo, boo, boo, boo, boo, crack, track, trr, trr,
trr, trrr, trrrrr, on, on, on, on, wooawooawooon, gog, magog, and
God only knows. . . .

Cosi gridai con la faccia levata—this I cried with lifted face,   *Inferno* XVI.76
from among the sodomites—

Inferno—facing Dante's theology—even a Roman
Catholic amen from childhood—of the immutable
and unchanging—recognizing that it is the vocabu-
lary of his cosmology—of creation and continua-
tion—in the body of thought—this entanglement
of language and death—mortality's speechless-
ness—repetitious or masquerading in our own vo-
cabulary of such territory—I walk into a crisis of
where Hell is—out of this cosmology—gone in the
teeth—among twentieth-century Constitutions and
religious pretensions—Yes! to be 'clean of these
hell-obsessions' in another world, as Pound said,
discovering Hell on the surface of the earth—where,

as in Dante, the present might be found—this sense
of exit and departure—'from the first canto to the
last, the poet's path was the path of the living
man'—at stake in the poēsis—finding the life of
form—in so vast a territory—*practices of the self and of
freedom within these games of truth*, turning round and
round in, say, your marvelous kitchen—to impart
relish—I read this great, vulnerable poem—materi-
ality of language—materiality of form—materiality
of men's and women's bodies envisioning—as if
they were my own—thus, to unravel *the Western para-
digm of one sole truth*—that cannot find the place of its
totality—founded on sacrifice—there or here—our
immortalities cannot help with this—Churches,
States, even Atheisms are given to personifications of
totality—exchanging bed linens—you can vote for a
water glass of democracy on the side-table—they
never apologize for time misspent, not even in the
theories of themselves—now and again, they reha-
bilitate some lives—

I was talking to Galileo the other day about his
rehabilitation—he was disdainful—we wondered
who or what is speaking in such ethics of thought—
certainly not time regained, let alone eternalized—
we were standing there in Rome—in the Campo
dei fiore—at the foot of Giordano Bruno's monu-
ment. He jumped right off his pedestal and said
'Listen, kid, it's better to burn.'

Ernst Kantorowicz,
Frederick II

Michel Foucault

Michel de
Certeau, *The
Mystic Fable*

'Hell,' I said, astonished, 'I'm 72.'—we three then
walked along talking about Bruno's dialogues and
sonnets, dedicated to Sir Philip Sidney, De gli eroici
furori, and of Plato's curious blending of the words
Eros and heros—'the name heros is only a slight alter-   Cratylus
ation of Eros from whom the heroes sprang'—of
what it was like to write of heroic frenzies—

in canto X of the Inferno, we come upon the open
tombs of those who questioned immortality—
Epicurus, who argued that happiness is the chief
good, 'and all his followers'—the last great Emperor
of the Holy Roman Empire (the title lasted until
1806), Frederick II (d. 1250)—of whom it is said
that he had a man imprisoned in a sealed wine vat
and left him to perish under watch to prove that
the soul died with the body, if it could not escape—
and among them Guido Cavalcanti's father and
father-in-law, so condemned while Guido was
still alive, neither of whom had so experimented
with human destiny—only Florentines in the midst
of religious and political strife, who questioned
immortality—the crown of such totality—where
in modern terms a fortuneteller paradises—

I think of the friendship and estrangement of Dante
and Guido, whom Dante names 'the first among my
friends' in The New Life, of whom, in Hell, he sends the
message to his father that he is still living, who is re-
called in the Purgatorio for the glow of his poems—   Purgatorio XI.97

Guido, i' vorrei che tu e Lapo ed io   Sonnet VI
Fossimo presi per incantamento . . .

in Shelley's beautiful sonnet, which translates it:

> Guido, I would that Lapo, thou, and I,
> Led by some strong enchantment, might ascend
> A magic boat . . .

in Robert Duncan's version from among the sodomites:

> Robin, it would be a great thing if you, me and Jack Spicer
> Were taken up in a sorcery with our mortal heads so turned
> That life dimmed in the light of that fairy ship . . .

there's an ancient prejudice to the effect that one is born and dies a human being
Robert Musil

A completed foundation of humanity should, however, signify the definitive elimination of the sacrificial mythogema and of its ideas of nature and culture, of the unspeakable and the speakable, which are grounded in it. In fact, even the sacralization of life derives from sacrifice: from this point of view it simply abandons the naked natural life to its own violence and its own unspeakableness, in order to ground in them every cultural rule and all language. The ethos, humanity's own, is not something unspeakable or sacer that must remain unsaid in all praxis and human speech. Neither is it nothingness, whose nullity serves as the basis for the arbitrariness and violence of social action. Rather, it is social praxis itself, human speech itself, which have become transparent to themselves —
Giorgio
Agamben,
Language and Death

'So!' Jack Spicer said, early in our friendship, 'you're one of those who eat their God.'
1945

in unmapped America, the Puritans had a ferocious
time with omniscience, which proposed predestina-
tion of human nature, one by one—now, when
you get down to brass facts, who in this community
should be allowed to receive the body and blood of
Christ?—the answer: the successful—speaking in
the voice of—the coherence of—capitalism—

---

in ESTHÉTIQUE DU MAL, Wallace Stevens writes:
The death of Satan was a tragedy / For the imagination—
and asks, *What underground?*—it was a dismissal
from usefulness—with the shift of Hell to the
surface of our own task, Purgatory and Paradise
also shift to the imagination of the *irreparable*—

like you, I walk *in contemporary culture—the movement of
perpetual departure*—I walk *the forest of innumerable sounds*—
I talk *with a haunted tongue*—how does *the body get
form?*—and clothe itself—

phrases from
Michel de
Certeau

the entire Comedy, Philippe Sollers writes, *is an apprenticeship
in thought, vision, and writing*—from the *frozen silence* to a
new poetry—*The Purgatory, in fact, is a continuous image of the
poetic condition*—Dante walks and questions—perhaps
the poetic condition is a matter of interrogation—
certainly, it is for us, as it was for him—he walks as
if he were in the place of language—in Sollers'
words, *to the discontinuity that rediscovers the silence and other-
ness of a new language*—the spontaneous, intimate lan-
guage that is opposed to Hell—and *approaches, through
successive ruptures the 'umana radice'* (human root)—*in other
words the root of a language exempt from guilt*—there in the

place where love dictates—I enter with you *la divina* Purgatorio
foresta spessa e viva—the divine forest green and dense— XXIV.54–56
in apprenticeship—so, Robert Duncan would cele-
brate Dante's seven hundredth birthday in 1965,
writing of 'the sweetness and greatness' of the *Divine
Comedy*—

we have been walking and climbing all the days of
our lives in a forest fire of language—one calls for
the good of the intellect—it is existentially given—
another calls for the grace note time can be in order
to know oneself—when suddenly a voice calls,
'O voi'—O, you there in your little barc—as one
might from the upper deck of a liner call, 'You there
in your dinghy, watch your shores before you lose
your bearings'—we enter the Odyssean language
of the *Paradiso* —*L'acqua ch'io prendo già mai non si corse*—
in waters that have never been sailed before—we are warned
that we may become lost in the *waves of the marvelous*—
among the light substances, if we do not have the
intelletto d'amore, as through smooth and transparent glass, this
discourse with cosmos—*the glorious wheel,* the radiance
speaking, horizon brightening, a swift fire in a cloud,
the sun-struck rubies of conjugated souls—the ladder
of splendours—(*La mente, che qui luce, in terra fumma*—
the mind, which shines here, smokes on earth)—the
mind that is the sky *ensapphired*—crystalline, where the
sewer of blood and filth is not forgotten but absent—sud- Inferno XXVI
denly, Dante looks down to see the earth—*il varco
folle d'Ulisse*—my mind looks back, as Dante's did,
to Ulysses in the *Inferno,* clothed in that which burned
him—who tells us, 'I could not conquer within me
the passion I had to gain experience of the world and
of the vices and worth of men'—he talked his com-
panions into making wings of their oars for their mad
flight—until, as he says, 'the sea closed over us'—
in the *Purgatorio,* the siren in Dante's dream sings of Purgatorio XXIX.22

Ulisse mid-sea—here, in the *Paradiso*, Dante looks
back through the dangers of language traveling,   *Paradiso* XXX.33
Odyssean, eager, and infinite—*come all'ultimo suo cias-*
cuno artista—as with every artist at his or her limit—
living sparks, rubies, the river of topazes—the laugh-
ter of flowers—to find this rose in the farthest petals,   *Paradiso* XXX.117
which Charles Olson calls *the longest lasting rose*—

Dante's Hell, Purgatory, and Paradise are signposts—
of tradition, which implicates us—of shifts in their
landscapes, which implicate us—in imagination
of language—Hell, where we are lost in the un-
redeemable time of our own century—Purgatory,
renames the poetic condition—the experiment of
writing—the feel of writing—Paradise, where words
wander in the *wildwood*—Dante's *Paradiso* remains in
the arms of Beatrice—for hers is the first name of the
love that moves his language among the stars—this
is, of course, heresy, as the Dominicans recognized
when they condemned him in 1335—

The gods prevent the supreme undecidedness of man; they close off   Jean-Luc Nancy,
his[/her] humanity, and prevent him[/her] from becoming   The Inoperative
unhinged, from measuring up to the incommensurable. . . . The   Community
gods forbid that man should be risked further than man. And most
serious of all, they take away his death.

What there is to say here can be said very simply: religious
experience is exhausted. It is an immense exhaustion. This fact is
in no way altered by the upsurge in the political, sociological, or
cultural success of religions (. . . Jewish, Islamic, or Christian
fundamentalism; sects, theosophies, gnosis). There is no return of
the religious: there are the contortions and turgescence of its exhaus-
tion. Whether that exhaustion is making way for another concern

for the gods, for their wandering or their infinite disappearance,
or else for no god, that is another matter: it is another question
altogether, and it is not something that can be grasped between
the pincers of the religious, nor indeed between those of atheism.

coming upon the inability of man, who is lost in time, to take
possession of his own historical nature

Agamben, *Infancy*
& History

poets who took the initial steps into our uncovered
Hell ran wildly into a dark forest—*una selva oscura,* say,

Shelley, living at Lerici on the Gulf of Spezzia in
1822, starting to write *The Triumph of Life*—beautiful
terza rima in honour of Dante—bring him into a
vision—he thinks he sits beside a public way where
he sees 'a great stream / Of people there . . . hurrying
to and fro, / Numerous as gnats upon the evening
gleam'— 'one mighty torrent'—a chariot comes 'on
the silent storm of its own rushing splendour'—and
in it sits 'a Shape, as one whom years deform'—and
the charioteer, 'A Janus-visaged Shadow,' drives the
'wonderwingèd team'—whose shapes are lost 'in
thick lightenings'—'a triumphal pageant of a captive
multitude' that becomes a 'sad pageant'—half to
himself, he asks, 'And what is this? Whose shape is
that within the car? And why—'—when suddenly
a voice answers, 'Life!'—so,

> *That what I thought was an old root which grew*
> *To strange distortion out of the hillside,*
> *Was indeed one of those deluded crew,*
>
> *And that the grass, which methought hung so wide*
> *And white, was but his thin discoloured hair,*
> *And that the holes he vainly sought to hide,*
>
> *Were or had been eyes—*

this is Jean Jacques Rousseau—displacing the fierce
dignity of Virgil in Dante's Comedy—Rousseau, whom
Shelley had revered as emblematic of 'political and
metaphysical transition'—of originary language—of
revolutionary possibility—of human liberty through
oppositional writing—of the stake in desire of any
one of us—

In Shelley's vision, we see the Chariot herd, tether,
and roll over the wise, the famous, age and youth—
now, Rousseau insists upon this endless passing on
of life—but Shelley interrupts:

> 'Mine eyes are sick of this perpetual flow
> Of people, and my heart is sick of one sad thought—Speak!'

Rousseau replies with the story of his own love—
when 'the bright omnipresence / Of morning . . . /
And the sun's image radiantly intense'

> 'Burned on the waters of the well that glowed
> Like gold, and threaded all the forest's maze
> With winding paths of emerald fire . . .

> 'A shape of light'

Rousseau tells us that he asked that she 'Pass not away
upon the passing stream'—she offers him a cup to
'quench his thirst':

> 'I rose; and, bending at the sweet command,
> Touched with faint lips the cup she raised,
> And suddenly my brain became as sand

'*Where the first wave had more than half erased*
The track of deer on desert Labrador;
Whilst the wolf, from which they fled amazed,

'*Leaves his stamp visibly upon the shore,*
Until the second bursts;—so on my sight
Burst a new vision, never seen before.'

shadows, phantoms, ghosts—'like small gnats and
flies'—'like discoloured flakes of snow'—which the
youthful glow melts and the snow extinguishes—
even Dante, whom the poem honours with its
rhyme, is seen on the 'opposing steep' and will
be swept away as the chariot climbs—Rousseau
continues:

'*Desire, like a lioness bereft*

'*Of her last cub, glared as it died; each one*
Of that great crowd sent forth incessantly
Those shadows, numerous as the dead leaves blown

'*In autumn evening from a poplar tree.*
Each like himself and like each other were
At first; but some distorted seemed to be

'*Obscure clouds, moulded by the casual air;*
And of this stuff the car's creative ray
Wrought all the busy phantoms that were there,

'*As the sun shapes the clouds; thus on the way*
Mask after mask fell from the countenance
And form of all; and long before the day

'Was old the joy which waked like heaven's glance
The sleepers in the oblivious valley, died;
And some grew weary of the ghastly dance,

'And fell, as I have fallen, by the wayside. . . .'

again Shelley cuts into this continuous flow of
despair, leaves us and the poem with only his
own question in six words—

'Then, what is life?' I cried—

before he drowned—

Shelley and Rousseau—like many of us—were en-
amoured of an absolute—the universal from which
human freedom might escape into a community of
meaning—

the shift of Hell to our own surface changes the be-
ginning and the end of time—the sacred powerline
of our totalies—alpha and omega reverse—unre-
deemed—into our own responsibility—the task of a
community of meaning—

———————

I think of Wittgenstein: 'to imagine a language means   *Philosophical*
to imagine a form of life'—   *Investigations* 1 9
and of his remarks to the heretics' club: 'and now I
shall describe the experience of wonderment before
the existence of the world, with these words: the
world thus is experienced as a miracle. I am now
tempted to say that the correct expression for the
miracle of the world, albeit as expressing nothing
within language, is the existence of language itself.'—

and I ponder Giorgio Agamben's reply: '. . . if the
most appropriate expression of the wonderment
at the existence of the world is the existence of
language, what then is the correct expression of
the existence of language?

 'the only possible answer to this question is human
life, as ethos, as ethical way. The search for a *polis* and
an *oikìa* befitting this void and unpresupposable com-
munity is the *infantile* task of future generations.'

———————————————

in this task of Hell—indebted to Dante—I hear
Ezra Pound's magnificent, poetic interrogation
of the great crystal—stained by anti-Semitism and
twentieth-century political shame—among us now,
as if they owned a percentage of the human mind
of—this viscid Western paradigm—transmuted into
silence—

'To what is the poet faithful?' Agamben asks, uncov-
ering a vocation—faithful to the immemorial, for
which we have used the word gods—faithful to the
emptiness of language—faithful to what is *first in
mind*, word by word and daily yet unformed—

in 1963, an Italian reporter named Luigi Pasquini met
Pound in the Tempio Malatestiano in Rimini:
 'When I reach him he is standing in the sacristy
of the church, a tiny room that formerly housed its
relics. Above the door is Piero della Francesca's fresco
depicting Sigismondo Malatesta as he kneels before
his patron saint. Pound is standing beneath it, sur-
rounded by people.
 'I approach him slowly, nervously, until I am
directly before him, face to face. I look him in the
eye, and inquire: "Ezra Pound?"

'He does not respond. He stares at me, silent, and his mouth hints at a smile.

'I insist, and repeat his name. He gazes at me, arching his eyebrows for a moment, but says nothing.

'I fear I must be mistaken and address my glance to the woman beside him. She peers up at him, then nods, reassuring me that it is him.

'I offer him my hand, and he takes it in his own. I do not tell him my name, but I make clear that I know his books. . . . He understands, it seems. He gives a sign of assent, but continues to remain silent.

'Our hands are still clasping each other. "This is the hand of the great American poet," I offer. ("La mano del grande poeta americano!")

'And at last his voice emerges, his first words, uttered in a tranquil Italian accent without a trace of an Anglo-American inflection: "I am not great." ("Non grande.")

'Swiftly I reply: "—you are among the greatest." ("Grandissimo.")

'But the conversation falters, and I grow uncertain. Through friends I had heard that he was living in Rapallo, but a stray remark from Miss Rudge indicates they have just come from Venice. I try to take up the topic: "Where are you living now: in Rapallo? Or in Merano with your daughter, or in Venice?"

'He will not reply. He looks at me again, with a mocking gaze.

'I persist: "Rapallo, Merano? Venice, Rome?"

'Nothing. He is still silent, his gaze fixed on me, like someone playing a guessing game.

'I press on: "So where are you living now?" I continue, "Where?"

'At last he lowers his head, slowly, and put his mouth to my ear so that no one can hear us. His voice is a whisper, rasping: "I live in hell."

'This leaves me bewildered. Here we are in church, in a sacristy in fact (even if it is the sacristy of a paganizing temple)—in a place, in short, as far as possible from Erebus or the underworld of Lucifer. And yet he says we're in hell. I fail to understand and want to pursue it: "Which hell do you mean? The hellish tourism? The inferno of the war, here in Rimini? The hell of Rome? Of Italy? Of the world?"

'He is silent again. At last he moves his hands: he places them before his stomach, and slowly lifting them to the level of his heart, as the traces of light in his pupils become like glowing coals, he whispers a suffocated scream. "Here is hell. Here."'

cited in L. S. Rainey, *Ezra Pound: The Monument of Culture*

25 August 1997

A Note

on my use of the word 'territory'—*territorio, zona*—to indicate the largeness each of us enters upon, which in contemporary terms seems to me mapless. We enter a territory without totalities of God, without totalities of spirit, Hegelian or otherwise, and without totalities of materiality on the record of Marxist practice in the 20th century. We have, as Lyotard has argued, paid far too much in terror for our totalities. The contemporary resurgence of religion, at least in North and South America, is exceedingly corrupt, and in its own terms blasphemous. This aging Roman Catholic looks across at the three great religions of Abraham—the Christian, the Jewish and the Muslim—and fears they are dying into violence. It is as if we were repeating the second century, ANNO DOMINI.

Dante is our contemporary in the *Comedy* and our guide to a poetics of interrogation. The *Comedy* is our greatest poem of interrogation, and the language of the *Inferno*, the *Purgatorio* and the *Paradiso* is Ulyssean. Although Dante did not know the *Odyssey* except through Virgil, Odysseus haunts him even in his dreams.

1997
Revised 25 January 2006

Wanders

2001–2002

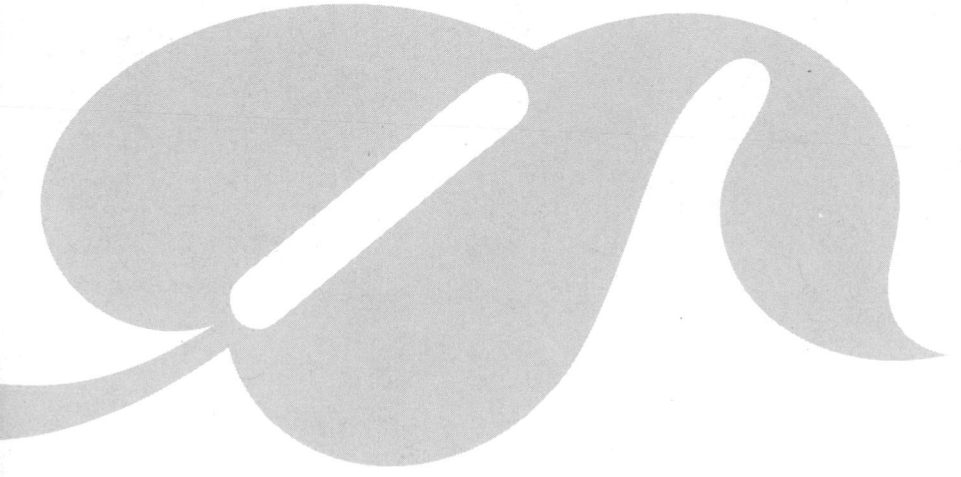

The Truth Is Laughter 20

The builders next door
call to one another in quick,
anxious Greek, their windbreakers
adorned with that beautiful alphabet—
suddenly, in English I hear
'cocksucker,' addressed, I suppose,
to a piece of wood—working on
the telephone pole, a woodpecker
answers: peck, peck, peck, peck, peck
striking the air of our peckerwoods
and intelligence

                                    6 March 2001

The Truth Is Laughter 21

'carte blank,' my horse, my horse,
so we goes dancing with radios, institutions,
traditions, creeds, and spirits
of vacuoles, wearing our *patent smallclothes*
and advertisements thissidedown,
up of, over of, in of, and out of considerable
nakedness snows

                                    27 March 2001

Oh!

I love the way crows walk,
a kind of strut ridiculing all
our bipedal, wingless
footings about—then winged
to divebomb any passerby
under the tree where a nest
enfolds in branches the consequences
of their sex—this, the first quickening
cry, perhaps, of Hitchcock's *Birds*—
to wit—to woo—to wound—
and last—

10 April 2001

Glass Road,

and there's my blue-green
parrot, perched on a roadsign
then another and another, squawking
'one body'—as I go along
this way to ancient antetalks—
how did this sweetpart of my journey
learn to yell 'no matter'—glistening
feathers, smiles in the sands
where glass starts

12 April 2001

Well, my dears, I knew there were shadows
around—rather, perhaps, a charade—my
beloved brother Jimmy died yesterday—12
years younger than I—haphazardly, David
and I went out and found a clock, which
we bought, French design, made in Germany
in the 1880's for export to China—here for
my return to the companionship of time,
lovely chimes—

15 April 2001

hail yah,

what would happen if the long history
of your appearances stopped
and god popped out
all new and differences,
sacrifices unsmoked and quenched
in young justice? What
laughter rumours in the circulation
of the blood uncaught
and the body tipped forward
to kiss the shatters of your hearts!

20 April 2001

'who, who, who, who,'
said Kissmequick,
and the owl in the boat
swore, 'whiskers,' whose dream,
like clouds of bisectors,
crossed eyes with blazed crystals.
Nomad smiled 'Hi!' his lips,
foot-loose and somewhere, wander
the commotion of oceans.

22 April 2001

half-you flown on a carpet,
the other-half caught in the treetops
and rooted—it is the multicolours
and intricate speech of the carpet
that I peeked over—O, a glisk
of this mind's flivver,
its glissandi whisper.

23 April 2001

'there, there, there,'
Somewhere said, offering

comfort that didn't comport, who is
dressed to the nines, who is
unaware of ten pins
to hold our sweetness up.
'there,' I said, 'is there, unshaped.'

24 April 2001

Among universals,

my piano collapsed into
a bonfire and wept—I'm
young again and return
to the curriculum—how
to open a bank account—how
to establish a credit rating and
self-esteem—the kid
at the next desk, like me,
playing with his marbles,
called his homework
on the tack of it 'self-steam.'

24 April 2001

Petty, vulgar, provincial,

O loves, to hell with it all,
look at it, but who would I leave it to?
but who would you?
The player piano is
out of tune—toodle-de-do.

play it again—toodle-de-do.
What is the meaning of this white garment?
What is the meaning of the scarlet inside it?
pounded quavers,
flowing semiquavers
before that chord F—A$^\flat$—D$^\flat$
releases the fugue of our form—out of tune.

for Mikhail Gorbachev,
1991, when he was 'worthy of Chekhov'
25 April 2001

Good morning,
here in this tunnel of creek-willows, curiously
near. Those erotic sands—great brushes of willow
resisting tangs of salt—one day, a gardener
crawled on his belly under them to cut out
the deadwood to make tunnels
so you could stand up and walk
twisting toward his domestic flowers—
beyond, the sea plashes its gaze of fierce
                                        companionship
when the moon, sudden as a bitten lip,
slips out of the haze, winds the threads of its light
in your mind and your body loses its footsteps
in this changeling place
of goodnight gates.

27 April 2001

So
you spend most of your time
digging in hearts? piles of them,
as if history were the truth
full of unpacked numbers
in this midst of happiness.
What if you commit unhappiness?
blame whom?
Well, that would be unhappiness
added to the excess of happenchance.
What'll you do?
with happenstance that ever so slightly
didn't happen to you.
There's a gasp in an angel's eye, who flits
from one to millions of eyes and looks
wide open and shuts, sighted only once.

28 April 2001

There's a wonder afoot,
loose with embroideries
among the leaves
and cherry blossoms imitate
raindrops flying on the winds
to stick on the windows,
but the raindrops run off
toward their destiny in thought.
big or little, visible or imperceptible,
the mind wrangles shapes for things
on the morning tides,

in the evening wiles
after thought.

29 April 2001

🦋

'like money in the gutter,' David said.
That was the best of luck,
pink petals stuck to the car's
tires, noted when we parked
near Dead Write Books
and the intense blue shirt
I wanted turned up.
a banner on a book in the window
read 'exciting as John Le Carré,'
rushed to the door, but Dead Write
Books was shut. '5 o'clock,' I said

29 April 2001

🦋

did you ever see an angel,
feet on the ground? I did.
she was of obsidian.
did you ever wrestle
with Jacob and the angel
in alabaster? I did.
a bit of a struggle
with volcanic glass

and compact translucence.
then, I steal their gypsum
gossip. lame words stalk it,
the soft iron of their magnetism
in us. angels reel their realism
in the where we stand under.

30 April 2001

forgot, *oubli*
et anamnèse
dans l'expérience vécue
de l'éternel
retour
du Même, recalled
here in Nietzsche's
typewriter, millions
of voices, rhythmic streets
their words pace, true
to the same multiplicity
tumbling word over words.
have you
touched the echoic shadows
as you read, their bodies
replete with calls. O,
give me our intensity,
our indebted discourse,
thinking of everyone
who is no one
gone, coming back.

1 May 2001

oubli, forgot
et anamnèse, loss
calls
dans l'expérience vécue,
calls you
de l'éternel, calls
retour, calls
du Même, the same
shouts here in the keys
of Nietzsche's typewriter
in rhythmic streets.
shadows of what echo
your wordage, call
quick selves
to surround quick words
in your parataxis
true to
the big Same that is—
never our selfsame calls.

2 May 2001

when Nietzsche said
'God is dead,'
he knew that words
are bits of our bodies,
big and little,
and the really
Big one is god.
we've thrown
everything

into it.
that's what
the 'eternal
return' is
going on about,
bits of our bodies
caught up
in it.

2 July 2001

a true story of
I'm 19—no, 20—
looking for watercress
in the mind's ditches
cold, running ripple of strawberry
creek

and Jack says
come on, let's go to the Trotskyite
meeting tonight—
a fold of 14 there
and one stood up:
'I move we ban supernaturalist
religions'
I elbowed Spicer and
said what if . . .
he said go for it
I stood up: 'Point of order.
I'm papal nuncio for the Bay Area.'
They kicked us out and changed
their meetings to a secret place.
Months later I ran into one of them.
I said how's it going, he said:

'Comes the Revolution, you'll hang
from a lamppost.' Unlikely as it may seem
his name was also Robin. A chill passed
over my joke—
now I'm 76 looking around for watercress.

6 July 2001

※

there were two accent
pillows embroidered
with dragonflies,
a favourite bug,
loved as much as
waterspiders capturing
tiny air bubbles
with their walking feet
to stride on water.
the clerk said you ought
to buy those pillows
before that 'motive'
goes off fashion.
how did she know,
was she listening in
on my mind
that I chase after the wings
and motivations of dragons
over hills, dales
and skygraphed streets
for their fiery sincerity?
no thanks, I said
to the pillows.

13 July 2001

the clock is back,
tick and talk—
time has such nonchalance
you can hear time walk
on rainbows
and bridges of believe-it-or-not.
that's how I caught
gravure of it in crystal
here on my writing-table;
a winged fairy
and Buddha, who refused
to become god.
           They gaze
in radiance and talk

                      7 August 2001

on page 61
of any book—
if your book
is smaller than that,
try page 1—
there's a grass angel
and your metaphysics
burns up
smiling like a kiss
with anyone at all—

                      13 August 2001

'I have lost track of the world,' Mahler said

oh! yes one does listen to Evil
when, especially, his personification
is appointed to speak to the American
people and, in his audience, all
the living exemplars of the Presidency
are present with kissing wives—
and war is being declared on, was it
Evil?—all, of course, in the name of love—
one must know what Evil is
doing—and how he's dressed—or
remain naked forever

14 September 2001

so eerie: 'must get rid of Halloween—
it's pagan,' say these clowns of
tailor-made, cardboard transcendence,
ignorant of Allhallows coming up,
deaf to this laughter with the ultimate
I know democracy means all-of-us,
but how did such ministers get it up
to swoop down from their perch
onto the scintillating forms
of life and death
in conversation
one night each year?
is their speculum all metal
mirroring honeys?
oh! give me a pointed hat,
let me laugh and whirl

with life and that
that I shall oneday meet
let me call out with thrills
and candy bars
and jelly beans
in the face of their whatnot.

1 November 2001

To: Colorado / Montana

Idaho man says
lava spills for miles,
the Craters of the Moon,
full of bowls
and caves reaching
the sagebrush of
imagining Denver
where imagination
was illegitimate
for five months,
hidden by Sacred
Heart nuns, who
are Jesuits—no wonder
Colorado seems out of
place in the moonshine
of fluid rocks
in the tree tops
of montane life
and lore—
c'était le prix d'alors

6 November 2001

imagine a map
when you're 1 to 5 months old—
every map has a heart-burn—
that's its town—
and when you're 1 to 5 months old
you've got bird-brains quick
in your kicking feet—
now, he was named Robin
after the heroine (the word now politically
incorrect) of a Frances Hodgson Burnett
novel about a war lover lost and
Francis Xavier, who flew over
the Mediterranean on magnificent carpets
and somehow landed in India—and
he of those months was watched over
by Sister Mary Madeleva, a Chaucer
scholar and Sister Seraphina alongside
heart-burn and bird-brain,
who knew this territory wasn't
on the map of burning directions,
of cross-purposes where
you-can't-go-back that's
the name of the town where you started

6 November 2001

I return to my meditations—explications—experiences
on Alcalay's page-one epigraphs—that strike me
as Supergraphs—from Jacques Derrida and
Edmond Jabès—I'm fascinated that we are

all cultural Judaists—Hebrews, Christians, Muslims—
floating on the turbulent stream of History—thus,
to cop Jabès, 'writing . . . the same waiting, the same
hope, the same depletion' just there at the edge,
which in Victor Hugo's terms, is marvelous—and
stains the mind and heart—perhaps best not
to go there—but poets do, willy-nilly, and
poetry must—now there lie prone the
political and social—dear WRITING
before and after September 1 1, I must—

19 November 2001

who's goose

what's your name?
puddin' 'n' tame
what's your other?
bread and butter
where do you live?
in a sieve
what's your number?
cucumber.

2002

everyday, the carpenter
on the new house next door
greeted me—'Morning Glory',

white hair standing straight up,
then, he found out
I was a professor and
said—'how are you, Sir'—
I said—'let's get back
to Morning Glory,
that's better than emeritus'

17 January 2002

Fingerspitzengefühl,

the i who am
recently uncovered
quakes
in the earth
of its finding
my strange forest,
oh, my *dragon candles*
of tourists at the tips of my fingers

for Tomas Marquard and
Ilonka Opitz
29 January 2002

Ruck and rot pucker in political thought
down south—fruit-fly larvae like it hot

13 February 2002

woke this morning
from a dream
of a dense forest
where
I was wandering
and met John Wieners,
seemed a greeting
among serried shadows
of trees

a real dream
2 March 2002

will be,
probably—
but don't rush it—
an apple of Sodom
resolving
into smoke
and ashes
over the nearest
rose garden

16 March 2002

what did I forget
when I first met
language in the womb—
there was no I—
a quarreling sound
and lullabye

21 March 2002

a dream that repeated during the night—each
time waking me—remaining awake for a while,
then back to sleep—repeat—on the landing of
my entrance steps—a large Lèger hand, palm
up, water bubbling up from the centre of the
palm and spilling through the fingers—all of the
sculpture the colour of lead—on top of it piled,
cut lumber—2 by 4's

———————————————

the hand appeared to be 5' long, 3' wide with
long slender fingers and thumb—resting on
a plinth about 2' high, round with a circumference
of 2'—the lumber about 3' high and heavy—

———————————————

repeat

11 April 2002

*

'oh,' I said to myself,
talking again to dragons
and strange birds—cocks
of the walks—on splendour
and such remisses—sending
the pardons for this beauty,
sending laughter to open books
and fantastic words that hold
heartbeats—hello—isn't it fun
that goodbye is never there?

3 July 2002

*

the Bible is as historical
as you or I
and feathered as our words
fly,
a crow there, a peacock,
a sparrow pecking sidewalk
crumbs.
We both know it takes centuries
to say that,
bumming it,
riding the rails of that railroad,
you and I whistling past
all stops.

8 August 2002

if you look at a table of minerals,
including water and mercury,
today is iron pyrite—glint
in the dusk of my mind—I sing
the footsteps meandering through
this dark and shine—Hi!
to every hard and liquid word
of it—Hi!

13 August 2002

the first imagination of god
was meant to stop the world dead
in its chances—stillness—
you and I there bounded
by the same old song—but
you and I unwound—let
out unheard-of sharps and flats,
trailing unreined horses
of the sun and moon and stars
and ongoing universes—oh, such smiles
in the mourning losses
of everybody-the-same—I said:
'Don't cry. It's destiny. Our history,
its possibility.' And added: 'No
presumptions of identity, god or not.'

13 August 2002

well, this old crow is making
a hook to dig out words
from the bottom and top
of things—thus, the middle
voice's myriad in definitenesses,
infinite circulations of
the body's mind—every sorrow,
every joy and in between crevasses—
every word of this and that

17 August 2002

I've caught the unease
of old age in my hands
and wrung it dry
in order to remain
within its kaleidoscope,
there to collide among all colours
of *kalos*—beauty
of *eidos*—form
of *skopos*—watcher of
lovers of
irreparables

21 August 2002

what i-densities
borders and rivers
ask for, oceans
keep their secrets
in order to *visit oneself,*
to show oneself as visiting,
to constitute oneself as visited,
active and passive,
he gets himself done.
the self is only a remainder,
reminder,
                  bearing witness
to the territory
where
one cannot dwell
and where
the mind dwells,
human and inhuman,
all at once
there and not there,
language
and *non-language,*
so to speak
of sacred hearts,
nude and once.

after reading Agamben
on Spinoza, Levinas, Keats
and Pessoa, for Peter
Quartermain.
1 September 2002

dear dusty moth
wearing miller's cloth,
Sophia Nichols' soft
voice calls wings
at dusk
      across railroads
and sagebrush
to lull me to sleep,
'Come to these window corners,
come, rest on my boy's dreams
and flight,
come tonight'

                2 September 2002

Robert Duncan said, 'Don't tell
anyone we loved *Butterfield
Eight*'

         comedic tears run
down my cheeks tonight
under the lamp of the sheer
romance of it

        of course,
I'll tell all these years later
and you're gone in your magnificence,
alarms of laughter
who dumped
my clothes in the wastebasket

whose teeth brushed with bourbon
whose fur coat
did I run home in

I'll leave out the car and the sorrow

28 December 2002

Ethel Merman,
that's a voice I like—
just roses—
from the top
and in the streets
there it 'is'
my plate
blow that kiss
put height
in your hair
and wait
you, love,
know,
morning
and night,
our song

29 December 2002

So

2003

Charles Watts,
you said, 'Please stay'
I said, 'I'll be back'
you said, 'I don't understand love'
I said, 'I'll be back'
but you had gone where love
is not so directed
though it is here
and there
in every poetic
step you left
just now at the kitchen
table staring across
from the unemptied
chair of conversations

29 October 2003

just out the door
a rainbow
so close
I could have
touched it
had I been
tall enough
I called 'Oh'
to life's prism
among wet leaves
a bird sang
note by note
red, yellow, violet

22 October 2003

begin the beguine

how many infatuations
how many charms
of staccato two-tone phrases
more or less than
four to the bar
jumping

> how many beautiful
> people smiled in
> The Five Spot,
> sat down, said
> 'let's dance'
> and the smile
> goes on
> bass
> in the heart
> years after

for Stan Pettigrove
21 September 2003

there
it goes
flying
like a crow
in the high winds
of this chaos,
              the MUST
of the practice of
outside
there's a way to walk blind
there's a way to talk blind
if you want to

                              2 November 2003

woke this morning
talking:
'operator, operator,
get the whole town on the line
I want to know who gives a shit'

                              2003

a song

there's a bluebird
in your eye,
a rainbow lines
your many lives
of Eroses.
I dedicate to you
all precious stuff,
all care-full lusts
that burn our lives,
I murmur,
   'luck'

2003

Oh!

2004

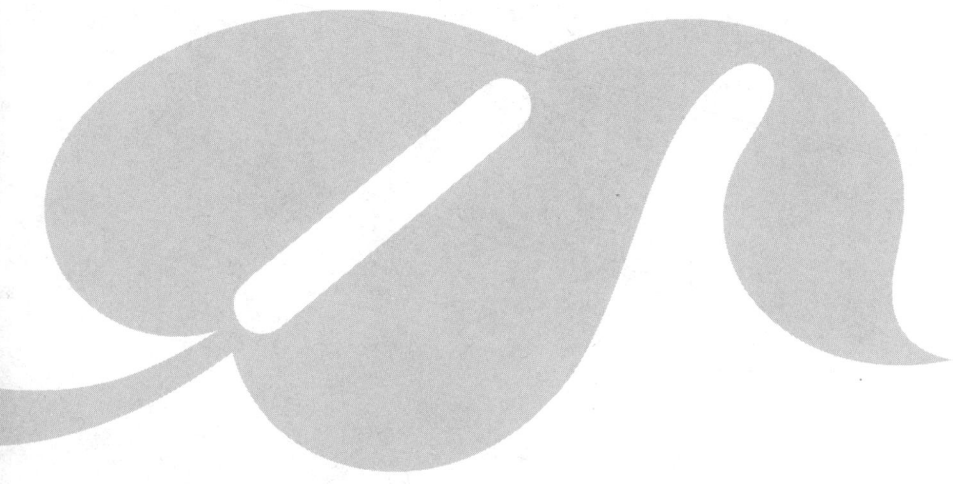

I don't remember this:
a kiss is just a kiss,
that's all I wanted,
sort of—
              was it
Pinocchio or some guardian
of the sparkling sidewalks
waving his staff of stars?
Was it only a creation of O?
or a thought in a gilded cage
whistling a 'wooden O'?
I verify it was anyone
breathing   O O O
that's what I wanted—O

                              24 January 2004

only the shadow knows
these footstep years, surprising thought
and loves so deep I keep them close
each day to wander their companionships
of wonder   oh! fly, come fly with me
in *an exaltation of larks*, and, yes, in *a murder*
of crows, in *the parliament of owls*, with
the eloquence of frogs—this poetry
one can't do without—murmuring clouds,
embrace of mountains—sunshining streets,
the wariness of skyscrapers—the longing
of steeples—out of this disarray of imagination
are dimmed sparkles where sorrow burns
in its ashes—hot as heaven.

'venery' from James Lipton
25 January 2004

comfortably
sit here by this fire of roses
and listen to your mind's canary
now then
leap on heaven
when it's roundabout
but rein in its tendency
to bite wild-things,
hold tight to the whiz-bang of it
and ride its whispers
well, you didn't expect just kindness
on the way to the danger-house,
did you?

29 January 2004

'*abstract monotheism and monism, which is its secularization as social philosophy, reveal a common totalitarian trend*'—Corbin

simplified mind
generalized human nature
freedom as aggregate
public without the private
source of witnessing
this perpetual interchange
of heavenish and hellish
exhalations
oh, I ask you in my grandmother's
phrase, 'be sensible'
where is the power of the heart—
in your breast—damn you—
not up there floating
like a careless alphabet
think of a real lemon
which is very intelligent
test everything everywhere
by your own physical event
then hang on to the heart of it
we're all lemons

29 January 2004

sea and sky
desiring
the boat with its vibrant
pink sail on English Bay
calls each of us to sail
those passionate adventures
out there   desiring,
I know it's the white
desire of the clouds drifting
when the moon rushes
into the game and drill
of actual language
loving it out there,
the particular peril
as desire trusts

8 February 2004

no body
so what shall we say of the soul
that it may be of space and of time
the self in the beyond
in order to exist somewhere
or it is arranged like music
the tune of it
epicurean and fiery
unafraid of the body
and its green moth
at the provisional door

2004

whose salted heart

we've met
it turns out
in a labour of form,
a cultural largeness
talking to itself,
its memory damaged
so the past
is over the hill
out of shape,
momentarily
tigerish disarray
of 'who made thee'
thus troubling
the lyric mind
with salt

2004

what would you do
if all the lovers of your years
passed by at midnight
dressed in the flesh
they wore when you
last loved them?
what do I do?
what do I say?
I loved you then,
I touch you now
with all the glow
you left in the palm of my hands.

9 February 2004

'Have you got a toybox?'
the question came out of the air,
puzzling the tiger among the leaves.
the cowboy in pieces fallen off
his celluloid palomino, its dove-coloured
tail somewhere on the cardboard bottom—
the dragon flaring—a water-gun
leaking specifics—an old cookie tin
for pens and pencils where Eros
swings on a crescent in the green sunset—O,
have you grown up to meet Igitur's
ancestral candle and the shake of the dice
of the Absolute, then the curtained room
opens, darker than most, breathing nevertheless
the blue flowering impossible   O, sleep
is impossible who just got there—or was it
something that stirred in the bananas,
pears, apples of the lights-out—sweetest
being or delicious somewhat of what I've
forgotten and remembered on the attic ladder
of this old house abandoned in the sagebrush,
imparadising

10 February 2004

divination by pebbles

come on, try it, one pebble,
two pebbles, three pebbles,
four   dropped in the pond
among the goldfish
there the logic went
there click the dear dice
of a life's swim for it
1001 letters of the alphabet
thunder in our footsteps
and the diaphanous heart
is at the door on the edge
of it here—there—where—
then—when   of it

for James Joyce
17 February 2004

language is love

Robin Blaser
2004

AFTERWORD

I dwell in Possibility—
A fairer House than Prose—

Emily Dickinson

Robin Blaser's poems are companions on a journey of life, a jour-
ney whose goal is not getting someplace else, but, rather, being
where you are and who you are—where *you* is always in the
plural.

In the plural might be a good motto for Blaser's courageous and
anti-declamatory poetics, his profound continuation, deep into the
darkening heart of contemporary North American poetry, of Emily
Dickinson's core value: "I'm nobody . . . Are you nobody too?"
For Blaser, it is not only nobody but also no mind, or "no" mind,
for this is a poetics of negation that dwells in pleats and upon folds:
pleating and folding being Blaser's latter day, Deleuzian manner of
extending his lifelong project of seriality.

One poem must follow instanter on the next, a next always out
of reach until in hand, in mouth, in ear.

Blaser celebrated his eightieth birthday on May 14, 2005, just
as this book was going into final production.

The present edition, an expanded version of the 1993 Coach
House Press publication of the same name—Blaser's first col-
lected poems—features a number of poems from the last decade
and also includes several important works not included in the
Coach House publication. Most significantly, Blaser has added a

recent long poem for Dante to his Great Companion series. This astounding work provides a bridge between Blaser's poems and critical writings, marking a direct point of contact to the University of California's companion volume of Blaser's collected essays.

Blaser's work constitutes a fundamental part of the fabric of the North American poetry and poetics of "interrogation," to use his term. Compared to his most immediate contemporaries, Blaser has pursued a different, distinctly refractory, willfully diffuse course that has led him to be circumspect about publication. As a result, it was almost forty years from his first poems to the time when The Holy Forest began to emerge as one of the key poetic works of the present. Indeed, Blaser's lyric collage (what he calls "the art of combinations" in a poem of that title, alluding to Leibnitz) seems today to be remarkably fresh, even while his engagement with (I don't say commitment to) turbulence and turbulent thought seems ever more pressingly exemplary. Blaser's work seems to me more a part of the future of poetry than the past.

Blaser's poems and essays insist on the necessity of thinking through analogy and resemblance—that is, thinking serially so as to move beyond the epistemological limits of positivism and self-expression. At the same time, Blaser has committed his work to everywhere affirming the value of human diversity, understood not only as sexual or ethnic difference, but also as the possibility of thinking outside received categories. There are some remarkably powerful and explicit political poems in the volume, notably "Even on Sunday." But the most radical politics of this work goes beyond any one poem: it is inscribed in the work's compositional practice. Even as Blaser questions the stable, lyric, expressive "I," he never abandons the possibility of poetic agency, through his generative recognition of language as social, as the "outside."

Blaser's "Great Companions" have now gone into the world of an ever-present no-longer-of-this-life: Jack Spicer, Robert Duncan, Robert Creeley, Charles Olson, of his immediate company; Dante, Nerval, Merleau-Ponty, Deleuze of his Imaginary. The poems of the Holy Forest are points on a map of a cosmos that does not exist in historical terms, that cannot exist, yet that must exist, if we are to make it to a Century 22 that is more than the name of a clothing store. The points form a constellation that we are not quite ready to apprehend but through which we are already formed. We grope and we stumble, but then, out of the blue or black or ultra suede, something unexpected happens: we are ensnared by the encounter.

Form finds us. Form founds us.

Blaser's *Holy Forest* is a blaze of allusion without symbols, quotation without appointment. In the forest of language, every tree is a poem, every leaf a word. The poet sings the songs of night, jumping, from branch to branch, to a syncopated beat; never, ever, finding home. "To wit—to woo—to wound—," Blaser writes in "Oh!" ("Wanders") one of his late, short, I want to call them anti-lyrics.

Citation, citation everywhere: the utter prism of his care.

No other moment exists but this one.

This one.

This one.

The Holy Forest is *wholly* secular, for only the secular allows the promise of an end to what Blake knew as the Totalizing Oppression of Morality. ("We have paid far too much in terror," Blaser writes in a note to his Dante poem, "for our totalities.") Each line of *The Holy Forest* is a glimpse into the unknown, each poem a new way of entering the holiness of the everyday. The frames are restless: no conclusion nor solution, the only resolution the necessity to go on. "We enter a territory without totalities where poetic practice is our stake and necessity."

"This World is not conclusion/A sequel stands beyond," writes Dickinson.

Neither is the poem the end of the poem, nor is the idea of the poem its origin.

The poem is the possibility of possibility.

In his exquisite articulations of the flowers of associational thinking, Blaser has turned *knowledge* into *nowledge*, the "wild logos" of the cosmic companionship of the real.

In Res Robin, Nibor Resalb
Inscripsit Mentastrum (XXC)

Matter over mind or anyway
mattering, muttering, sponge
warp, cup, meld, then again

clutched, shred, shrift. Blister
origins (orangutans) in souped-
up monkey-wrench. Prattling
till the itch in pines becomes
gash (sash) in the pluriverses
of weft & muck (wept). Pleat
as you may, fellow traversers
on the rippled road to hear &
however, ne'er so near.

Charles Bernstein
New York
October 2, 2005

INDEX OF TITLES
AND FIRST LINES

Titles appear in roman type. First lines appear in italics.

Text: 10/13 Joanna
Display: Joanna
Compositor: BookMatters, Berkeley
Printer and binder: Thomson-Shore, Inc.

LL DATE DUE J

GAYLORD · PRINTED IN U.S.A.